2

C

CRPYK

Developing Teachers Professionally

The process of professional development in teaching is, or should be, a continuous one, beginning in the initial training phase and lasting for a professional lifetime. In the last few years, from the 1988 Education Reform Act through to the 1992 White Paper *Choice and Diversity in Schools* and beyond, arrangements for lifelong training have changed almost beyond recognition. More people than ever before in schools, in higher education and in local authorities are responsible for teachers' professional development.

Developing Teachers Professionally is a provocative collection of articles by authors involved in the pre-service and continuing education of teachers. The contributors look critically and constructively at the changing world of teacher education. Each contribution shows how a commitment to collaboration and quality can produce truly professional development for teachers throughout their careers.

Drawing on the experience of one Local Education Authority and of the University School of Education serving the region, the contributors to *Developing Teachers Professionally* consider such issues as coherence and continuity across the various phases of teacher education, the evaluation of in-service work and the search for quality.

This collection of some of the latest and most positive thinking in the field will appeal to everyone responsible for developing teachers' professionalism.

David Bridges is Professor of Education at the University of East Anglia and Director of the Eastern Region Teacher Education Consortium (ERTEC).
Trevor Kerry was formerly Senior General Adviser for In-service and Further Education, Norfolk LEA, and is currently Staff Tutor (Education) for the Open University and Visiting Fellow in Education at the University of East Anglia.

Developing Teachers Professionally

Reflections for Initial and In-service Trainers

Edited by
David Bridges and Trevor Kerry

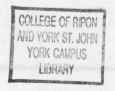
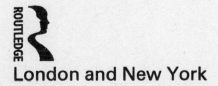

London and New York

First published 1993
by Routledge
11 New Fetter Lane, London EC4P 4EE

Simultaneously published in the USA and Canada
by Routledge
29 West 35th Street, New York, NY 10001

© 1993 David Bridges and Trevor Kerry

Typeset in 10/12 pt Garamond by
NWL Editorial Services, Langport, Somerset

Printed and bound in Great Britain by
Mackays of Chatham PLC, Chatham, Kent.

British Library Cataloguing in Publication Data
A catalogue record for this book is available from the British Library

Library of Congress Cataloging in Publication Data
Developing teachers professionally. Reflections for initial and in-service
trainers / edited by David Bridges and Trevor Kerry.
p. cm.
1. Teachers – Training of – Great Britain. 2. Teachers – In-service
training – Great Britain. I. Bridges, David, 1941– .
II. Kerry, Trevor.
LB1725.G6D48 1993   93–6981
370.71′0941 – dc20   CIP

ISBN 0–415–09295–7
     0–415–09296–5 (pbk.)

Contents

Figures and tables

Contributors

Roger Aspland is a lecturer in education at the University of East Anglia where he teaches courses in the management of education. He is particularly interested in the process of professional learning and the management of staff development, both in schools and in commerce and industry.

Geoffrey Brown is Professor of Education at the University of East Anglia and an educational psychologist. In addition to his abiding interest in the initial preparation of teachers and the further professional development of practising teachers, he is concerned with theoretical models of human learning, the nature of adolescence and the dyslexia debate.

John Elliott is Professor of Education in the School of Education at the University of East Anglia. He was a founding member of the Centre for Applied Research in Education (CARE) in 1972. John is currently directing a joint CARE/Open University ESRC-funded research project on children's talk in the context of computer mediated learning activities, and he is a consultant for the OECD. He is also directing an action research-based management development programme for the Norfolk Police.

David Bridges is Professor of Education at the University of East Anglia and Director of the Eastern Region Teacher Education Consortium. He directed an early (1979–81) project on School Centred In-service Education and a series of evaluations of in-service programmes in Suffolk, Norfolk and Cambridgeshire. He has been consultant on teacher education to overseas governments in Ethiopia, Guyana and Belize.

Susan Halliwell works in the field of in-service and pre-service courses for primary and secondary teachers of modern languages in this country and of English as a foreign language overseas. She has a long-standing research interest in the processes of teacher education as provided by school-based and higher education based courses.

Les Tickle lectures in education at the University of East Anglia. He was responsible for designing and developing programmes for initial teacher education between 1981 and 1986 and research associated with that work led to the publication of *Learning Teaching, Teaching Teaching* (Falmer Press, 1987) and *Study of Partnership in Teacher Education*. He has recently been awarded a Ph.D. for his study of teachers in their first year of teaching.

Michael Ransby is an advisory teacher with management responsibility for the induction of newly qualified teachers, licensed teachers, teacher-tutors, curricular and professional mentors. He is a member of a management team which offers training, development, support and consultancy to teachers, deputy headteachers, headteachers and governors within and beyond Norfolk.

Chris Husbands is lecturer in Education at the University of East Anglia. His research interests include school-based teacher education and curriculum development in history. His recent publications include *Whose history? School history and the National Curriculum* (History Education Group, 1992) as co-author.

David Wright taught in schools in Stevenage, Herts. and in Pittsburgh, USA, and now lectures at the University of East Anglia. He is author of eighty-two articles and of sixteen books; his *Philip's Children's Atlas* has sold half a million copies worldwide. His interests include walking, railways, flying, hymnology and environmental issues (local and worldwide).

Parts of the chapter in this volume are adapted from articles by him in *Education, The Author, British Journal of In-Service Education* and the *Times Educational Supplement*.

Terry Cook is General Adviser (INSET Development) and Head of the County INSET Centre, Norfolk Inspection Advice and Training Services. In addition to countrywide roles involving Inspection and Advice, and the managerial oversight of the County INSET Centre, he has been responsible for the co-ordination of the LEA's advisory teachers and related support staff. Previously he was first deputy headteacher in a high school, an INSET consultant, and has run curriculum projects and published curriculum related materials.

Joni Cunningham taught in an FE college in London before becoming the advisory teacher in further education with Norfolk LEA. In 1991 she was appointed principal lecturer responsible for staff development at Harlow College.

Trevor Kerry is staff tutor in education for the Open University (East Midlands), is a Visiting Fellow of the University of East Anglia and was, until recently, senior adviser (INSET and FE) in Norfolk LEA. He has taught in the primary, secondary and FE sectors and has published a wide range of practical education texts and research articles.

Chapter 1

Introduction

Trevor Kerry

The nature and climate of education have seen more changes in the last three years than in the previous fifty. Following the Education Reform Act in 1988 major developments in schools have included massively increased responsibilities for governors, the introduction of a National Curriculum, new assessment and reporting arrangements, and financial accountability delegated directly into schools. Colleges of further education and sixth form colleges have become incorporated and have left Local Education Authority control. The range of roles and the power of Local Authorities themselves have been significantly denuded, and those of governors extended.

Inevitably, these changes have had a knock-on effect on both initial and in-service training of teachers. On the initial training front we have seen the introduction of schemes to train teachers 'on-the-job', and even the college/university-based PGCE has become more vocationally orientated. Teachers trained through Articled, Licensed or PGCE routes have all previously served a probationary year: but this, too, has given way to status as Newly Qualified Teachers (NQTs). Employing institutions are having to accept more responsibility for these NQTs and for their further professional development.

In-service training for teachers has, over the last five years, been delivered through grants from government to LEAs who have had to provide a proportion of the costs. Schemes have changed at a bewildering pace: through GRIST (Grant-Related In-service Training) to LEATGS (LEA Training Grant Scheme) and ESGs (Educational Support Grants) to GEST (Grants for Education Support and Training). This last, GEST, has itself changed in nature over its short life-span and now requires substantial devolution of the training moneys more directly into schools. For the further education sector the grants are now paid direct to institutions; and Grant Maintained Schools receive separate and preferential funding for staff training.

In this climate of rapid change a group of experienced trainers – some employed by Norfolk Local Education Authority as in-service specialists, and some concerned with initial and in-service education in the University of East

Anglia – decided to come together to produce a book of papers on aspects of initial and in-service training.

This book was seen as serving a number of distinct purposes.

First, the authors believed that within the region they had developed several models of good practice. Some of these models had attracted national attention, and it was felt to be opportune to disseminate them to a wider audience.

Second, the book marks an underlying philosophy and belief. This is a philosophy of collaboration. Although staff employed by the two institutions spent part of their time on quite discrete jobs, for both groups of staff the initial and in-service clientele substantially overlapped. In this context staff from the LEA and from UEA developed close working relationships: a professional proximity which we believed had informed the thinking and practice of both, and which we believed should be, of itself, a model.

Third, these groups of trainers numbered within themselves individuals of national stature, whose work within the rapidly changing educational context described above made a significant contribution to the current debate on initial training and professional development.

So why is this book important to the reader, and what can s/he expect to find within it?

Though the views expressed in this book are personal views of individual authors, they are born out of the collaborative context. The contributions take up issues of immediacy, trying to analyse and retain the best of existing practice and to see it alongside critically evaluated innovation. It is intended that each paper should be both rigorous and provocative.

The cynic might say that, in juxtaposing writers from the politically constrained LEA advisory services and from the maverick university sector, we had married ill-assorted partners. There may be an apparent tension between open-ended research into teaching or teachers' skills on the one hand, and LEA policy (immovable but often unresearched) on the other. One could caricature the extremes of the two approaches thus: university lecturers have all the questions but never get beyond looking for the answers, while LEA officers assume they know all the answers but seem to have forgotten the questions! But part of the model here – and one we believe to be of crucial importance – is precisely that the writers trade perspectives in a quest for something nearer truth than dogma.

The contents of the book reflect a wide range of current issues in initial and in-service education: a process which is seen here as a continuum, not as divisible into compartmented phases. Thus, the first two contributions to the book deal with issues connected with the concept of professionalism. Roger Aspland and Geoff Brown, in Chapter 2, confront the crisis of confidence between the teaching profession and the public, and the resulting interventionist stance of government. They voice fears about the emerging mechanistic view of the teacher's role. A contrasting view, the social market view, is expressed; and the nature of 'competency' in teaching is examined as a factor in the continuum of professional development. They then take the argument on to evaluate Elliott's 'practical science' model which has its roots in action research.

In Chapter 3 John Elliott provides his own contribution to the professionalism debate. He begins by examining the government's 'market model', and argues that it shifts the debate from educational to fiscal realms, and is thus a diversionary tactic. Indeed, of the latest White Paper, he concludes that its mission is 'to further the construction of an elaborately stratified social market as a basis for cutting public expenditure through the selective and unequal distribution of resources'. Elliott then goes on to propose a view of the teacher-as-researcher and of action research in classrooms and schools which uses these insights and techniques to reflect critically on government-imposed innovation itself and to bring 'parents, employers and others into the discourse about what education means in a democratic society'.

Elliott's contribution bridges the gap between concepts of professionalism and the process of professional development. The next four chapters deal with issues largely in the context of initial teacher training. David Bridges overviews some recent changes which have led to increased institutional responsibility for, and involvement in, training. He is concerned to explore the role of classroom teachers as trainers and some reservations about how this might work in practice. The place of experiential learning in teacher training is discussed. He draws up an agenda of characteristics of effective components of training drawn from both traditional practice and the future needs of the profession.

In the next chapter Susan Halliwell scrutinises the concept of creativity in teacher education against a background of reform which seems to present the process of teaching in narrow, mechanistic terms. Mischievously, she contrasts the message of a recruitment advertisement – are you creative enough to be a teacher? – with imposed curricula and centrally controlled education structures. She uses evaluative feedback from students to look at creativity in PGCE courses. There is strong emphasis on the need for students to learn flexibility and responsiveness. Learning teaching is, she argues, about taking risks in a context in which confidence can be built, and in which critical and self-critical approaches can be acquired. But the reader is left to ponder whether school-based training can provide an appropriate context for these criteria to be met.

Les Tickle, who has had long and unique experience of continuing professional development of teachers in their first years of teaching, contributes the next chapter. In it he examines critically the experience of a group of teachers who have followed UEA's B.Phil. (Teaching) degree after completing a probationary year in the profession. Based on the personal reports of individual B.Phil. students, the chapter investigates the processes through which teachers have to go in order to acquire their professional skills. Tickle's work gets inside the minds of his subjects to research and reflect upon professional growth and warns against the assumption that learning a simplistic battery of strategies to be trotted out in a Pavlovian response to classroom events can ever be effective.

From an LEA perspective Mike Ransby contributes the next chapter on the theme of support and training for Newly Qualified Teachers. He describes some innovative practice in Norfolk, and offers a strategy to develop competency profiles based on guidelines from the National Curriculum Council. He reinforces the argument for the continuum of professional development, from initial training to career-end. Bridges' discussion of support for teacher-tutors is amplified in an LEA context.

A slightly different viewpoint on profiling of teachers' professional development is offered by Chris Husbands in the next chapter. He examines two broad approaches to profiling. The first draws extensively on the competency-based approach to teacher education, and Husbands describes and critiques this approach. A second methodology, based on the designation of broad generic areas of performance, is also analysed and criticised. He concludes that, despite the difficulties, profiling does offer a mechanism for the tighter management and assessment of entrants to the profession. But he does put the caveat, too, that profiling is still chimeric, with the debate open for further research and elucidation.

Chapter 9 begins with vignettes describing in-service training in progress, and opens the debate about professionalism in the specific context of in-service work. David Wright casts a quizzical glance at some cherished but uncritical practice in, and attitudes towards, professional development. His thesis is that teachers deserve more respect and better treatment than they have been given recently.

So far, the book has dealt with the continuum of professional training from initial training to established professional. Chapters 10 and 11, by contrast, look at the further training of professionals who have reached a level which might be described as managerial. Chapter 10 reviews the support which can, and should, be given to those people who are charged with supporting teachers in schools. Terry Cook is responsible for the professional development of advisory teachers in Norfolk – who in turn work alongside classroom teachers to develop them. With the roles of LEAs changing and diminishing, Cook explores the problems schools will face in providing training to their own staff, some strategies using advisory teachers, and the ways in which these trainers can themselves be updated and be equipped with role-specific skills. Cook's work arises from his research into advisory teacher induction; and while recognising that this group of trainers may need to adopt new descriptors and a fresh *modus operandi* in a rapidly changing world, he develops a policy for advisory teacher support and a model for their operation.

Chapter 11 turns the spotlight on further education teachers and is the vehicle through which Joni Cunningham describes an innovative approach to training FE managers: never so important as with incorporation operating from April 1993. The scheme, adopted by all five Norfolk colleges as well as by the Adult Education and Youth and Community Services, applied insights from existing schemes and from the School Management Task Force Group reports to FE. The result was an 'on-the-job' training scheme with institutional mentor support, some centrally organised activities and optional accreditation to master's degree level.

Chapter 12 draws together the threads of the argument of the book by seeking that most elusive phenomenon: quality. With millions of pounds and countless person-hours expended annually, how can one assess whether all the professional development effort is producing an effect or whether its intentions are being fulfilled? Trevor Kerry works over some of the issues of quality assurance with reflections drawn from an HMI conference. He examines criteria of effectiveness, motives for evaluations, some kinds of measurement and the potential audiences for evaluation. The responsibility for evaluation placed on individual institutions such as schools in the changing world of education is noted, and its implications explored.

This is a book which will be indispensable to all who have a direct concern to deliver professional development to initial and serving teachers: advisers, inspectors, education officers, HE lecturers, headteachers, education consultants and teachers or trainee teachers themselves. Other audiences are implicit, too: school or college governors who have a duty to ensure effective professional development in their own institutions, government officers, and politicians involved with education both locally and nationally.

Throughout we have tried not only to keep the text readable but also to sustain the nature of its scholarship so that it will be directly useful to those using it as a text in working towards accredited qualifications.

The popular press has tended to present educationalists as a group consumed with a biased and secretive self-interest. We have tried to redress the balance, and to present the issues in a spirit of open enquiry informed by knowledge and experience. In an educational world currently dominated by instant legislation and controlled by those who lack professional training and insight, we would all do well to recall the old Red Indian proverb:

The tribe can slay the Redwood sewn by
Nature in antiquity,
But a man can replace it
Only with the seedling.

This book is by no means a plea for the status quo, but is a plea for a regeneration which is planned and which is informed by the best possible intelligence that can be gathered.

Chapter 2

Keeping teaching professional

Roger Aspland and Geoff Brown

Recognition of a need for a systematic pattern of professional development for teachers throughout their careers is not new. The 1972 James Report, *Teacher Education and Training*, began thus:

> This report describes the reform in the education and training of teachers which we wish to recommend. Its argument for fundamental change is not based upon any false assumption that the present system has, in some total sense, failed or is in imminent danger of doing so . . .
> Nevertheless there is abundant evidence that the system is no longer adequate to its purposes. That inadequacy arises from an over-dependence upon initial training, as distinct from continued education and training . . .
> (DES 1972, p. 1)

Whilst advocating a radical proposal that initial training be reformed towards an all graduate profession (identified as training cycles one and two), the bulk of the James Report was concerned with the need for career-long professional education and training, what it called the 'third cycle'.

> To commit energies and resources to the development of a third cycle . . . would be the quickest, most effective and most economical way of improving the quality of education in schools and colleges, and of raising the standards, morale and status of the teaching profession.
> (p. 72)

The Report was never implemented, and twenty years later there would perhaps be those who would be more willing to opine that the system is failing. There is little doubt of an accelerating pace of change in the needs of teachers, of schools, and of the society which they serve. It is easy to associate these changes with interventions of an ideologically radical government aimed at improving the quality of schooling. But anxieties and calls for change in the education and training of teachers transcend the boundaries of political parties.

The rapid growth of degree courses in initial teacher training and education following the James Report made significant contributions to an upsurge of scholarship in the colleges and university departments, and to intellectual study in the field of Education generally. But patterns of training in classroom practice remained largely unchanged from pre-degree courses, and the theory-to-practice relationship, as in many professions, was a source of growing concern. Lawrence Stenhouse (1975) was the earliest and most influential amongst advocates of an alternative model based on teachers developing professional knowledge and understanding through practical enquiry in classrooms. This work was largely focused on in-service rather than initial training, but by the early 1980s several institutions were exploring innovative forms of initial training in partnership with schools. However, despite the move to an all-graduate entry and the gradual demise of theory-led training, no clear or pervasive model of professional learning established itself across the largely autonomous training institutions.

The James Report also insisted:

> What is needed is firm action ... initiated by government and carried through by all branches of the teaching profession, by institutions of higher education and by the LEAs.

> (DES 1972, p. 1)

The intervening period, particularly the past decade, has seen significant action related to teacher education and training initiated by a government which has systematically established centralised power through legislation over the education system as a whole. Arguably these interventions and restructurings of the system are informed as much by ideological and managerial precepts as they are by concerns for the process of developing and motivating a professional teacher force. Nevertheless, cumulatively they represent and reflect an identifiable model of teaching and teacher professional development. The main purpose of this chapter is to examine the possible impact of this model on professional development.

THE EMERGING PARADIGM

The White Paper *Teaching Quality* (DES 1983) set the scene for change, arguing the need to match teacher appointments with their training. In particular it identified 'the teachers' need for subject expertise if they are to have the confidence and the ability to enthuse pupils and respond to their curiosity in their chosen subject fields' (p. 19). It recognised the need for courses to give 'adequate attention to teaching methods', but advocated a much closer involvement of experienced practising teachers in the conduct of courses. The Council for the Accreditation of Teacher Education (CATE) was established to bring some standardisation to widely varying patterns of initial training (Circular 3/84; DES 1984). Accreditation was, however, dominated by a prescription for the content of courses which did little to clarify a process of professional learning, other than the need to involve people of proven practical expertise. This view of 'expert-led' practical skills training was reinforced by the requirement that 'a sufficient proportion of each training institution's staff should have enjoyed success as teachers in schools, and their school experience should be recent, substantial and relevant'. This became the underlying model set out in detail in the criteria for accreditation laid down in DES Circular 3/84. CATE undoubtedly gave impetus to the demise of theory-led training and resulted in more substantial attention to partnership with schools in the development of professional skill and practical knowledge. A major problem for training institutions seeking to develop a more significant collaborative role for schools in partnership arose from the lack of financial resources. Initiatives were still largely dependent on the goodwill of schools in devoting their time and increasingly strained resources to work with initial training, though many acknowledged that there were reciprocal benefits to the school. Paradoxically, it also led some institutions to constrain innovations, as courses were subject to formal inspection against the criteria, and proposals for change were subject to lengthy bureaucratic scrutiny.

The introduction of the Licensed Teacher Scheme (DES 1989a) encouraged the provision of largely classroom-based skills training. The scheme required that entrants hold adequate, though not necessarily graduate, qualifications in an appropriate subject, and that professional training be developed on-the-job, based on identification of individual learning needs against a model of classroom competence.

Circular 24/89 (DES 1989b) strengthened the powers of the CATE, to include a tighter specification of content related to the National Curriculum and Assessment, and for the first time ventured into a tentative identification of exit criteria. The National Curriculum Council (1991) produced its own similar schedule of exit criteria. At the 1992 North of England Education Conference, the Secretary of State indicated that 'CATE have [sic] suggested that many of the criteria relating to the courses can be recast in the form of competence statements, setting out what employers expect of newly qualified teachers' (Clarke 1992, para. 36), and that he had asked CATE to pursue the development of these competences as an agenda for initial training. He proposed that experienced teachers acting as 'mentors' be charged with providing the 80 per cent of the initial training for student teachers that was now to be based in classrooms, and with primary responsibility for their assessment. This was later reduced to 65 per cent by his successor in Circular 9/92 (DFE June 1992), Annex A of which is dominated by the specification of 'Competences expected of newly qualified teachers'.

It is clear that the Secretary of State's statutory powers to determine the form and nature of initial training are to be exercised to radical effect, and that the link between professional training and Higher Education will be seriously weakened, if not broken.

In parallel with changes in initial training the structure of provision for in-service education and training has been subject to reformulation over the past decade. The Advisory Committee on the Supply and Training of

Teachers Report, *Making Inset Work* (DES 1978), began a significant move away from traditional course-based provision towards an increasingly school-based approach. DES Circular 6/86 (DES 1986) established the LEA Training Grants Scheme (LEATGS), a mix of structural, financial, statutory and accountability imperatives, which replaced the old 'pool' scheme that offered LEAs considerable autonomy in in-service provision. LEATGS redefined the relationship between the DES and LEAs, giving increased power to the centre. As the ability of Local Authorities to raise finance has been progressively restricted under financial 'capping' legislation, the dependence on centrally controlled funds for provision of in-service education through Grant Related In-Service Training (GRIST) and Educational Support Grants (ESGs) has increased. Funding for training provision is increasingly prescribed by centrally determined national priorities, and by the requirement for DES approval of LEA plans on an annually changing basis. Long-term systematic planning for professional development by LEAs has been made more difficult, following the 1988 Education Reform Act (DES 1988), by government pressure to devolve ever higher proportions of their overall education budget direct to individual schools (see various chapters in McBride, 1989). The effect of this shift is an increasing emphasis given to staff development addressing short-term institutional deficit needs within a framework of an annual financial cycle and tight budgetary control. Longer term needs for the professional development of individuals are understandably not accorded highest priority by school managements coping with rapid change, and having scarce resources.

In parallel with these developments in initial and in-service training, the conditions of service and salary structures for teachers have been revised to enhance managerial control of the service. Teachers' contractual obligations have been clarified with a specification of 'directed time', and include provision for compulsory in-service training through five annual professional development days. Following a long and turbulent gestation a formal performance-appraisal system is finally to be introduced from 1992.

The 1980s have seen a cyclical crisis of confidence develop between the profession and the public, in which the government has sought an increasingly interventionist stance towards reform across the educational spectrum. Policies to control and manage the professional training and development of teachers are one part of this wider process. There is no doubt that both initial and in-service training have been galvanised into increasing activity during the past decade, and that these activities are subject to growing public and political scrutiny. The question at issue is whether the substance of these interventions reflects a model of professional development which will be effective in recruiting and retaining a professional, well motivated teacher force, capable of meeting the challenge of providing a quality service, and able to adapt to the accelerating pace of change. Is the professional training and education of teachers moving closer to meeting the aspiration of the 1972 James Report?

Table 2.1 A mechanistic view of the role of the teacher

Issue	Characteristics
View of education	Utilitarian, instrumental, positivist.
Control of system	Centralised bureaucratic regulation, plus social market forces.
Teaching profession	Technical delivery system for prescribed curriculum.
Initial training system	Subject knowledge plus basic classroom skills, minimum competence criteria.
Professional induction	Socialisation plus skills reinforcement. Some protection from overload desirable to consolidate classroom competence.
Professional development	New or additional competences, based on imposed change and identified school development needs.
Career development	Hierarchical differentiation, based on role definition and increased responsibility.
Quality control	Appraisal, performance criteria and quantified outputs.
Motivational system	Individual self-interest, material reward plus compulsion/sanction.

Evidence of the effects of this emerging framework of regulatory, legislative and structural changes can be interpreted as indicating a predominantly mechanistic view of the role of the teacher. The dominant characteristics of this perspective may be summarised as shown in Table 2.1.

This analysis of the government's view is confirmed with some clarity in the Secretary of State's address in January 1992. Brought together these characteristics form the web within which the debate about professional development is currently being conducted. It is essentially this ideological framework which is the driving force towards what Elliott (in press) describes as a 'social market' view of teacher education and development.

THE SOCIAL MARKET MODEL

The major characteristic of the 'social market' model of professional learning is that it views appropriately trained teachers as products which may be valued by consumers (in the form of school managers, governors and parents). Such valuing is informed by immediate short-term institutional requirements to meet specific needs, through either appointment or provision of appropriately targeted training. The needs-driven market assumes that required outcomes can be prespecified in performance terms. The logic of this perspective is thus to seek to identify the desired outcomes, and define with increasing precision those practical behaviours which lead to successful outcomes.

Interest in what have come to be termed 'competences' began in the vocational training area of FE in the early 1980s, and received a significant impetus from the establishment of a graduated award system under the

National Council for Vocational Qualifications set up under the Training Agency in 1987. Initially concerned with technical training for employment in commerce and industry, NCVQ soon aspired to explore competency-based approaches to professional training as an extension of the semi-skilled/skilled continuum. This has proved a more difficult area to analyse in behavioural competency terms, probably because of the prevailing view within the professions that the skilful exercise of professional expertise relies *inter alia* upon judgements made in complex contexts which cannot be clearly prespecified. Nevertheless the search to translate higher order professional performance into identifiable competences for purposes of assessment has persisted. As Norris (1991) points out:

> Everybody is talking about competence. It is an El Dorado word with a wealth of meanings and the appropriate connotation for utilitarian times. The language of competency based approaches to education and training is compelling in its common sense and rhetorical force. Words like 'competence' and 'standards' are good words; everybody is for standards and everyone is against incompetence.
>
> (Norris 1991, p. 331)

The 1989 CATE criteria and 1991 NCC document on initial training signalled increasing interest in this direction. The most recent proposals, outlined earlier, place teacher training firmly within the competency model. There is, of course, a strong rational argument for a competency-based framework for training. Teaching undoubtedly requires appropriate knowledge and skill, and training must ensure that these are acquired. Such a model offers clear potential benefits:

- It establishes clearly identifiable goals for the training process for both trainers and students;
- It offers a framework for course design to meet the need for practical classroom skills;
- It offers a framework for performance assessment based on clear (and preferably objective) criteria;
- It emphasises the practical skills nature of teaching;
- By focusing on demonstration of performance competences, it eliminates the need for a fixed training period or programme. Students can proceed to QTS at the pace at which they can demonstrate the necessary classroom competences (as in Licensed Teacher Schemes).

For many years most training institutions have had some form of framework for giving feedback to students and others on classroom performance, usually developed in consultation with schools. However, they vary extensively in format and content, and are rarely adopted without reservation. This illustrates the difficulty of identifying and agreeing suitable competences, and in applying such an approach to teaching.

After surveying the existing situation in a range of initial training courses, Whitty and Willmott (1991, p. 310) were forced to recognise both narrow and more general interpretations:

> Competence characterised as an ability to perform a task satisfactorily, the task being clearly defined and the criteria of success set out.

and

> Competence ... encompassing intellectual, cognitive, and attitudinal dimensions as well as performance; in this model neither competences nor the criteria of achievement are so readily susceptible to sharp and discrete identification.

The distinction between these two competing views goes to the heart of the issue of the nature of professional action and development, and to the implications for future developments in the professional development of teachers. The second, more general view of competence recognises the significance of understanding and judgement in the performance of classroom teaching. But the logic of the social market model leans towards the narrow definition of performance competences with a concern for behavioural outcomes. Knowledge requirements for teachers are largely identified with the necessary 'subject' knowledge required by the curriculum. Within this model professional development involves simply acquiring additional or perhaps more complex competences or 'new' knowledge. More importantly, it ignores the role of experience in the development of the situational knowledge and value base which inform intelligent professional judgement. It is an essentially narrow instrumental view of teaching performance, advocacy of which may be a classic case of sacrificing validity for the reliability of a simplistic model. It is this lack of valid representation of skilled performance which underlies the rejection of the competency-based model by many professionals.

It is not insignificant that the competency debate is being conducted with greatest urgency over initial teacher training and QTS rather than INSET. There are obvious reasons why this should be the case:

- The development of the 'competency movement' is tied to assessment and certification through NCVQ;
- Initial Teacher Education is the only compulsory period of training which is formally assessed;
- There is a need to ensure minimal practical competence for new entrants to the profession;
- It can be argued that some aspects of basic teaching performance can be reduced to behavioural task analysis (for example, using an overhead projector or administering a standardised reading assessment);
- There is a need to match initial training with first appointment and induction;

- Initial training programmes are currently the one area of teacher education and training over which absolute statutory control is possible.

These characteristics also provide the strongest support for the more precise and narrowly defined view of competency. Whilst initial training may provide the immediate forum for the debate about the nature of professional competence, the outcome of that debate may have far-reaching impact. If a narrow view of professional competence becomes established for initial training, it may rapidly permeate the professional socialisation and culture through appraisal and performance-led in-service training.

THE IMPACT OF THE MODEL

The aspiration of the competency-based 'social market' model is for improved standards, to be achieved through improving the quality of teaching. We must therefore ask what impact this model might have on 'raising the standards, morale and status of the teaching profession' (DES 1972), for the two must surely be related.

The quality of teaching

The history of the 'competency movement' derives from a craft skill definition of performance. Critics of the competency model normally focus on its inadequacies in reflecting the cognitive nature of professional activity (see Norris, 1991). They point to the unstable and unpredictable nature of social situations such as classrooms, and the inadequacy of mechanistic routines or behavioural recipes in handling the complex dynamics of interpersonal action. Expert response to such situations depends largely on actions based not on formally trained skills but on the exercise of intelligence, reflection and deliberative judgement developed through experience. The emphasis on defined output competences need pay little heed to how they are acquired, save that some processes may be more economic than others.

Behavioural competences are derived from task analysis of successful performers. They are predicated on an 'expert' model which prescribes how the task should be performed. Whilst not defined with the kind of analytic precision espoused by current advocates of competency, the shortcomings of such expert-led emulative training have been well exposed in the history of teacher education. The underlying assumption is of an identifiable 'correct way' to act, which takes little account of the variables in the situation, or of the strengths, weaknesses, or personal needs and goals of the performers. Neither does the model address seriously the complex question of transfer of skill from one context to another. Each classroom situation is unique, and there is an obvious danger of maladaptive behaviour if the salient features of one set of circumstances are deemed, because of their reappearance, to be equally salient in another situation. Yet rigid competency-based systems offer little by way of insight into adaptive response, precisely because they fail to examine the knowledge or value basis upon which the prescription is formulated. The endemic difficulty of this approach is that the 'right way' all too frequently is exposed as inappropriate or inadequate to deal with the realities of the classroom. The teacher is therefore required to behave in a particular way which does not work, but with no training in developing intelligent alternatives.

If teachers are not expected to develop their own adaptive behaviour to meet situational realities there is a danger of a form of 'learned helplessness' in which they become dependent on external expertise, rather than their own capabilities to solve problems. Evidence of such dependency is not uncommon in current forms of initial training as student teachers are faced with tasks which are beyond their knowledge and experience. This is an understandable and natural response. There is evidence that even experienced teachers, particularly when faced with the current plethora of changes, may respond in this way when confronted with situations for which they are ill-prepared. Teachers frequently feel deskilled when their established practices are rendered redundant. Yet improving the quality of teaching implies changes in what teachers do in classrooms. There is therefore a danger of implementing a model of training and development which fosters dependency by failing to recognise the centrality of teachers as independent learners. When the learning of practical skills focuses on acquiring behaviours, rather than on cognitive processes, deskilling becomes endemic in the context of change.

Morale, motivation and professional status

One of the most significant shifts under the 1988 Education Reform Act has been to relocate control of curriculum and assessment firmly at the centre. By doing so, the government has placed itself in the position of determining the value base of the education system, establishing goals according to its ideological position. It has set about ensuring that these goals are attained by creating regulatory and monitoring bodies, and by establishing procedures for enforcement. The effect of these systemic changes has been to control from the top what teachers do. It is a classical bureaucratic managerial response to crisis.

Such 'bureaucratic managerialism' is primarily concerned with goal achievement as determined by the dominant power group at the 'top' of the system. Morale, motivation and professional status, on the other hand, are human experiences and perceptions of groups and individuals operating 'lower down' the system. Such bureaucratisation also inclines towards a particular managerial view of employees. McGregor (1960) identified two contrasting sets of assumptions which might inform the actions of managers. These he termed Theory X and Theory Y perspectives (Table 2.2).

McGregor argues that managers will tend towards one or other of these

Table 2.2 Assumptions which might inform the actions of managers

Theory X	Theory Y
1 Most people inherently dislike work and will avoid it if possible.	1 Work can be a source of stimulation and satisfaction.
2 People must be directed, closely supervised, and monitored in their adherence to organisational goals.	2 People will exercise initiative and self-direction if they are committed to the goals of the enterprise.
3 Effort is related to the material reward system, backed up by coercion.	3 Material rewards are only one of several factors influencing effort.
4 The average worker will avoid responsibility and seek formal direction from superiors.	4 Under favourable conditions most people will willingly seek additional responsibility.
5 Most workers value security above ambition or autonomy.	5 People value the opportunity to make decisions, and to operate independently.

Source: McGregor (1960).

views. This formulation was drawn largely from experience in commerce and production industry, but has considerable resonance with the current situation in education. In attempting to trace some consistency in managerial developments in the education system there is ample evidence which might be interpreted as a disposition towards a Theory X perspective on the part of both the government and some of the Teacher Unions. Much of the current demoralisation of the teaching profession might not simply be a response to the scale or pace of change which is being imposed on the system, as is most frequently argued. It may be more related to the implicit messages about management's perceptions of the teaching force that are embodied in the way in which these changes are being managed. It is well recognised that employees (in this case teachers) come to behave in ways which reflect the expectations of them as demonstrated in management actions. If there is substance in the Theory X analysis, then in broad terms we might expect an increase in the unwillingness of some teachers to take initiative or seek responsibility (e.g. headships), an increasing dependence on directive management, and continued pressure for greater material rewards.

McGregor's model represented one of the early steps in the development over the past three or four decades of 'Human Resources' thinking about organisational management. The main thrust of this movement has been to attempt to shift management perception and action towards a Theory Y view. The focus of managing human resources centres therefore on concern for ways in which people's commitment, energy, intelligence and initiative might be channelled towards the goals of organisations. It is difficult in general terms to see how a system of professional training, predicated on a craft skill model, will raise the morale of the profession or engage the aspirations or commitment of an all-graduate workforce.

Just as raising the quality of the educational service is ultimately dependent on influencing the performance of individual teachers in the classroom, so raising the commitment of the profession as a whole depends upon the motivation of the individual. The effect of an 'exit competency' emphasis is to give rise to a 'minimal competency model' of the trained teacher. That is, a sufficiency of skill for effective classroom practice can be achieved; a deficit view. The notions of 'reflective practice' and 'experiential learning', on the other hand, invoke a model that sees the skills of the practitioner as amenable to infinite development. This has much in common with Maslow's 'abundance motivation', and his hypothesis of the process of self-actualisation (Maslow 1970).

Herzberg (1976) used similar ideas when studying the motivational patterns of large samples of professional workers. He concluded that a number of work-related features produced dissatisfaction, but that these were separate from, and could co-exist with, factors which people found positively motivating. The task of management, he suggested, was to eliminate the former, which related to the work environment, line management practices, confused policies, conditions of service, and so on, and to enhance and develop the latter. It is reasonable to suppose that clearer policies, such as the National Curriculum, clarification of teachers' Conditions of Service, better salaries, and a higher priority for management training, will make positive contributions to ameliorating the discontent and demoralisation of many teachers. However, there are other positively motivating factors identified by Herzberg which relate to the nature of the work itself, and these function independently of the work environment. They include a sense of achievement and personal and professional fulfilment, a feeling of doing a valued and worthwhile job, and opportunities for autonomy and responsibility. The vivid and sensitive description offered by Lortie (1975), of the intrinsic and extrinsic rewards of teaching based on teachers' own accounts of their experiences, well illustrates this complex and varied pattern of motivation amongst teachers.

Under devolved management school managers have been given substantial new powers over their budgets and policies. The upsurge of management training for senior and middle-management staff in schools and colleges rightly reflects the need for new knowledge and skills in discharging these responsibilities. It also emphasises the need to develop structures and processes which will encourage and harness the motivation of individuals, departments and institutions. Characteristically such training focuses on developing suitable roles, responsibilities and relationships which relate to job-satisfaction and enrichment for teachers. But teaching is also a value-laden activity in which a sense of what is desirable is reflected in the decisions and actions which teachers take. A sense of achievement or fulfilment requires that the task is consonant with the personal and professional values which the individual brings to the task. This area of accommodation between nomothetic institutional values, and the idiographic value-base of the individual represents a major challenge for managers. Failure to secure this *rapprochement* risks demotivation and conflict. 'Quality' like 'competence' is a 'good' word to which those with a stake in the education system must aspire. But quality is an amorphous concept capable of multiple interpretation. The assumption or imposition of a unitary interpretation may place considerable strain on attempts to manage individual schools.

Perhaps the greatest danger of the positivist orientation on management thinking lies in its assumption that people are motivated only by self-interest (Habermas 1971). The argument denies the possibility that people might act from humanistic or altruistic motives, let alone issues of principle. In such a view individual beliefs and values, if subjected to deeper analysis, will be interpreted simply as reflections of the individual's affective structure and emotive dispositions (Hodgkinson 1983). Teachers can thus be caused to teach those things, and in those ways for which they are materially rewarded by the 'system'. Questions of value, of what is desirable, become the exclusive province of policy makers. They are assumed to be either non-problematic and consensual, or subject to control by the politically powerful. Evidence of the imposition of an ideological value-base is overwhelming in the current proposals for reforms in teacher education, and in the systematic campaign to discredit or excise dissenters from the system; not only the 'educational establishment' in LEAs and HE institutions, but also civil servants and members of quangos such as NCC, SEAC and CATE, who seek alternative or more pluralist resolutions.

Whilst the above argument may appeal largely to a philosophical level of debate, on a practical level it translates into two issues for emerging patterns of professional training and development. The first of these is whether an exploration of the relationship between practical classroom action and the goals or values which inform practical judgement is to have any place in the initial or in-service training of teachers. The second is the extent to which assumptions about a unitary value-base are justifiable, and whether they are in harmony with the needs of individual teachers.

The definition of what constitutes 'quality' in terms of teacher performance in secondary schools is illustrated in the proposals for identifying 'training schools' which are to be accredited as being 'of the right quality'.

> It is my intention to move as soon as possible towards the use of performance indicators for the choice of partner (training) schools – such as academic results, staying-on rates, and the destination of pupils in terms of employment, Further and Higher Education.
>
> (Clarke 1992, para. 32)

Leaving aside questions of whether the currently dominant rhetoric of quality and value is the most appropriate for meeting the needs of the whole population of pupils and students, the intention that new teachers should be trained and socialised in contexts of a particular value orthodoxy is clear. If one subscribes to the positivist view that individual values are not a significant influence on behaviour and motivation, then there is no problem. All that is needed to secure the commitment of teachers is better salaries and conditions, and a clear and differentiated ladder of career advancement. If, however, there is substance to the humanistic view that individuals are motivated by a complex of needs, wishes, beliefs and values, the likely effects are unpredictable. We do not know whether such a system will have the power to attract, motivate and retain the commitment of the majority of an intelligent and thinking workforce, but the evidence of young graduates withdrawing from the profession and of the early retirement of experienced teachers are not optimistic signals.

DELIVERING PROFESSIONAL DEVELOPMENT

Reforms of the education system during the 1980s, aimed politically at both a social and educational agenda, created sweeping changes to curriculum policy and the manner in which the system was structured and managed. Local education authorities became caught between increased centralisation by statutory and financial control on the one hand, and devolution of management to individual schools on the other. Support services, including those concerned with professional development of teachers, are being re-formulated on a market-led basis. The established infrastructure for initial and in-service training provided by higher education and LEA advisory services is shifting, and new forms of provision are emerging. This reform, whilst an obvious threat to established practice, offers new opportunities to remodel provisions for professional development. If those opportunities are to be seized, change must be on the basis of a realistic and sensitive analysis of what constitutes professional development.

The signal message of the 1972 James Report was the recognition of a need for systematic career-long support for a teaching force faced with continuous change. This was, and still is, a challenging proposition. Teachers who enter the profession in the early 1990s may still be teaching in 2030, though that may not be as common as hitherto, with career shifts replacing the traditional expectation of a career for life (Handy 1989). Hence provision must be made not only for the development of those within the profession, but also for increasing numbers of new entrants who will bring with them a variety of different experiences and new skills.

Notwithstanding this changing pattern of recruitment, the progress of the life-long career teacher is not characterised by steady, cumulative growth, any more than that of those in other professions. Steady, systematic development is the stuff of textbooks, normative patterns derived from analysis of cohorts of cases. For the individual teacher, career development is punctuated by externally devised curriculum changes, the impact of new technologies, changing responsibilities and variations in personal circumstances.

As we have argued, the basic 'competency' model of professional learning addresses discontinuities in career progress in terms of a need to acquire those new or additional skills which have been deemed necessary. It would be perverse to deny that such requirements exist, but pertinent to enquire whether they alone constitute adequate provision. We believe that this deficit model is inefficient, and that assurances about minimal competence do less than justice to the sophisticated judgements required of advancing professionals working in complex situations. The point at issue is whether the demands of a professional career can, at any time, be defined in terms of narrow, prescribed behaviourally construed skills. We suggest that it cannot. It allows for no appeal to progress from 'adequate' to 'expert' performance. Yet developing the capacity to optimise learning from experience is of central concern for professional development. It is within this context that the ideas of 'teacher as researcher' (Stenhouse 1975), 'action research' (Carr and Kemmis 1986), 'the reflective practitioner' (Schön 1983) and experiential learning (Kolb 1984) have been developed. They are notions with currency across the professions, reflecting widespread concern for a means of fostering adaptive and high quality professional performance.

Elliott (in press) develops the idea of a 'practical science' model of learning based on practical experience, suggesting stages of development which mark the transition from novice to expert. The principle underlying this process of change is that of 'situational understanding' which 'implies that practice is grounded in interpretations of particular situations as a whole, and cannot be improved without improving these interpretations' (Chapter 3).

Elliott argues that it is the capacity to recognise the components of the situation, and their relative salience, which should be the goal of professional education, and that analyses of real-life professional experience might be the means for its attainment.

This view of professional performance, embodied in the 'practical science' model, propounds a view of teaching as practical action informed by knowledge and judgement. It is not inconsistent with the development of identified competences, but the nature of those competences relate to the development of perception, analysis, understanding and judgement as a basis for action, rather than simply to the behaviour itself.

We believe that an outcome of employing such a model would be a form of professional training with greater potential for growth and self-determination than that offered by a competence model. It would be disingenuous to suggest that its adoption would eliminate the feelings of dependency and deskilling which many experience when faced with necessary change, but in so far as such training as we envisage would aim to produce adaptive behaviour with which to address practical problems, we believe it would have a better chance of success. In many respects Elliott's model builds upon ideas of 'action research' which are already current in much in-service provision (see Somekh 1989). What is new is the suggestion of a pattern of phases of development from novice to expert.

It may well be found that the different demands made upon the novice and the expert require different combinations of narrowly defined behavioural competences and 'practical science' activities. Stenhouse anticipated this possibility in respect of training based on action research:

> the business of educational methods [in initial training] is to distil the best from the tradition and interpret it to students. The study of methods should produce, in the first place, intelligent and competent conformists; and it is important that teachers beginning their careers should be capable of intelligent conventional work. One wants a student who can step into a school, take over a class from another teacher, and run it as a going concern.
>
> (Stenhouse 1967, pp. 149–50)

Kenneth Clarke, as Secretary of State, expressed similar views:

> It is vital that the young teacher . . . should have the competence to do his or her job effectively – right from the very first term, because children have no second chance.
>
> (Clarke 1992)

But we would emphasise, as did Stenhouse, that the difference between initial teacher education and in-service training should be in the balance of competences and 'practical science' in the programme. Intelligent behaviour is required at all levels; adherence to a formula, even if such could be identified, will never suffice. The introduction of new curricula and technologies, and career-induced changes in roles and responsibilities, will mean that the balance will need to be addressed, even with experienced teachers. For example, the introduction of a National Curriculum, with all its attendant assessment requirements, clearly demanded that serving teachers access new knowledge and skills. But the 'practical science' model would, we believe, encourage and enable them to take control of and develop that learning process.

CONCLUSION

We have explored briefly some of the recent history of change in the education service in England and Wales, and acknowledged the argument that the profession may have been slow to recognise and respond to the pace and scale of change in the wider social, economic, technological and political environment. The service is now confronted with discontinuous change in which established structures and processes for professional training and development are being dismantled. New patterns of provision need to be developed. It is crucial that such patterns recognise the need for highly motivated professionals capable of self-development and adaptability throughout their careers.

We have presented a view that the 'training' model dependent upon tightly prescribed behavioural competences, which is in the ascendant, reflects an inadequate view of the nature of teaching as intelligent activity; and through its concern for 'minimal competence' does not aspire to, and cannot deliver, a profession committed to the development of quality and excellence. Neither does it respond to the need for adaptable and flexible professional learning. But of equal concern is that this model of professional learning arguably holds the seeds for an increase in demoralisation, deskilling and dependency amongst many teachers.

The model of professional development as 'practical science' that is presented by Elliott offers a way forward which, we believe, is more compatible with the demands placed upon professionals and their practice. It argues for a continuum of learning process through initial training and subsequent professional development which is aimed at encouraging and developing self-initiated, intelligent action.

We can begin to see a much more varied pattern of provision emerging for the support of professional development for teachers. School-based staff development is progressing rapidly, existing patterns of external provision are being redefined, distance-learning and the use of consultants are burgeoning. The increase in professional development activity is matched by greater diversity of provision, much of it driven by a 'social market' pattern of demand. Against this background, the need for a coherent model which can inform and offer some continuity to the professional development of teachers is urgent. The 'practical science' model offers the prospect of meeting both the short-term 'deficit' needs of teachers, and the long-term development needs of the profession. Determining this balance, and creating a coherent model for supporting the professional teacher throughout his or her entire career, is an essential quest upon which those committed to developing the quality of teaching should embark without delay.

REFERENCES

Carr, W. and Kemmis, S. (1986) *Becoming Critical*, Lewes: Falmer.
Clarke, K. (1992) 'Speech delivered to North of England Education Conference', January, London: HMSO.
Department for Education (1992) *Initial Teacher Training* (Secondary Phase), Circular 9/92, London: HMSO.
Department of Education and Science (1972) *Teacher Education and Training* (the James Report), London: HMSO.
DES (1978) *Making Inset Work: a basis for discussion*, ACSTT Report, London: HMSO.
DES (1983) *Teaching Quality*, Cmnd 8836, London: HMSO.
DES (1984) *Initial Teacher Training: Approval of Courses* [established Council for Accreditation of Teacher Education, CATE], Circular 3/84, London: HMSO.
DES (1986) *Circular 6/86*, London: HMSO.
DES (1988) *Education Reform Act*, London: HMSO.
DES (1989a) *The Education (Teachers) Regulations 1989*, Circular 18/89, London: HMSO.

DES (1989b) *Initial Teacher Training: Approval of Courses*, Circular 24/89, London: HMSO.

Elliott, J. (in press) 'Three perspectives on coherence and continuity in teacher education', in J. Elliott (ed.) *Reconstructing Teacher Education*, Lewes: Falmer.

Habermas, J. (1971) *Knowledge and Human Interests*, Boston: Beacon.

Handy, C. (1989) *The Age of Unreason*, London: Hutchinson.

Herzberg, F. (1976) *The Managerial Choice: To be efficient and to be human*, Homewood, Calif.: Dow Jones-Irwin.

Hodgkinson, C. (1983) *The Philosophy of Leadership*, Oxford: Basil Blackwell.

Kolb, D.A. (1984) *Experiential Learning: Experience as the source of learning and development*, Englewood Cliffs, NJ: Prentice Hall.

Lortie, D. (1975) *School Teacher*, Chicago, Ill: University of Chicago Press.

McBride, R. (ed.) (1989) *The In-Service Training of Teachers*, Lewes: Falmer.

McGregor, D. (1960) *The Human Side of Enterprise*, New York: McGraw-Hill.

Maslow, A.H. (1970) *Motivation and Personality*, 2nd edn, New York: Harper & Row.

National Curriculum Council (1991) *The National Curriculum and the Initial Training of Student, Articled and Licensed Teachers*, York: National Curriculum Council.

Norris, N. (1991) 'The trouble with competences', *Cambridge Journal of Education*, 21 (3): 331–41.

Schön, D.A. (1983) *The Reflective Practitioner*, New York: Basic Books and London: Temple Smith.

Somekh, B. (1989) 'Action research and collaborative school development', in R. McBride (ed.) *The In-Service Training of Teachers*, Lewes: Falmer.

Stenhouse, L. (1967) *Culture and Education*, London: Nelson.

Stenhouse, L. (1975) *An Introduction to Curriculum Research and Development*, London: Heinemann.

Whitty, G. and Willmott, E. (1991) 'Competence-based approaches to teacher education', *Cambridge Journal of Education* 21 (3): 309–18.

Chapter 3

Professional development in a land of choice and diversity

The future challenge for action research

John Elliott

THE GOVERNMENT WHITE PAPER AND THE ONWARD MARCH OF THE MARKET METAPHOR

More diversity allows schools to respond more effectively to the needs of the local and national community. The greater their autonomy, the greater the responsiveness of schools. Parents know best the needs of their children – certainly better than educational theorists or administrators, better even than our most excellent teachers. Children themselves, as they grow older and mature, often have a well developed sense of their needs and a good grasp of the quality of the teaching they receive.

(DFE 1992, p. 2, sect. 1.6)

Educational 'theorists' continue to have a bad time in the latest deliberations of the Conservative government. Their future looks very gloomy indeed. But who are they? They are certainly 'baddies' but largely defeated ones. In the White Paper, *Choice and Diversity: a new framework for schools*, they make an occasional appearance as ghosts from the past. We are told that some of them at least were responsible for the 'misguided notion ... that if work is graded some children and parents will think of themselves as failures'. This is not untypical of the ways in which the government represents educational issues. The issue, to my knowledge, was about the standards against which pupils' work was best assessed – whether such assessments ought to be norm, criterion, or pupil referenced – not about whether it should be assessed at all. But the whole tone of the White Paper dismisses such issues as unreal and beyond the world of common sense the government claims to inhabit. Assessment information will be given to parents 'in a straightforward and simple way – characteristic of an open society – rather than in jargon-laden, inward-looking and technical language suitable only for the professional'.

The 'theorist' appears as a source for the mystifying language employed by professional educators, whether they be teachers or LEA administrators and inspectors. The marginalisation of 'the theorist' is part and parcel of the government's mission to demystify and deprofessionalise education and open it up as an intelligible object of parental choice. Teachers are no longer presented as under the dominion of theorists, thanks to the sweeping reforms inaugurated through the 1988 Act. Most teachers are now portrayed as existing in a state of 'blessed excellence'. With respect to pupils needing to be told when they are doing badly, 'most of our excellent teachers recognise this'. Moreover, the principles underpinning the National Curriculum are no longer a matter for debate.

> What was hotly contested in the mid 1980s is now widely accepted. Debate is no longer about the principle of a national curriculum but about the detail. It is about how subjects should be developed within the National Curriculum and about the crucial testing arrangements associated with them: it is not about whether subjects should form part of the National Curriculum ... The government will keep the curriculum under review and ... will consult widely about the case for further refinements if necessary.
>
> (DFE 1992, p. 3, sect. 1.12)

From this point of view the remaining issues are largely technical in character, about means rather than ends, and their resolution will require no more than fine tuning here and there. There is little room for the educational theorist in this scenario because there is little room for the idea of the professional educator as someone possessing a body of knowledge about 'the ends' of education. The price of teachers' emancipation from the influence of theorists is their 'deprofessionalisation' into operatives of a state-designed technology which is shaped as a national curriculum and assessment system. One of the few remaining contaminating influences appears to be that of the LEAs and their inspectors who continue to refuse to make a distinction between 'inspection' and 'advice'. The White Paper, armed with the Audit Commission's 1989 Report, castigates inspectors who 'tell schools what to do and then check up to see if they were doing it' (p. 3), and states that it could not allow such a state of affairs – inspectors who feel that they know what education is about – to continue. In this way the new proposals for 'independent inspections' is justified: 'all schools will be subject to regular and rigorous inspection under the watchful eye of the new and powerful Chief Inspector of Schools' (p. 3, sect. 1.14).

No mention is made of the radical reductions that the government has made in the numbers of HMI, and of the details of the new 'privatised' inspection arrangements. The national inspectorate also need, like teachers, to be given a boost in morale at a time when their direct involvement in inspection has in effect been very much lessened. Their diminished role is rationalised in terms of a need to speed up the number and frequency of school inspections in order to provide parents with the comparative data they will need as a basis for choice.

The immediate task for it [the new inspectorate] . . . is to complete for the first time ever a Domesday Book-like survey of the quality and achievements of all of England's schools, and to do so within four years. Six thousand schools a year will be examined . . . Under the Parents' Charter, parents have the right to expect such information . . . At the prevailing rate of inspection by Her Majesty's Inspectorate of Schools before the changes introduced in the Education (Schools) Act 1992, it would have taken some sixty years to cover every secondary school in England, and two hundred years to inspect each of our twenty thousand primary schools.

(DFE 1992, p. 8, sect. 1.37)

Exactly what sort of data the new inspection teams will gather is not specified in detail. But it is clear that it will relate to school ethos and management variables which are believed to explain differences in school performance as this is measured by indicators such as 'test results' and 'attendance rates'. A good ethos is associated with the capacity to transmit a 'strong moral code' – 'a clear vision of those things they and the community hold to be important' – and with strong leadership on the part of the headteachers, which means 'articulating a clear academic mission for the school, setting standards and creating a recognisable ethos'. What all this basically adds up to is that 'the good school' is one which effectively exercises coercive power over the conduct of its pupils. It is an efficient instrument of containment and control as measured by 'attendance rates' and 'test results' respectively. It is not an institution in which teachers reflect about both the ends and means of education jointly, because the ends are fixed and given by the state and separated from decisions about means. In this context ends are construed as measurable performances rather than human qualities, and means as instruments of production rather than ethical processes which enable such qualities to develop. By construing educational 'ends' as consumable commodities the government aims to transform the educational process into a control technology and thereby 'liberate' teachers from any imperative to ground their practices in educational theory.

The commodification of education not only 'liberates' teachers from educational theory. It also 'liberates' citizens from any need they may feel to participate in theoretical discourse about education. The Education Reform Act (DES 1988) bestows no such rights of participation on parents or any other citizen. They cannot choose a school on the grounds that it articulates a particular vision of education and demonstrates its ability to realise this vision in practice. Parents cannot choose to have their children's schooling grounded in a particular philosophy of education. The grounds of their choice are restricted to considerations of a school's instrumental effectiveness as a production system. Government policy disenfranchises not only teachers but also parents from participating in a discourse about the aims and processes of education. Such is the price of its 'demystification' policies. As Ball (1992) has recently pointed out:

> The market setting and the instrumentality it fosters produce a version of that confusion of relations between people that Marx called 'commodity fetishism'. A confusion of social relationships with exchange relationships that is basic to the ideological thrust of Thatcherism and the hegemony of 'consumer' politics.

In the market setting parents are viewed not so much as partners in the common task of educating children, with all the 'collaboration', 'dialogue' and 'reciprocity' this entails, but as distanced from each other by a form of one-way accountability which characterises relations between 'producers' and 'consumers'. The government's preference for parental choice as opposed to participation may have little to do with democratising and demystifying education in a free and open society as the White Paper asserts. The construct of 'choice' may simply provide an ideological peg on which to legitimate 'cutting costs'. In other words, 'choice' operates as a basis for rationalising the allocation of funds and getting rid of surplus places.

'Choice' does wonders to shift the concerns of headteachers away from educational issues. Ball richly documents the extent to which many headteachers feel that their role of educational leadership is rapidly becoming subordinated to fiscal control and marketing functions. He points out that the new relations of 'production' and 'consumption' between teachers and parents leave little room for the idea of professional leadership. When head-teachers transform themselves from leaders to managers in a social market dominated by the government's construct of 'choice', they 'distance' themselves from the professional concerns of their staff. School management is 'driven by context, by the realities of per capita funding, "rate-capping" ... and it relates closely to ... entrepreneurial management ... the market is to the fore, image, hype and PR'. Such are the consequences of 'reform' for the organisational culture of schooling.

The strong headteacher responsible for school ethos, envisaged in the White Paper, must not be confused with the educational visionary who has formerly served as a role model of professional leadership in schools. The White Paper lays emphasis on school attendance, discipline, and the inculcation of a strong moral code, which can all be viewed as dimensions of a marketing rather than an educational ethos. The White Paper gives this away through a significant 'Freudian slip', in which it unthinkingly dissociates ethos from the quality of teaching and learning.

> There is little point in having good, regularly inspected schools, first rate teachers and the National Curriculum well taught and assessed, if all of our children do not attend school, remain there and learn throughout the whole of the school day.

(DFE 1992, p. 5, sect. 1.22)

The autonomous, self-governing schools depicted in the White Paper may give headteachers new 'managerial' powers but not with respect to educational decision-making. The government disenfranchises headteachers, as well as teachers, inspectors, educational theorists and parents, from participating in the determination of educational ends and the means appropriate to them. Power to determine ends, albeit in an ideologically distorted form which translates them into performance indicators and disconnects them from any consideration of educational processes, is reserved exclusively for the Secretary of State and sanctioned by legislation. The government's reforms defy the old contrast between centralised and decentralised educational systems (see Elliott 1992a). The reconstruction of the system in the ideological clothing of the market empowers the State to 'steer it at a distance' (Ball 1992) through its control of performance targets and indicators and the structural mechanisms governing its assessment and monitoring of performance. The proposal outlined in the White Paper to merge the National Curriculum Council (NCC) with the Schools Examinations and Assessment Council (SEAC) is a further enhancement of this steering by remote control. The tensions between the two bodies are well known. The former, charged with implementing the National Curriculum, has revealed a tendency to accommodate the values of professional educators and has reinterpreted it accordingly, while the decisions of SEAC in the sphere of national assessment have aroused hostility amongst professionals precisely because they appeared to lack an 'educational dimension'. The proposed restructuring will ensure that the curriculum experiences of pupils are shaped by the performance measures specified by the State rather than the qualitative indicators of professional educators (see Elliott in press).

The use of the market metaphor in education implies a divorce between power and responsibility. What gets decentralised is not power but responsibility for making the system work and accountability for anything which goes wrong. Several educational researchers (e.g. Ball 1992, Elliott 1992a) have suggested that the government's reforms are a device for dissociating power from responsibility in the educational system. Power over performance in the system accrues to the Secretary of State while accountability for it accrues to the schools and teachers who work in them. Power is centralised but responsibility and accountability decentralised. What gets devolved to the schools is punishment and blame for deficiencies in performance. The White Paper's talk about school autonomy (one of its 'Five Great Themes') may simply be a smoke screen to mask the totalitarian enterprise of divorcing the power of the state from responsibility for what happens to children in schools. Ball suggests that 'once the rhetoric of devolution is accepted then it becomes possible to blame the schools for the faults and difficulties inherent in or created by the policies'. At best, he argues, the only substance that can be given to the government's rhetoric of school autonomy is a certain financial flexibility which they gain through LMS and to a greater extent by opting out of LEA control altogether. Certainly the school autonomy envisaged by the White Paper cannot be linked to the idea of corporate professional autonomy for the staff of schools.

The major thrust of the White Paper is to establish further structural conditions which will encourage more schools and their governors and parents to opt out of local government control by seeking grant-maintained status. As yet only about 300 have done so. By appealing to a need for enhancing 'greater diversity' within the system as a basis for parental choice, the Secretary of State may simply be trying to legitimate proposals which further advance the totalising power of the state in education to the detriment of LEAs and local democracy. These proposals include the creation of such structural conditions as:

- Establishing a National Funding Agency for GMS which will share responsibility for school admissions with LEAs once more than 10 per cent of pupils are in opted-out schools;
- Accelerating the process of applying for GMS, making it easier to achieve, and allowing (a) clusters of primary schools with or without a linked secondary school, and (b) voluntary schools to apply;
- Giving the Secretary of State the power to dismiss Governors in GMS schools;
- Enabling schools to specialise in certain subjects rather than others, particularly in the areas of technology, business studies, and languages, while at the same time maintaining conformity to broad national curriculum requirements; whether entry will be based on academic selection criteria will be for the school governors to determine, but the White Paper is keen to point out that access should be parent rather than selection-driven although its rhetoric of 'school autonomy' enables it to leave the door ajar for an increase in selective schooling – in other words, it is highly ambiguous about its position;
- Establishing Education Associations, or 'Hit Squads' (as *The Times*, 29 July 1992, described them), to take over and sort out low-performing LEA schools. After this has been accomplished the 'normal expectation is that the school will then become grant-maintained'.

The leader in *The Times* on these proposals was headed 'State Knows Best' and comments:

This is one of the most dramatic extensions of Whitehall power since the war. This is no free market in education. The White Paper is filled with new powers to be conferred on the funding agency and other quangos, whose officials will fill office blocks the length and breadth of the land . . . This is a devastating vote of no confidence in local democracy.

(*The Times*, 29 July 1992)

Even that great advocate of the 'free market' in education, Stuart Sexton, is concerned by what he perceives as certain 'worrying bits of centralisation creeping in'. He exhorts the Secretary of State not to contaminate the market with them:

> Yes, a funding agency to distribute the cheques and, yes, give them the authority to place the child that no school really wants, but no to controlling admissions generally, no to deciding which GM schools should expand and by how much, no to deciding which schools are surplus. That would be central control all over again . . . Come on, Patten, having set up a market system, leave it to the market. GM schools will expand in response to parental demand, will decline in response to lack of it, will specialise where parents want it.
>
> Specialisation and selection will come, not because Patten says so but because once you remove the political imposition of comprehensive schools, the market will dictate a diversity of schools to meet a diversity of needs. The White Paper is ambiguous on this point.
>
> (Sexton 1992)

Commentators on the government reforms are increasingly unmasking the massive transference of power to the State which accompanies each wave of government 'reform' under the cover of a free market rhetoric. The market metaphor is becoming increasingly over-stretched as a legitimation device and no longer functions as the perfect disguise for the construction of totalising power. This is evidenced in the White Paper's attempt to legitimate helping schools to achieve GMS in terms of a rhetoric about enhancing 'diversity' as a basis for choice. The options appear to be extremely loaded in favour of GMS and it is not hard for the reader to discern that the primary intention underpinning the proposals is to enhance the power of the Secretary of State to construct an educational system which rationalises reductions in public expenditure. This implies a 'stratified' as opposed to a 'diversified' system of schooling (see Pring 1989, pp. 65–6). Parental 'choice' constitutes a politically constructed mechanism for achieving such stratification; shaped and constrained as it is by the economic imperatives of the State.

Diversification as a basis for genuine choice implies a variety of options that people are equally free to choose between. Stratification implies an absence of equal freedom in two senses. First, the incentives for choice are politically loaded in favour of some 'options' rather than others, so that the 'consumer' feels that he or she has no option but to 'choose' A rather than B. Second, if the stratified system is to be maintained, some people have to be denied their preference in favour of others. Within a highly stratified system 'choice' is neither free nor equal. A totally free and unconstrained educational market characterised by a variety of open options is no basis for rationalising reductions in public expenditure.

Sexton is surely right to feel that the White Paper shows signs of betraying the principle of the free market when it gives the proposed funding agency for

GM schools the functions of controlling admissions, deciding which schools should expand and by how much, and which schools are surplus to capacity. What he fails to appreciate is that the whole mission of the White Paper is to further the construction of an elaborately stratified social market as a basis for cutting public expenditure through the selective and unequal distribution of resources. The centralised elements Sexton finds objectionable in the White Paper, and this includes encouraging specialisation in GM schools through industrial sponsorship, are all ways of rationalising the selective and unequal distribution of resources by the State. Sexton fails to understand the difference between the ethical and ideological uses of the market metaphor. Where he uses it to articulate his vision of schooling in an open and free society, his political 'friends' use it to legitimate a new form of totalitarian intent, in which the intention is hidden from view by distancing its source from the social mechanisms through which it is enacted.

Such are the problems of using an essentially economic metaphor to articulate a vision of social relations. It lends itself to this kind of ideological distortion by casting citizens in the passive role of consumers, and their relations with public institutions as matters of production and consumption. As consumers, people are acquisitive and possessive individuals whose wants and desires are defined in terms of things which exist in their external environment but are produced independently of their own agency. The 'needs' of consumers are the things they want and desire but do not have or possess. Since they can be expected to know what things they want or desire they are usually aware of their 'needs' as consumers. And it is this awareness that provides legitimation for the idea of consumer-driven markets which are responsive to consumers choosing 'goods' in the light of their needs. However, the idea of the economic free market ignores an important dimension of relations between production and consumption. Producers cannot only respond to markets. They can also create them. They manufacture not only products but also the desire to have and possess them, through image-creation and 'public relations'. The idea of a free economic market is largely a myth to hide from consumers the extent to which their needs are not so much the products of the soul as the products of power operating in the soul.

Viewing people as consumers can be contrasted with viewing them as active citizens capable of changing and transforming the public institutions which govern and regulate their lives through the development of their powers and capacities as human agents (see Giddens 1984, Elliott 1992b). In this context what people value, want and desire are not things produced beyond the sphere of their agency to be passively acquired and possessed, even in response to consumer demand and choice. They are qualities of living which are defined and realised through their active participation with others in shaping the institutions of society.

The use of the market metaphor to structure people's relationships to their social institutions totalises their identities as consumers and denies them opportunities to develop those human powers and capacities which are central features of human agency. By confusing the 'citizen' with the 'consumer' the metaphor ideologically legitimates the covert operation of State power on the souls of the citizenry, i.e. by masking the role of the State in 'manufacturing desire' within the sphere of social relations.

There is a world of difference between parents viewing education as a desirable commodity which they can acquire or possess ('buy') for their children, and viewing it as a process in which they can actively participate in partnership with teachers to realise worthwhile learning experiences for them.

The market metaphor, with its emphasis on relations of production and consumption, distances parents from schools and thereby reinforces the power of the State to define for them what they need and desire from schools. What the metaphor of the free market, extended into the field of schooling, masks is the tendency in advanced capitalist societies for the desires and needs of the citizenry to be shaped by the economic imperatives of the State. The transformation of parents into consumers of education is yet one more indicator of the covert encroachment of state power within the domain of schooling.

THE GOVERNMENT'S REFORMS AND CHANGING CONCEPTIONS OF THE THEORY–PRACTICE RELATION IN HIGHER EDUCATION-BASED TEACHER EDUCATION

Higher education institutions are being shaped by the same 'free market' ideology as schools. There appears to be little future role within those institutions for schools of education as agencies of initial teacher education, of in-service education for serving teachers, or of educational research. What conceivable market could schools of education cater for in these respects within an educational system 'reformed' and 'constructed' in the light of the market metaphor? Control over initial teacher education is being devolved to the schools, and responsibility for student trainers to 'mentors' in them. Even the higher education based 24 per cent is to be 'led' by the staff of schools. This scenario, it seems to me, is the logical culmination of the kind of provision higher education institutions have been forced to make within the framework of the CATE criteria. As Pring (1992) has pointed out:

> These conditions make little mention of theory. They require no philosophical insights. They demand no understanding of how children are motivated; they attach little importance to the social context in which the school functions – unless it be that of local businesses and of the world of work; they attach no significance to historical insight into the present; they have no place for the ethical formation of those who are to embark on this, the most important of all moral undertakings.
>
> (Pring 1992, p. 17)

The source of this rejection of educational theory, Pring argues, is not simply the contemporary political context but also the models of theory generated within academia itself. He traces the similarity between the attack on educational theory conducted by the philosopher D.J. O'Connor in the 1950s and the more recent pronouncements of politically influential 'new right' intellectuals who operate under the banner of the Centre for Policy Studies. The disconnection of means from ends which is implicit in the government reforms is legitimated by the kind of philosophical positivism O'Connor propounded.

> According to O'Connor, theory refers to a set of principles which organise what we observe in a systematic and coherent way, which explain why things happen, and predict what will happen in particular circumstances . . . a clear theoretical account would thus be open to falsification . . . But, according to O'Connor, there simply are not these well-tested theories. Instead we have two sorts of statements – statements about desirable goals to be pursued . . . and statements about the means to achieve these goals. Whereas we can sensibly argue about the latter, we cannot do so about the former . . . Theory, if there is theory, must be confined to method, not to purpose.
>
> (Pring 1992, p. 12)

But, Pring argues, even in the realm of method O'Connor believed that there was no 'respectable theory'; only 'hunches, drawn from many theories arising in psychology and sociology, and these hunches are not so organised as themselves to constitute a theory or prescribe with confidence a practice or be falsifiable in experience'.

> In the light of such criticism the 1960s brought an attempt within colleges and departments of education to achieve academic respectability by grounding educational studies in established university disciplines which appeared to be relevant to education: philosophy, psychology, sociology and history. Leading academics in these fields with a concern for education accepted O'Connor's view of the status of educational studies and, while dismissing it as undifferentiated mush, attempted to provide it with the kinds of theoretical foundations and academic rigour that O'Connor was sceptical about achieving.
>
> (Pring 1992, p.9)

According to Pring, this mission to endow educational studies with academic respectability increased the number of voices raised against its irrelevance to practice.

> Again and again one could see in departments of education how the separation of thought from action, of theory from practice, of thinking from doing, had been institutionalised. A questionable theory of knowledge, according to which we have thoughts and then translate

thoughts into action – we develop theories and then put theories into practice – had become (under the impulse to be respectable) part of the framework within which we prepared students to be teachers and those already teaching to be better teachers.

(Pring 1992, p. 15)

The coming of CATE in England and Wales put an end to the quest for academic respectability in initial teacher education and replaced it with the quest for practical relevance that would be acknowledged in the schools. It put an end to academic careers in the philosophy, psychology, sociology and history of education, at least as far as those involved in initial teacher education were concerned. It left room only for the employment of 'good practitioners', as these were defined by the 'common sense' judgements of experienced practitioners operating in the schools. And, in order to reinforce this subordination of theory to practical common sense, CATE insisted that tutors returned regularly to schools for periods of 'recent and relevant' experience.

According to Pring, the 'relevance' achieved by higher education institutions could take a variety of forms:

It might, for instance, consist in sharing one's own practical expertise with teachers – as a kind of adviser (but employed by the university, not by the local authority) in the practical matter of teaching history or geography or any subject. The university might be seen – indeed with some gratitude by school teachers – as a place to which they can repair for advice on diagnostic tests for slow learners, the most up-to-date textbooks on French grammar, the shrewdest legal advice on how to avoid needlework classes for boys, the most attractive printing of work-cards, or the latest gossip on the machinations of the National Curriculum Council.

(Pring 1992, p. 16)

In other words, they became providers of 'technical services' for schools; repositories of 'techniques' for supporting 'good practice' as this was tacitly defined and understood by teachers.

The 'new right' thinkers who have influenced the shape of government reforms around the Centre for Policy Studies were slow to appreciate the extent to which initial teacher education programmes had become 'decontaminated' from the influence of theory. They attacked 'useless' and 'irrelevant' theory in teacher education well after the attempt to ground it in 'the disciplines of education' had failed. Such an attack was used to justify the removal of teacher education from the higher education sector altogether in order to ensure that practice in schools was shaped by 'market forces' alone. The transfer of teacher education to the schools, however, needed no such justification. If institutions of higher education were merely supplementing the technical resources available to teachers, then more adequate resourcing within schools of the necessary technical expertise would have removed the need for such institutions to exercise this function. It is a logical outcome of the subordination of teacher education to the criterion of 'practical relevance'.

What the 'new right' attack on theory in teacher education seems to have done is to have diverted attention away from the resource issues. It publicly legitimated a transfer of initial training to the schools without raising the question of resources. This is why the 'new right' thinkers have remained 'blind' to the defence of teacher educators that they had already banished 'irrelevant theory' and instituted 'practical relevance' within their courses. Any acknowledgement of such a defence would shift attention to the problem of redistributing resources from the 'training institutions' to the schools. John Patten has somewhat modified Kenneth Clarke's original proposal to transfer 80 per cent of initial teacher education to the schools. It now stands at 66 per cent and the major reason for this is not unrelated to the costs of a total devolvement of training resources to individual schools.

The prospect of schools of education continuing into the future as centres for administering and rationalising the distribution of training resources to schools is not one that higher education institutions will find attractive. It is bound to increase problems at the interface with schools, and the government will tend to delegate the blame to higher education rather than accept responsibility itself. Increasingly one can envisage a scenario in which initial teacher education is administratively co-ordinated and resourced through a higher education system which is able to exert little influence on the formative learning experiences of student teachers, and training processes in schools. Other than a small core of managers, the staff of such 'training centres' are likely to be serving teachers seconded from link schools on short-term, part or full-time contracts. Staff may well be selected on the grounds of their reputations as 'good practitioners' in schools but, as Pring argues, 'There must be more to professional preparation than being "good at practice" '. What that 'more' might be and what higher education's responsibility for it might be, I shall return to a little later.

There is an apparent paradox in the government's policies for initial teacher education. On the one hand it talks about the need to raise standards in schools, while on the other hand it devolves responsibility for initial training to the schools. One solution to this paradox is the proposal to locate students only in 'good schools', as these are defined in terms of such performance indicators as 'good test/exam results' and 'low truancy rates'. However, as some headteachers have been keen to point out, such 'good schools' may have some very weak subject departments, and the so-called 'poor schools' may have some good ones. The overall effect of the government's proposals might well be to locate large numbers of student teachers in privileged school settings, such as private schools and others operating in social environments where the teachers hardly need to teach well in order to secure 'good results'. And this raises the question of whether student teachers will be prepared at all to operate intelligently and effectively in 'less privileged' schools.

However, the government is impatient of such complexities. It rests its faith on market forces to shape good practice. The 'good schools' as measured by the kinds of performance indicators cited in the White Paper – 'results', 'low truancy', 'strong moral ethos', 'strong management' – will be the schools parents want their children to go to. The motivation to succeed in these terms in a highly competitive climate will, according to the government, reinforce those 'common sense practices' which have been so undermined in our secondary schools by progressive methods based on the ideas of left-wing theorists (a myth promoted by Professor Antony O'Hear and accepted by the Prime Minister).

It does not occur to the government that the problem of standards in our schools might be at least partially due to the persistence of well-established, highly routinised and unquestioned 'common sense' approaches which are deeply rooted in the traditional 'craft culture' of teachers. If the problem of 'standards' and indeed of 'non-attendance at school' is linked in any way to the persistence of unquestioned and unreflected upon practices endorsed by the 'craft culture', then the devolvement of initial training to the schools is going to do little to resolve it.

However, there appear to be signs that the government is not simply leaving the question of what constitutes good teaching to the operation of 'market forces'. It is engaged in an attempt to specify minimal performance standards which student teachers will need to satisfy in order to be deemed competent to operate independently in a classroom with children. In other words, the common sense practices into which student teachers will be inducted will need to conform to certain explicit behavioural requirements, organised in the technical language of competences. And here we see the intrusion of a technology of knowledge acquisition and pupil control into the domain of teaching: one which frames – limits, circumscribes and constrains – the repertoire of behaviours on which the student teacher can legitimately draw from the teacher culture. The problem attending this quest for minimal performance standards is that the quest through 'educational' research, to link teacher performance variables causally with pupils' learning outcomes, has been inconclusive. It is therefore likely that 'the standards' will be derived from the common sense practices adopted by teachers operating in those schools which best succeed in 'the market place'. In other words, the source of performance standards is less likely to reside in the domain of educational theory and research than in the domain of the social market. However, the government may well attempt to legitimate such 'standards specifications' or 'competences' through commissioned research. What it could do is to commission a research agency to describe 'good practice' as it operates in schools which score high on the currently fashionable school performance indicators. It can then argue that the behaviours or 'competences' identified are the causes of such high scores. Such inferences may be invalid and the researchers may protest as much, but the deed will have been done for a 'few pieces of silver'. The operations of the social market may after all be the source of competency specifications. If this happens, and certain elements in the common sense practices of teachers become transformed into the functional equivalent of the ten commandments on 'tablets of stone', then the possibility of teachers themselves recreating and reconstructing their practices becomes slighter.

Of course, such explications of teachers' tacit conceptions of 'what works' in successful market orientated schools constitute a kind of 'educational theory'. It is a theory that is, in the words of Carr (1986), 'articulated from within the world of practice'. Carr has argued that it is an approach 'fast gaining acceptance by members of the teaching profession, teacher educators whose allegiance is to a particular subject and many members of HM Inspectorate'. But he fails to acknowledge sufficiently the possibility that the need to articulate the common sense beliefs embedded in 'good practice' stems from a concern to ensure that pedagogy is shaped and driven by the market context of schooling. The logic of market-driven educational theory is, however, well illustrated by Carr when he points out that 'the idea that educational theory can be devised independently of practice and then used to access practice is replaced by the diametrically opposite view that theory must itself be tested and corrected in the light of its practical consequences'. Such an idea, Carr contends, renders the question of what constitutes an educational practice 'a largely uncontentious issue'.

The common sense approach to understanding 'good practice' leaves little room for any discussion about the ends to which the practice is directed. This makes it highly adaptive to a market-driven system of schooling, since what constitutes 'good practice' is simply that repertoire of behaviour teachers use in those schools which succeed in the market-place. Such an approach pre-empts any consideration of educational ends, and discussion of educational values. It offers the possibility of reducing value-complexity in education, and of limiting the pedagogical options open to teachers.

When Pring argues there is more to professional preparation than 'good practice', as this is defined within a framework of common sense judgements, the 'more' refers to being able to teach 'critically, thoughtfully, experimentally, and reflectively'. In other words, the aim of teacher education is the development of teachers as 'reflective practitioners' who are able not only to articulate the beliefs and assumptions which shape their practices, but also to question and test them in the light of evidence and argument and to reconstruct them accordingly.

The 1980s saw the increasing influence of Schön's (1983) model of the professional as a 'reflective practitioner' on higher education based programmes of initial teacher training; in spite of the constraints of CATE. But long before Schön's work crossed the Atlantic, the in-service training of teachers in many higher education institutions had been influenced by a form of educational research which sprang out of the transactions between curriculum theorists in higher education and teachers during the school-based curriculum reforms of the 1960s and 1970s. Stenhouse captured the essence of the emerging paradigm in his idea of 'the teacher as a researcher', developing curriculum in classrooms and schools experimentally and reflectively through self-critiques grounded in systematically gathered evidence about practice.

Stenhouse and his colleagues at CARE in the University of East Anglia transferred this form of educational action research, in which teachers actively participated in the research process, from the context of the national curriculum projects in which they were involved (e.g. The Humanities Project) to in-service education courses operating at Masters degree level. During the 1970s other higher education institutions in England and Wales followed, particularly those whose schools of education had established 'Curriculum Studies' as an integrated field of educational inquiry. Many of the key personnel had previous experience of collaborative curriculum development with teachers and schools through national projects sponsored by the Schools Council, and they tended to confine their teacher education activities to the in-service domain.

The 'action research' movement which emerged in the UK embodied a totally different view of the relationship between theory and practice to the theory-driven model which underpinned the attempt to achieve academic respectability through the 'foundation disciplines'. Its low transfer from the field of curriculum studies in schools and colleges of education, which emerged from collaborative attempts to develop curricula with serving teachers, to initial training programmes is perhaps a major reason why the 'new right' thinkers have been able to ignore it in their attack on theory-driven approaches. It also offers a different account of the theory–practice relationship to the common sense view propounded by the 'new right' thinkers. In Carr's account of the practical approach to educational theory (in contrast to both the 'common sense' approach and the kind of 'applied science' of education O'Connor was sceptical about), he articulates a view of educational practice which underpins the form of action research that emerged from the school-based curriculum reform movement. Educational practice is viewed as:

> an open, reflective, indeterminate and complex form of human action which can be neither governed by theoretical principles nor guided by technical rules ... it is an essentially ethical activity guided by basic educational values rather than narrow instrumental or utilitarian concerns ... these are construed not as 'ends' to which practice is the technical 'means' but as educational commitments that can only be realised *in* and *through* practice. Practice, therefore, is not seen as an instrumental process serving fixed educational ends, but as a fluid activity in which the choice of both means and ends is guided by values and criteria imminent in the educational process itself; criteria which serve to distinguish practice which

is educational from practice which is not, and good educational practice from practice which is indifferent or bad.

(Carr 1986, p. 182)

This view of educational practice, Carr argues, implies that the aim of educational theorising is to:

rehabilitate the art of 'deliberation' as a basis for making educationally defensible judgements about how to intervene in the complex on-going life of the classroom and the school. To this end, it offers practitioners interpretative theories which describe their practical situation in ways which are intended to help them to uncover their underlying values and to reveal the tacit and previously unacknowledged assumptions inherent in their work ... theory relates to practice by enlightening practitioners, it aims to educate practitioners, deepen their insights and enliven their commitments so that they may see more deeply under the surface of their ideas and practices.

(Carr 1986, p. 182)

The theory–practice relation offered here is an interactive one. Theoretical ideas and insights are tested by teachers deliberating about how to realise their educational values in practice, and in turn are modified and developed as a result of such deliberations. Central to the development of both educational practice and theory is the 'teacher as researcher'.

The 'teacher-researcher' not only participates in the development of educational theory and practice but also, through such participation, develops him or herself as a person who becomes committed to certain educational values and their realisation in practice. Hence, Stenhouse's contention that there can be 'no curriculum development without teacher development', and his belief that in-service education should help teachers to undertake 'applied research' in their classrooms and schools.

Carr's account of the view of educational practice which underpins 'the practical approach' echoes Stenhouse's 'process model' of curriculum development, as exemplified in his Humanities Project (1967–72). The Humanities Project aspired to help teachers to explore how they could handle controversial issues as curriculum content in an educationally worthwhile way within a democratic society that espoused respect for different points of view. In the light of a certain interpretation of democratic values Stenhouse suggested that an educationally worthwhile aim was 'the development of an understanding of human arts, social situations, and the controversial issues they raise'. Rather than analyse such an aim into fixed objectives he argued that it implied certain principles of procedure for the teacher, e.g. 'discussion,' 'protection of divergence and minority opinions', 'refraining from imposing one's own personal commitments on the class', and 'representing critical standards of evidence and reasoning'. The conception of a worthwhile aim and process was informed by values and, in deliberating about how to realise the aim in practice, teachers were asked to collect and analyse evidence about the relationship between their teaching methods and the educational values implied by the aim. In doing so, reflection about means could not be dissociated from reflection about worthwhile ends. It was indeed in the context of developing such a process orientated curriculum that the 'teachers as researchers' movement in the UK emerged. It is a very different curriculum context to the one the State is now imposing through a National Curriculum structured by specifications of fixed objectives or targets. The latter exemplifies the very model to which Stenhouse sought an alternative through the 'process model'; on the grounds that an objectives model distorted the relationship between educational ends and means.

THE SOCIAL AND POLITICAL CONTEXT OF ACTION RESEARCH

The government reforms appear to leave little room for the kind of action research which is rooted in a conception of curriculum development as educational innovation. However, as Noffke (1989) points out, action research movements evolve in different social contexts and shape up differently in them. They address different themes and not all variants are underpinned by the view of the theory–practice relationship Carr depicts as 'the practical' approach. Could the current educational context, shaped by the 1989 Act and the 1992 White Paper, provide the setting for the emergence of yet another variant? The origins of the term 'action research' are normally associated with the work of the social psychologist Kurt Lewin in the 1940s , although Noffke identifies its use to describe the 'applied anthropology' of John Collier, the US Commissioner for Indian Affairs in 1933–45, with whose work Lewin was familiar. Noffke suggests that the work of Collier and of Lewin embodies different themes derived from rather different social contexts. Collier's themes were 'progressive education', 'field study', the 'community', 'democracy' and 'ethnic relations', and it was the values embedded in them that he sought to realise for the Native American communities for which he was responsible. Through a form of 'action-research, research-action' (Noffke), research became responsive to a 'need for change' which was experienced by communities themselves who used the data it generated to change their lives. The basic aim of Collier's version of action research was that of democratic self-determination on the part of a minority group.

A concern for the realisation of democratic values and progressive educational methods was shared by Collier's friend, Kurt Lewin. But the latter's connection with research for industrial efficiency included 'management' as a major theme. Such research, Noffke argues, tied industrial productivity to increased worker participation in decision-making. Thus, action research constituted a form of investigation into the most 'effective' and 'democratic' ways of socially organising the means of production. It involved 'carefully collecting information' on the effects of social action and 'then evaluating them'. The whole process might be interpreted as a management strategy for social engineering – of manipulating people's motivations and commitments to achieve pre-determined outcomes – rather than of enabling them to participate fully in the determination of both outcomes and processes in the light of democratic values. As Noffke points out:

> Much of action research can be seen as being 'on' or 'for' people somehow 'disadvantaged'. Yet this fact also raises the contradiction between the uses of 'democratic' methods for 'worthwhile democratic ends' and what Collier considered the undemocratic spectre of social engineering.

Noffke argues that, post-Collier, the 'desire for both democratic means and social improvement guided by principles from "outside" the field setting, was to remain a central tension in later developments in action research', particularly those inspired by Lewin. She does, however, acknowledge the latter's awareness of the issue, and his attempt to resolve it, and quotes him as saying: 'We do not want group manipulation . . . but we do need that amount of management of groups which is necessary for harmonious living together. We want this group management to be done "by the people, for the people".'

But we can argue that such a 'resolution' fails because the group members are given no control over what constitute desirable aims for them to pursue.

A third strand in the emergence of action research, according to Noffke, stemmed from educational developments in the US, especially that of Curriculum Study under the influence of John Dewey's ideas. The emergence of action research in the UK, stimulated by Stenhouse and others working with teachers to realise curricula innovations in the schools of the 1960s and 1970s , can be seen as a recent development within this particular strand. As Noffke argues, the theme it has emphasised is the role of the teacher as a researcher. In my view, such an emphasis in the UK tradition stems from a concerted attempt to strengthen the dialectical relationship between theory and practice by dissolving the division of labour between teachers and researchers that operated even within the 'applied anthropology' and 'social psychology' strands. The focus of the academics' research becomes displaced from the first-order problems of developing practice in classrooms and schools to the second-order problems that the academic faces as a facilitator of teachers' research.

One of the most persistent second-order problems that these academic facilitators have failed to resolve is the contradiction which Noffke identifies as common to all the strands of action research, albeit taking different forms; namely, between 'the democratic impulse' and 'social engineering'. With respect to recent developments in educational action research, she claims that the tension 'continues to be worked out'. The 'social engineering' element 'can take the form of changing teachers' attitudes towards research, developing hypotheses about the ways teachers develop, or "facilitating" the research process'. Since these purposes are carried out 'above' the action research conducted by teachers, for Noffke they carry the potential for 'socially engineered' change.

I have frequently encountered this tension in my own experience of educational action research (see Elliott 1985, 1991) and have argued that it stems from a commitment to certain ends, which are defined in terms of educational values, whether this refers to children's learning in schools or their teachers' learning. This vision of educational ends is something the academic facilitator of teachers' research needs to represent, particularly at a time when the government 'reforms' are promoting an instrumental view of schooling in which teachers become technical operatives 'manufacturing' results, rather than moral agents responsible for the development of human capacities and potential.

There is of course a strand in the development of action research which the government might find attractive as a strategy for 'socially engineering' its reforms. The kind of operational or technical action research advocated by Lewin could well be employed to enhance teacher motivation and commitment towards the implementation of its curriculum and other policies. The government, anxious to raise morale and commitment to its policies amongst a disaffected and dispirited profession, might well find a 'democratic' process, which involved teachers in the management of change through action research aimed at developing and testing 'implementation strategies', an attractive prospect. Such an approach to the implementation of government policy might work wonders for maximising productivity but do very little to raise teachers' awareness of the educational issues at stake in implementing government policy.

In the current 'market setting', academics in schools of education must struggle to help teachers to maintain an educational vision of their practice and to find ways, through action research, of realising it in spite of the constraints imposed by the government's restructuring of schooling. And, since higher education is also being restructured in terms of the market metaphor, teacher educators must also struggle to maintain an educational vision of teachers' professional development, and attempt to develop, through their own action research, ways of realising this vision in their own institution.

In my view, such a stance does not necessarily imply an alternative and oppositional form of 'social engineering', because it is quite consistent with the dialectical relationship between theory and practice which underpins educational action research. If the interpretative frameworks ('theories') academics use to help teachers to analyse data about their practices are embedded in value-assumptions about the educational ends they should serve, and if, in the light of such analysis, carried out under conditions of free and open dialogue with teachers, the frameworks used are further modified and developed, then it follows that the value-assumptions underpinning them will be questioned and redefined. Educational action research, as a dialectical process of testing theory against practice and developing theory through practice, acknowledges no 'fixed visions of educational ends'. The presence of elements of 'social engineering' constitutes a constraint on the dialectical relationship between theory and practice. Although it is important for the academic facilitator to represent a vision of educational ends, it must always be represented as a provisional one capable of being revised and developed through dialogue with teachers. Moreover, since the latter are alone accountable for their decisions and actions in classrooms and schools, they must be given the freedom to draw their own conclusions from the data, albeit in the light of the analytic dialogue with a facilitator and other interested parties.

The action research facilitator represents a vision of educational ends not only to teachers but also for teachers, as it is manifested in his or her own practices. But here again s/he need not succumb to a form of 'social engineering', if s/he treats this second-order vision as provisional and open to revision and development in the light of an analytic dialogue with teachers about the educational value of his or her facilitation practices for them.

Educational action research is simply an educational discourse between academics, teachers and others, which is grounded in the field study of educational practice. But it involves two dimensions of discourse which are based in the study of two practical domains: the first-order domain of the teacher and the second-order domain of the teacher educator or facilitator. The dialectical relation between theory and practice can only be maintained if these two dimensions of practical discourse are sustained. If they are not then there is a very real danger that the action research process will become distorted by 'elements of social engineering', whether they be introduced by a government 'hijack' of action research as a strategy for securing compliance to its policies or by academics using it as a strategy for manipulating teachers to resist and oppose such policies.

THE FUTURE CHALLENGE FOR EDUCATIONAL ACTION RESEARCH

The major theme that has underpinned the emergence of all the strands of action research to which Noffke refers is that of 'democracy'. All the strands represent various interpretations of what democracy means for the organisation and conduct of human affairs in different spheres of social action. In the field of education, action research represents an attempt to work out the implications of democratic values for educational decision-making. In doing so it has been preoccupied with democratising the relationship between teachers in schools and educational researchers in order to give teachers more control over the social conditions which shape the generation and use of educational knowledge. Although educational action research has revealed a persistent tendency on the part of academics to use the process as a subtle form of 'social engineering', its development also reveals an increasing awareness of such elements in its progressive sophistication and refinement through the incorporation of the second-order dimension of reflection and action.

However, the project is unfinished and I would suggest that the government initiated reforms, rather than simply threatening it, provide it with new possibilities for development. If a contradiction between 'democratic values' and 'social engineering' runs through the development of the educational action research movement it also runs through the development of government policy, as I attempted to point out in my analysis of the 1992 White Paper. Many advocates of 'the market' approach to reform see it as a means of realising democratic values in education by opening up education to the influence of parents and employers. What I tried to do was to show how those values are partially misrepresented by the market ideology and conceal undemocratic elements that constitute a subtle form of social engineering of the interests of parents and employers in education.

In the context of the government reforms I would suggest that the task of educational action research is not so much to resist as to transform them by reinterpreting the democratic values which underpin them, albeit in distorted form. And this must involve bringing parents, employers and others into the discourse about what education means in a democratic society and how these values can be realised in classrooms and schools. The challenge for action research presented by the government reforms is for teachers and researchers to broaden their own self-understanding of who should participate in the determination of educational ends and processes. They should free themselves from any temptation to collude in maintaining a form of esoteric professional discourse which excludes parents, employers and other members of the public from having a say in the determination of educational ends and means. What I am advancing is the development of educational action research into a process capable of constructing public visions of educational values, fitting for a democratic society, by involving the citizenry in that process. It will be grounded in the study of the educational issues teachers and schools confront under the influence of government policies, and will aim to strengthen the public accountability of the state for those policies.

I am not suggesting here that parents, employers and others should simply be the recipients of research reports on action research programmes carried out by teachers and academics working collaboratively. The continuing 'democratisation' of action research has more radical implications than that. It will involve teachers, academics, parents, employers, administrators and others collaboratively gathering and analysing data about educational practices in a context of free and open discussion. And, in order to minimise the possibility of 'social engineering' on the part of any of these parties, it will also involve the second-order activity of collecting and analysing data about the role and influence of each of these parties on the process itself. Such 'democratised' action research groups could be established at school, local, regional, or national levels and linked through forms of networking.

How would schools of education in higher education institutions have to change to become facilitating agencies for developments along these lines? In the recent past the higher education institutions have supported the 'teachers as researchers' movement in two major ways. The first is through nationally or locally funded research projects which involved teachers in addressing certain practical issues in classrooms and schools. Such projects resulted in publications and materials for a largely professional audience of teachers and teacher educators. They include projects with which I have been associated, such as the Ford Teaching Project (1972–5) with Clem Adelman, the Schools Council 'Teacher–Pupil Interaction and the Quality of Learning Project' (TIQL 1981–3) with Dave Ebbutt, and more recently the NCET funded 'Pupil Autonomy and Learning with Microcomputers' project (PALM 1988–91) with Bridget Somekh. Second, the movement has been supported through part-time, award bearing in-service courses for teachers at Diploma or Masters level. Although some of these programmes have been school-based (e.g. the University of York initiative), the vast majority have continued the tradition of recruiting individuals and operating seminars and discussion on 'campus' rather than in the workplace. Although the focus of such courses has been on the 'workplace', and tutors sometimes visited schools to assist with data-gathering, they had to leave it to individual teachers largely to negotiate with headteachers and colleagues the level of their involvement in the process. In spite of the individualised nature of action research based in-service courses, they have not been unsuccessful in supporting the institutionalisation of this process in many schools. This is because headteachers and their deputies were often members of such courses, and used them subsequently to build up a critical mass of 'innovation orientated' staff in their schools. This was at a time when schools were being encouraged by LEAs to develop coherent curriculum policies, and managers to secure a more collaborative and less privatised approach to curriculum decision-making within the teaching profession. Much of the financial support for teachers who participated in such courses was provided by the LEAs.

In this context of LEA supported school-based development, both the funded projects and in-service courses maintained what Susan Noffke (1992) has called 'the inter-relatedness of curriculum, pedagogy, and "management"' that was characteristic of 'the early action research era' in the US in the educational field. However, times have now changed and Noffke reminds us of what could happen to action research during a period when educational policies are 'deskilling' the work of teachers. Commenting on the re-emergence of action research in the US during such a period, in the late 1970s and early 1980s, she argues that 'there was an implicit narrowing of the teachers' role that made it difficult, if not impossible, to unite practices with guiding curricular principles . . . there was a clear view that teaching is a matter of discerning and acquiring a set of specific competences and techniques.' The outcome appears to have been not so much the collective empowerment of teachers as educational innovators but rather 'increased confidence in their professional skills and heightened self-esteem' as technical operatives.

In England and Wales, curriculum initiatives have passed from the schools and the LEAs to central government. It is highly unlikely that policy-driven research funding through government agencies will support action research programmes that involve the kind of interconnectedness between curriculum, management, and pedagogy to which Noffke refers. The LEAs, under conditions of financial delegation to schools through the mechanisms of LMS and opting out into GM status, have little money to support traditional award-bearing courses.

One can imagine a scenario where the National Council for Vocational Qualifications takes over as major accrediting agency for in-service teacher education and defines it in terms of the development of technical competence at levels 4 and 5 ('professional grades'). In this context higher education might well 'sell' to schools NCVQ accredited, school-based 'action research' programmes that involve teachers in 'reflectively' acquiring specific skills and techniques. In so doing they will collude in a redefinition of teacher professionalism which is consistent with a 'market' driven school system. In some such way the in-service education of teachers in higher education could 'survive'. Moreover, the costs of such a provision to schools might be ameliorated through special support grants from central funds that have been diverted away from local government control.

There is, however, an alternative possibility to this depressing scenario. There are signs that many teachers are willing to pay for higher education based courses themselves, in a search for learning experiences that are both intellectually demanding and professionally illuminating; in the sense of enabling them to construct professional identities that they can justify to themselves in their present circumstances.

MacLure (1992), drawing on a recent empirical study of 69 primary and secondary teachers (see MacLure *et al.* 1990), notes that:

> We found some general trends – most of them depressing – in the cumulative impact upon teachers of the educational reforms ... we also found variation in teachers' reactions to the reforms according to their contexts and circumstances.

She points out that part of that context is the teachers' own 'biographical project', namely 'the network of personal concerns, values and aspirations against which events are judged and decisions made'.

The effects of the government reforms on teachers will in part be mediated through contextual variables operating in their work and lives and the biographical projects they have constructed for themselves within their particular circumstances. MacLure argues that many teachers have come to find 'teacher-hood' increasingly problematic. In other words, they find it increasingly difficult to sustain their biographical projects in the face of the 'reforms' sweeping through the country. Many teachers in the study testified to what she describes as 'spoiled identities', namely 'a deep sense of alienation from the values and practices of their institution, or the LEA, or central government'. She suggests that the traditional virtues which defined 'teacher-hood' – vocation, care, dedication and self-investment – are becoming increasingly eroded 'while the new identities of "professionalism" which are being offered by employers and policy makers are becoming ever more difficult to believe in'. She concludes that if teachers' needs for professional development were to be truly catered for then a less restricted range 'of culturally endorsed professional identities' should be available to them.

I would hypothesise that, as the 'problematics of teacher-hood' are exacerbated by the current wave of government initiated reforms, many teachers will look to higher education institutions for support in reconstructing their biographical projects within their present working circumstances. And those of us who work in schools and departments of education within those institutions must be careful that we do not simply reinforce the limited and restricted range of identities teachers perceive to be on offer within the system. It is my view that the educational action research tradition that has been established can do much to help teachers to construct and realise 'biographical projects' which are appropriate to the circumstances they now face.

Teachers may well be prepared in greater numbers than we think to pay for action research based in-service courses. However, as the 'problematics of teacher-hood' become increasingly evidenced in schools, we may find headteachers and school governors willing to use their new 'financial flexibility' to sponsor key personnel for action research programmes and 'courses' co-ordinated through higher education. The task of such personnel might be to facilitate within schools the kind of 'democratised' action research process – involving teachers, parents, employers, etc. – which I have outlined.

In responding to the opportunities that 'the problematics of teacher-hood', generated by the government reforms, could present, teacher educators in higher education must ensure that they rethink the structures which govern the relationship between higher education and the school system. For example, the structures which have in the past shaped teachers' access to and experience of higher education have tended to reinforce highly individualised notions of professional development. Although action research based award-bearing courses have often emphasised the importance of teachers involving their colleagues and their institution as a whole in the research process, and have achieved more success in this respect than is commonly realised (see Dadds 1991), it nevertheless has constituted an achievement in spite of the constraints imposed by the course structures in higher education. In my view we need to move towards the integration of our 'research projects' with our in-service work, so that our research increasingly takes the form of action research with schools, and the teachers who play significant roles in the process are academically accredited for their contribution. Somekh, for example, went some way to achieving this integration of research with in-service work through awarding significant teacher contributions with a Certificate in Educational Research. Research degrees already on offer could also be deployed in this manner. And there is no reason why those who are now actively involved in decision-making in schools – governors and parents' representatives, for example – could not also become candidates for academic accreditation in some form.

This kind of integration of research with in-service work would enhance the possibility of attracting funding for the kind of 'democratised' action research process that I am advocating. Not only might teachers and others be prepared to make personal contributions through 'the course fee' mechanism, but other contributions might be found from school budgets and non-government organisations, ranging from traditional sources such as charitable foundations to the world of business and industry itself. The development of action research through the involvement of higher education in the work of teachers and schools is not necessarily terminated by the 'drying up' of government or local government financial support.

A refusal on the part of higher education institutions to modify their individualised course structures and to involve schools as partners in their educational research programmes could result in a distorted response to 'the problematics of teacher-hood'. On the one hand they will produce numerous studies of 'teacher stress', 'burn-out', 'low morale' and 'identity crisis', which may be read but do little to alleviate the problematics. On the other hand they may develop courses for teachers which respond to their problematic identities according to what MacLure calls 'a holistic ideology of self-discovery or self-improvement', which aims to help teachers to 'recover', 'restore', 'reintegrate' or 'emancipate' a lost professional self.

MacLure is sceptical of a process which focuses on 'identity itself', abstracted from the social and political context in which teachers conduct their jobs and lives, and argues on the basis of data collected during the 'Jobs and Lives' study that notions such as 'the reflective practitioner' and the 'self-actualising professional' are as problematic for teachers as the restricted range of options currently being peddled by central government. Since these ideas have also been employed to articulate aspects of the professional development dimension in action research, I wondered whether MacLure was tacitly including the latter in her remark that such ideas 'mark a narrowing down of the range of options as to what a person may be or become, into a small set of coercive identities'.

I hope that the account of the educational action research movement provided here is ample demonstration that it has not developed as a process of privatised and solitary reflection on a 'self' abstracted from the social context of teachers' jobs and lives. What I have attempted to portray is a process which enables teachers continuously to construct and reconstruct what MacLure calls their 'biographical projects' in relation to the circumstances which shape their jobs and lives. The action research projects on which I have worked with teachers have not, in my view, emphasised the particular ideology to which MacLure refers. Noffke points out in her paper, 'The work and workplace of teachers in action research' (1992), that Stenhouse, although he emphasised the development of 'a capacity for autonomous professional self-development through systematic self-study', added that this was to be 'through the study of the work of other teachers and through the testing of ideas by classroom research procedures' (Stenhouse 1975, p. 144). Professional self-development on this view is grounded in a discourse about practice in which ideas and experiences are shared and analysed. Noffke concludes that, as in the earlier curriculum-based action research in the US, 'the teacher's workplace and the conditions for change play significant roles in Stenhouse's writings'. With respect to the Ford Teaching Project, which was heavily influenced in its conception by Stenhouse's ideas, Noffke claims that the publications of the teachers involved contained 'the most fully developed picture of the workplace'. Especially salient in those reports she believes 'is a need to see the work and workplace issues in action research in terms of the larger social context in which they are enacted'.

The educational action research movement might indeed lapse into the kind of 'privatised' and 'solitary' reflective process to which MacLure refers, if higher education institutions insist on maintaining course structures that reinforce an individualised conception of the teacher's role. But the Stenhouse tradition of action research has always emphasised collaborative deliberation on practice between teachers, and indeed between teachers and children, as well as between teachers and academics. What is now being proposed in response to the effects of government policy on the practice of schooling is an extension of these collaborative relationships to include parents, employers and others whom the government wants to have a say in education. This in no way undermines the individuality and creativity of the teacher's role. To think that it does is to confuse, as Andy Hargreaves has argued, individualism with individuality (see Hargreaves 1990). Drawing on Lukes, he argues the former implies social 'anarchy and atomisation' whereas the latter refers to 'personal independence and self-realization'. He reminds us that 'the principled dissent and disagreement of individuality is commonly presented in the pejorative language of individualism'.

The action research process has always respected the individuality of teachers in classrooms, but has always presupposed that it is best fostered by giving them access to a variety of perspectives on their practices and opportunities for dialogue about them; particularly those of their peers, their children, and educational researchers. What I am proposing is an extension of the range of perspectives and opportunities for dialogue open to teachers within the action research process. Rather than restricting their individuality such a process should enrich it. It may indeed further erode the individualism which has traditionally shaped teachers' practices in schools and Hargreaves warns us of strategies which do this while undermining individuality at the same time. The alternative to individualism in the teaching profession is not a form of managerially imposed collectivism which suppresses and denies individuality but the construction of the individual's biographical project through the collaborative study of practice in its contemporary social and political context. In this manner the teaching profession might well discover a way of reinstating, in new clothes, its traditional virtues of vocation, care, dedication, and self-investment.

REFERENCES

Audit Commission (1989) *Assuring Quality in Education: The Role of Local Education Authority Inspectors and Advisers*, London: HMSO.

Ball, S.J. (1992) 'Changing management and the management of change: educational reform and school processes; an English perspective', Paper prepared for the Annual Meeting of the American Educational Research Association, 'National Educational Reforms and School Processes: international perspectives', San Francisco, 21 April, mimeo, London: King's College.

Carr, W. (1986) 'Theories of theory and practice', in *Journal of Philosophy of Education* 20 (2): 177–86.

Dadds, M. (1991) 'Validity and award-bearing teacher action-research', Unpublished Ph.D. thesis, School of Education, University of East Anglia.

Department for Education (1992) *Choice and Diversity: a new framework for schools*, London: HMSO.

Department of Education and Science (1988) *Education Reform Act*, London: HMSO.

Elliott, J. (1985) 'Facilitating educational action research in schools: Some dilemmas', in R. Burgess (ed.) *Field Methods in the Study of Education*, London: Falmer.

Elliott, J. (1991) *Action Research for Educational Change*, Milton Keynes: Open University Press, Ch. 5.

Elliott, J. (1992a) 'Centralisation and decentralisation of education in England and Wales', in P. Posch *et al.* (eds) *Bildungsforschung: Schulautonomie in Osterreich*, University of Klagenfurt, Austria.

Elliott, J. (1992b) 'What have we learned from action research in school-based evaluation?' Paper delivered to Conference on School-based Evaluation in Lillehammer, Norway.

Elliott, J. (in press) 'Are performance indicators educational quality indicators?', in J. Elliott (ed.) *Reconstructing Teacher Education*, Lewes: Falmer.

Giddens, A. (1984) *The Constitution of Society*, Cambridge: Polity Press.

Hargreaves, A. (1990) 'Individualism and individuality: reinterpreting the teacher culture', Paper presented to the Annual Meeting of the American Educational Research Association, Boston.

MacLure, M. (1992) 'Arguing for yourself: identity as an organising principle in teachers' jobs and lives', mimeo, Norwich: Centre for Applied Research in Education, School of Education, University of East Anglia.

MacLure, M., Elliott, J., Marr, I. and Stronach, I. (1990) *Teachers' Jobs and Lives (Phase 2)*, End of Award Report to the ESRC, mimeo.

Noffke, S. (1989) 'The social context of action research: a comparative and historical analysis', Paper presented to the Annual Meeting of the American Educational Research Association, San Francisco, March.

Noffke, S. (1992) 'The work and workplace of teachers in action research', *Teaching and Teacher Education* 8 (1): 15–29.

Pring, R.A. (1989) *The New Curriculum*, London: Cassell.

Pring, R.A. (1992) 'Academic respectability and professional relevance', Inaugural lecture delivered before the University of Oxford on 8 May 1991, Oxford: Clarendon.

Schön, D.A. (1983) *The Reflective Practitioner*, New York: Basic Books and London: Temple Smith.

Sexton, S. (1992) 'A bridge not far enough', *Guardian*, 4 August.

Stenhouse, L. (1975) *An Introduction to Curriculum Research and Development*, London: Heinemann Educational.

Chapter 4

School-based teacher education

David Bridges

INTRODUCTION

The 1980s saw a substantial shift of attention and resources in in-service education from higher education based courses to school based in-service programmes and from LEA held and managed in-service budgets to budgets under the control of schools. The most visible manifestation of this was the introduction of five professional development days when staff were required to attend school, when pupils were not present, for staff development. The 1990s have seen the extension of this shift in responsibility to the initial training of teachers, with the introduction of the articled and licensed teachers schemes and in 1992 of the requirement for substantial proportions of initial training courses for secondary schools (24 weeks of the 36-week postgraduate course) to take place in schools (DFE 1992).

These developments in the in-service and in the initial training of teachers are separable in recent history and have tended to be treated separately in the literature, but they appear to express several common principles concerning, for example, the school as a unit of educational responsibility, the extended professionalism of teachers and the nature and sources of teachers' professional knowledge; and they raise many common questions. For these reasons and because I count it as desirable in any case to view the initial and in-service training of teachers as part of a continuous process, I propose to discuss school-based initial and in-service training together.

Some rather different arguments and programmes for change underlie the development of school-based teacher training. Three which have been especially significant and which I want to discuss more fully in this chapter are:

- The political and to some extent professional programme to strengthen the school as the unit of educational responsibility;
- The professional concern to enhance or to acknowledge the enhancement of teachers' professionalism;
- The political promotion of and professional sympathy for what one might loosely label as experiential learning.

Certain features of these arguments or programmes for change are worth noting straight away. The first is the intertwining of educational arguments about learning, of programmes of change related to professional aspirations of teachers (and indeed the aspirations of people not directly involved in teaching for the professional advancement of teachers) and of explicitly political programmes. In this field, as in most others today, political arguments dominate more strictly educational discourse.

This is partly why many of those in and around education feel ambivalent about the changes. For teacher educators based in higher education this ambivalence is particularly acute since the enthusiasm they may share for the enhanced professionalism of teachers and their interest in experiential learning requires them to associate themselves with developments publicly presented as designed to 'slit the throats' (in the delicate expression of one government spokesperson) of their own institutions.

Sober consideration of the rationale for school-based teacher training requires us, therefore, to separate some of the underlying arguments and consider them in their own terms.

THE SCHOOL AS THE UNIT OF EDUCATIONAL RESPONSIBILITY

Partly as a reaction against the disappointments of earlier attempts at centralised curriculum change generated by the Schools Council, the late 1970s saw the repeated affirmation of the centrality of teachers and of the school in the processes of educational development. This was reflected in the language and practice of 'school-based curriculum development'; 'school self-evaluation' and 'the self-accounting school' (see Elliott *et al.* 1981).

Comfortably associated with all these was the notion of school-based in-service education. As early as 1972 the James Report had recommended:

> In-service training should begin in schools. It is here that learning and teaching take place, curricula and techniques are developed and needs and deficiencies revealed. Every school should regard the continued training of its teachers as an essential part of its task, for which all members of staff share responsibility.
>
> (DES 1972, p.11)

In the 1980s political commitment to the devolution of extended managerial responsibility to schools strengthened. This was informed by a management philosophy which supported the devolution of financial responsibility and empowerment to units closest to practical working realities. It was primarily this philosophy which inspired, for example, the early piloting of local financial management (LFM) and local management of schools (LMS) in Cambridgeshire and elsewhere. The shift was also explicitly motivated as far as central government was concerned by its desire to 'free' schools from what it presented as the burdensome bureaucracy and political tutelage of the local education authorities. This desire was reinforced by the government's undeclared determination to destroy what were in practice all the significant and informed sources of independent criticism or 'subversion' of its educational programme – the LEAs, colleges and departments of education and HMI.

With LMS came the requirement for schools to produce school development plans, and these were expected to incorporate staff development plans. At the same time the provision for five 'non-contact days' gave schools a resource in terms of teachers' time roughly equivalent in value to the whole of the previous national INSET budget though happily at no extra cost to the Exchequer. With delegated in-service budgets, staff development plans, non-contact days and, in most larger schools at least, a senior teacher holding direct responsibility for staff development, school-based in-service training had apparently come of age. However, the coincidence of these developments with training required to support the government's introduction of the National Curriculum, which was provided on the whole by local authority trainers, meant that schools did not get quite the sense of ownership of in-service training that they might otherwise have done.

The twenty-year span covered by this brief historical review also saw significant shifts in the location of the financial resources available to support INSET, with first an expansion of in-service provision within colleges and departments of education (filling the vacuum left by the reduction in the number of students on initial training programmes); then a shift in funding from the higher education institutions to the local education authorities, which could then choose whether or not to buy in training from higher education; and then most recently a shift in funding and responsibility from LEAs to schools which, similarly, might or might not choose to purchase the services of LEA advisers.

One principle associated with and underpinning the development of school-based in-service training is, therefore, a commitment to the increased responsibility or even empowerment of schools at the expense of LEAs (directly) and higher education (indirectly).

Associated with this has been the increasing corporatism of schools and attempts to strengthen the professional identity of teachers with their place of employment rather than a wider professional group. An early evaluation of school-based INSET illustrated the contrasting emphasis evident in some secondary schools between the desire of some teachers (and in particular of senior management) to give priority to whole staff INSET on whole school issues and the preference of other teachers (notably subject heads of departments) for INSET through professional networks of teachers working within the same subject area (Bridges 1981).

Recent government measures (for example, the publication of examination results, the freeing of constraints upon admissions, parental choice of schooling and the award of grant maintained status) have deliberately encouraged competitiveness between schools, have provided a disincentive to collaborative work and have identified the individual school, rather than the group of schools operating in a district or the LEA, as the unit for the delivery of educational service. Of course, the sense that this represents an impoverished vision of educational service leads many teachers and others to oppose such developments. Nevertheless, while these remain firmly on the political agenda it is clearly the case that they reinforce the notion of the school as the unit of professional identity, the school as the focus for the identification of staff development needs and the school as the base for the delivery of the staff development which flows from that identification.

Initial training has been slow to follow in-service training either in being sucked into what have been, with the rather important exception of curriculum determination, the expanding responsibilities of schools or in reflecting their developing corporatism. In 1984, and again in revised form in 1989, the Secretary of State published criteria which all teacher training courses had to satisfy (DES 1984, 1989). These established a minimum requirement for the amount of school-based work and set clear expectations for the involvement of teachers in, for example, the selection of students, the supervision of their practical work and the assessment of their classroom competency. But these expectations required little change in most initial training institutions (the criteria relating to the substance of academic programmes in the B.Ed. created more problems) and did little in themselves to transform the roles of schools in initial training.

In a significant sense the impetus towards a closer partnership with schools in initial training was growing out of a maturing relationship between schools and initial training institutions and was a consequence not of new regulation but of collaboration in school development programmes, advanced courses, classroom action research and school-based INSET. These relationships provided the foundation for what in some cases were adventurous collaborations between individual tutors in higher education institutions and individual heads or teachers in schools, and in other cases some of the early pilots in systematic versions of school-based training.

By 1991 HMI were able to report on a variety of developments in 'school-based initial training' (DES 1991) including the recently established articled teachers and licensed teachers schemes. The report makes explicit the shift in control ('influence' and 'determination' to be precise) bound up in the concept of school-based training.

> The extent to which a course is school-based cannot be determined adequately just by counting the hours students spend in school; the more influential role for teachers implied by the criteria needs to be evident, too. It would be hard, for example, to think of a course as being school-based if teachers had only a marginal voice in determining its content, or were not

significantly involved in its delivery and in deciding whether, at the end, students were fit to join the profession or not.

(DES 1991, pp. 6–7)

This same association between the location of training in schools and the control of training by schools was evident in the Secretary of State's consultative document and in his successor's revised criteria (Circular 9/92; DFE 1992) – though there remained some ambivalence between the rhetoric of 'partnership', the assertion that schools should be in the lead role and the proposal that higher education institutions should be the validating bodies.

Circular 9/92 makes it clear that the new partnership is between higher education institutions and schools as institutions, not just with teachers as individuals or as a wider professional group (see especially paras 12–14). It is schools that should approach their local teacher training institution; the contribution of schools that will be described; schools that will carry the responsibility and schools that will receive their share of the financial resources. On the face of it, therefore, this development will, like those already described, strengthen the corporatism of schools.

But the reality is not as simple as this. Some universities have already developed plans to work with clusters of schools. Both headteachers and university staff recognise that within schools some departments are much more suitable than others in terms of their ability to provide acceptable training. Different schemes place different kinds of emphasis on the range and variety of schools which students will encounter during their initial training. In fact one of the interesting features of the variety of responses to the new requirements can be expressed in terms of the strength or weakness of school corporatism in the training model. The following headteacher, for example, is clearly concerned that her school's role in initial teacher education should support rather than undermine her corporatist strategy for school improvement. Considering a Leeds approach to school-based training which concentrates five students in one department with time allowed to an individual member of staff, she observes:

> This apparently works well . . . for those schools involved. The view at Fearnhill [her own school] is that the whole staff are working together to improve their delivery of education, and this arrangement would place an emphasis and recognition on one department at the expense of another; it would be difficult to justify the involvement of such a large number of students within a limited area to parents and staff.

(Monck 1992, p. 21)

A strongly corporate model of school-based training (stronger certainly than Monck was advocating) would be one which treats the individual school as the central unit for the delivery of training, provides for the tightest association between the trainee teacher and that school and allows that school the greatest opportunity to promote its own professional culture through the training process. In rather the same way some of the old teacher training colleges left their own distinctive mark – and major corporations such as ICI or Sony would reckon to provide management or sales training programmes which bear their own distinctive corporate style. Such a strongly corporate model of school-based training contrasts with what one might call a more collaborative professional training in the ways indicated in Table 4.1.

In practice the licensed teacher scheme, in particular, and the articled teacher scheme, to a lesser degree, have reflected the features of the more strongly corporate model and in this way have echoed some of the characteristics of school-based INSET. However, other forms of school-based initial training, which retain strong associations with higher

Table 4.1 Corporatism in school-based initial training

	Strongly corporate model	Collaborative professional model
Selection of students	By the school in which they will do their main practice or, more strongly, by the school in which they will be employed.	By trainers and teacher/mentors, for the course but not necessarily for training in their own school.
Contract	Between HE institution and an individual 'training school'.	Between HE institution and a cluster or consortium of schools.
Placement	(i) School has major role in determining which student(s) it has; (ii) Students placed in a *school* with a variety of departments involved in training.	(i) Schools accept students allocated by HE; (ii) Students placed with a selected *department* in one school or with the cluster.
Training	Largely focused on one school; strong socialisation into the ways of that school.	Provides wide basis of experience and comparison across schools; weak socialisation into the ways of any one school.
Assessment	Students assessed by training school on its own criteria of success.	Students assessed collaboratively by those participating in training on common criteria of success.
Employment	Within school in which trained.	Anywhere.

education institutions, seem likely to reflect the broader collaborative professional model. This is not only because the institutions themselves have traditionally had a commitment to a broader or more liberal conception of the professional socialisation of teachers but also because, in spite of the several pressures towards a more isolated and competitive corporateness already described, many teachers in many schools continue to affirm their identity with a larger educational service and to recognise the regenerative benefits of communication and collaboration across a wider professional community. A letter from forty-five staff to the governors of a Cambridgeshire school which was contemplating the move to grant maintained status asserted these principles succinctly:

> As teachers we believe we share collective responsibility for the education of pupils in this LEA, and that the school is part of a community of schools ... We would be unhappy to isolate ourselves from other schools in the area. The LEA enables us to communicate, share ideas, and collaborate with other schools.
>
> (Snapper and Charles 1992)

There remains an important choice of identity for teachers (though it is not obvious that the choice lies any longer with teachers) and an important decision concerning the focus of the professional socialisation of new teachers: are they to be socialised into a department; a school; a school district; or a wider educational profession? The narrower the focus of this socialisation perhaps the more powerful ('effective'?) it can be. But it would be sad, in a decade in which even international obstacles to the mobility of professional competence are being pulled down, if school-based teacher training were used to legitimate professional parochialism.

THE ENHANCED PROFESSIONALISM OF TEACHERS

The attribution to teachers of responsibility for their own professional development is presented and perceived both as a recognition of their extended professionalism (see Hoyle 1974) and as a contribution to that extension. It fits comfortably with two decades of development which have provided a fertile range of possibilities for the expansion of teachers' roles as:

- Curriculum developers;
- Researchers – notably within the framework of classroom action research;
- Self-evaluators – within the context of school reviews and personal appraisal;
- Self-developers – within the context of school-based staff development;
- Advisers – either formally as advisory teachers or less formally as 'consultants' available to support development and training across schools.

It is difficult to resist the implication that if teachers have come to be able to handle these complex responsibilities for professional and educational development, then they ought also to be able to play a prominent and effective part in the initial training of teachers. As Hargreaves was able to observe, in arguing for school-based initial training, 'a striking change of recent years is the growing confidence and skill of heads and teachers in all aspects of training and professional development' (Hargreaves 1989).

The argument presented is a combination of the view that teachers' extended professionalism now equips them to provide initial as well as in-service teacher training with the view that they should be providers of initial as well as in-service teacher training because this will enhance their professionalism.

Recent debates have tended to qualify rather than to contradict this comfortable conjunction, but the qualifications offer important cautions for the way in which school-based initial and in-service training develops. The main qualifications are as follows.

The first reservation is to acknowledge that whatever one's admiration for the professionalism of teachers, the training of adults as teachers requires some different skills from those involved in successful classroom teaching. These arise partly out of the different requirements of teaching adults, some of whom may well be older than the classroom teacher and have all sorts of child rearing and work experience outside schools. They arise too out of the different subject content. The classroom teacher may (a) teach mathematics and do it extremely well, but does s/he also (b) communicate to someone else how s/he does it and does s/he (c) help them to develop an approach to the same task which will work for them? Plainly, a high level of competence in (a) is not sufficient for (b) nor (b) for (c). Indeed it is questionable whether (a) is even necessary to (c) though no doubt this sort of personal competence in the classroom adds credibility and authority to the trainer.

This argument amounts only to a caution, however, since it is generally acknowledged that practising school teachers do need support and training if they are to function effectively either as in-service trainers or as trainers or mentors of students in initial training. Norfolk LEA has worked actively to provide training for those with responsibilities for staff development in schools (see, for example, the resource pack for INSET co-ordinators distributed to all schools, Norfolk LEA 1991), and all school-based initial training schemes are required to make provision for mentor training. There is considerable evidence (e.g. Furlong et al. 1988) which suggests, however, that the task which practising teachers have in communicating and explicating their own craft knowledge to students is a complex one which defeats many teachers and leads others to avoid even trying.

A second reservation to teachers' assumption of the role of teacher trainer is linked to one of the more negative sides of extended professionalism. At its worst the strengthening of the professionalism of the delivery of a service to any community is a reinforcement of the exclusivity of that service. In the case of teachers' roles, the greater the span of activity which is deemed to fall within the province of teachers' professionalism, the narrower the range of agencies or voices involved in the delivery of that service. In medicine, in law and in the church the protected professionalisation of the sphere of activity has served to disqualify or invalidate a whole range of 'lay' contributions to its discourse and practice. In any context in which the professionalism of one group is extended, it is important to ask – at whose expense? In many ways the parental role in the education of their children has been diminished by the widening professionalisation of child rearing and education (or perhaps it is the other way round). Recent administrations in England and Wales have hardly been marked by their enthusiasm for the enhanced professional status of teachers, so why are they so supportive in this instance? The reason is not difficult to find. Whatever the government's distrust of classroom teachers, it is even more suspicious of the perceived ideological predilections of what successive ministers continue – ignorantly or bloody-mindedly – to refer to as 'the teacher training colleges'. Teachers may or, more likely, may not be flattered by the idea that government finds their opinions safer than those of colleagues in higher education, but either way it would be a betrayal of some profoundly important educational and indeed democratic principles if the extended professionalism of teachers in the area of initial as well as in-service training were acquired at the cost of excluding educational voices perceived fairly or unfairly to be dissonant with those of the government in power.

Fortunately the notion of partnership described in DFE Circular 9/92 does give scope for students to have contact both with teachers and with staff from higher education. There remain, however, influential right-wing ideologues who insist that government has not yet gone far enough in taking initial teacher education right out of the hands of the universities. It will in time diminish teachers' professionalism and constitute a quite unwarranted restriction on student teachers' access to alternative ideas if this is allowed to happen.

A third reservation to the extension of teachers' professional roles into initial teacher training is of a quite different kind. It stems from concern about the distraction of teachers – and especially successful teachers – from their central and overriding commitment to the teaching of their children in the classroom. There is considerable evidence, which in this case supports what common sense would surely suggest, that children learn best when (i) they themselves spend the maximum time on task and (ii) when their teachers spend the maximum time on task. If successful teachers are to give significant attention to the training of student teachers, then this must surely be at the cost of their classroom pupils. If they give whole-hearted attention to their pupils then this must surely be at some cost to the students? Not surprisingly, therefore, a significant portion of the resistance to the extension of school-based training has come from parents and teachers alarmed about its potential impact on children's learning. 'It will be impossible for a school to take the leading role in the training of teachers', wrote Lynne Monck, head of Fearnhill School, Letchworth, 'because schools must be first and foremost concerned with education of pupils in their care. The student teachers will always take second place to this' (Monck 1992).

The equation in terms of costs and benefits to schools of involvement in initial teacher training is by no means as simple as is described here. Schools recognise that student teachers can contribute positively to the life of a school and to pupils' learning. For a considerable part of their training they may be working alongside the experienced teacher rather than taking his or her place. The presence of small groups of students can provide for individual attention for pupils quite beyond the scope of a single teacher. And experienced teachers commonly acknowledge the boost to their own enthusiasm, the fresh ideas brought in by student teachers or the benefits of collaboration with staff from higher education (see, for example, Benton 1990 on the Oxford Internship Scheme).

These kinds of arguments have application too in the context of in-service teacher education, except that here the provision of school-based training is seen as less disruptive of pupils' learning than the away-based course which requires the regular teacher's absence and the deployment of a supply teacher.

I have indicated three sets of considerations which qualify our enthusiasm for extending the professional role of teachers to include the initial and in-service training of their fellow professionals. But these suggest conditions for the implementation of programmes of school-based training rather than overwhelming objections to that implementation. With proper safeguards, training and support and developed in a context of partnership with higher education, such programmes should be able to enhance the professionalism of teachers and to contribute to quality of learning in the classroom.

SCHOOL-BASED TRAINING AND EXPERIENTIAL LEARNING

I have so far couched the arguments relating to school-based training rather narrowly in terms of the location of control and the professional interests of teachers. A spectator to recent government and allied pronouncements could be forgiven for imagining that this is what the debate is all about. However, intertwined with these arguments are other considerations regarding how teachers acquire or develop their professional knowledge. Plainly what school-based training (and in particular initial training) most readily provides is the opportunity for learning through practice and through observation of practice, in other words (though we should not lose the distinction between practice and observation) experiential learning. If we regard experiential learning as a particularly potent form of learning, or even an essential condition for the development of practical competence, then we must clearly welcome developments which maximise the opportunity to found professional learning in professional practice (see Jamieson 1992 for a discussion of 'Experiential learning in the context of teacher education').

There is, of course, no contest to the argument that the initial, let alone the continuing, training and development of teachers should include a significant and central ingredient of practice of teaching. Nor does anyone seriously maintain that practice is by itself sufficient for the professional development of teachers. The real issues are located inside this framework of assumptions. There are four which have particular relevance to the context of teacher education and which I will comment on briefly.

The first issue concerns the conditions under which people best learn from experience or indeed the conditions under which they properly experience something at all, since it is evident that two people, who are equally well equipped with healthy sensory organs, can be present in the same place at the same time, attending to the same events, and have totally different experiences and that the time spent can constitute for one of the two a rich experience while for the other it barely constitutes an experience at all. Experience awaits the experiencing mind, that is, one motivated by interest, curiosity or purpose; one equipped with sufficient conceptual apparatus to allow it to discern, to discriminate, to analyse and to interpret; also one receptive to having ideas and assumptions challenged or expanded by what is beheld.

These conditions of experience-based learning were well appreciated in the classical works of the Chicago pragmatists, which are the progenitors of much contemporary thinking (see Bridges 1991). In pragmatic theory, practical experience provides the challenge or testing ground to the assumptions or hypotheses which inform our attempts to do things. Our attempts are frustrated when, from time to time, those assumptions or hypotheses are not adequate to the world in which we attempt to act. Experience challenges our beliefs and we have, through our imagination and intelligence, to refine or adjust those beliefs to experience so that we are once more able to go about our business.

This is a crude summary of a complex set of theories which were developed in different ways by Dewey, Pierce, James and others (see Rucker 1969, Scheffler 1974) and revived in recent times in the popular but philosophically less sophisticated form of Kolb's 'experiential learning cycle' (Kolb 1984), but it will serve to illustrate the active and informed intelligence which is brought to experience, which wrestles to interpret the significance of experience and which constantly refines belief structures so as to allow the individual to function effectively in the experienced world.

In the context of in-service teacher education already, and in initial training increasingly, there is plainly no shortage of participation in school and classroom events. However, if 'participation' is to contribute to teachers' professional development, it must be rendered as richly as possible as 'experience', as articulated here; that is, as something which engages our interest and curiosity, as something to which we bring a sophisticated and appropriate conceptual armoury and as something to which we are sufficiently receptive that we allow it to modify our assumptions. Notions of 'the reflective practitioner' (Schön 1983) and of 'teacher as researcher' (Elliott 1991) provide important foundations for this kind of dynamic and conceptually laden notion of experience-based learning, though perhaps neither notion has yet been represented in a form which adequately captures the interplay between the understanding which a teacher brings to classroom practice and the understanding which he or she takes from engagement in or observation of that practice.

These last considerations bring me to my second reservation about school-based learning, in so far as this takes the form of experiential learning. This echoes similar criticism of pragmatic theory of knowledge from which, I have suggested, it is derived. Pragmatism – and theories of experiential learning – work reasonably well when they are applied to the domain of technology in which the test of whether 'it works' or not is the singular significant consideration and in which the determination of whether 'it works' or not is firmly grounded in experiment and experience. But, as we have become increasingly aware, we run into all sorts of trouble if we take technological decisions on technological grounds without reference to, among other things, moral and social principles. This is especially the case in the context of the education of children, which is an activity governed at every turn by moral and social considerations. But neither pragmatism nor any experiential theory of learning provides an adequate account of, and still less an adequate justification for, the moral framework which has to be applied to our experience of teaching and has to be interpreted within the context of that experience but cannot plausibly be derived from it.

The problem extends wider than this. Many teachers today observing a classroom in which boys were engaging in 'hands on' work with the computers while girls stood back to offer occasional supportive advice would identify this as an instance of sexism. Similarly a student spending a term in a school in which Christian festivals were marked with intensive activity while those of other faiths were unselfconsciously ignored would recognise this as one of the ways in which the cultures of minority ethnic groups in Britain were structurally devalued and discriminated against. In so far as this awareness is abroad, however, it is only because the wider significance of features of school and classroom work, to which practising teachers had managed to remain oblivious for many years, was repeatedly brought to their attention by critical theorists, most of whom stood at some distance from the classroom but had a wider perspective on social structures. Critical theory developed in this way and communicated to teachers mainly through university departments has come to provide a significant part of the conceptual apparatus which now informs their observation and the way in which they experience classrooms. It is theory which has in some sense to stand the test of experience, but it is not theory which (in any simple sense at least) is going to be derived from experience. Thus, the professional education and development of teachers must continue to include engagement with challenging conceptual structures, not as an antidote to experiential learning but as a condition of experiential learning properly understood.

A third set of reservations about experiential learning are of a more elementary but no less important nature. They are neatly summarised by the nineteenth-century historian Froude (1877): 'Experience teaches slowly, and at the cost of mistakes.' In a sense the fundamental rationale of education and training is to quicken a process of learning which, if it were left to experience alone, would be interminably slow. So we quite sensibly expect teachers to be familiar with, to collect together and to communicate to others the lessons of experience of previous and contemporary workers in the field under consideration. Learning derived at second or third hand like this may not have the immediacy of one's own experience and may be less powerful in modifying one's actions, but access to it is nevertheless a condition of any serious kind of social progress. More especially in areas like education, where the mistakes of teachers can have damaging consequences for children, we have plainly a particular obligation to provide education and training in advance of the practice of teaching, which will at least limit the damage resulting from the otherwise stumbling and inadequately informed efforts of new practitioners. The principle applies both to pre-service training of classroom teachers and to that of headteachers, though only relatively recently has its application to the second case been taken seriously.

This discussion of experiential learning sets out not to challenge the importance of experiential learning in teacher education but to describe (i) the conditions under which learning from experience becomes even intelligible, (ii) some of the limits to what can be derived from experience in the ordinary sense of the term (i.e. setting aside the consideration that all learning is derived from experience of something even if it is only the monotonous drone of someone dictating the declension of a verb), and (iii) some of the limitations on what we sensibly rely on experience to teach.

In the context of teacher education all of this argues for:

- The collecting together and passing on of the fruits of other people's experience to new entrants to the profession and to people taking on new responsibilities in their professional careers;
- The development (by pre-service and in-service teachers) through discussion, reading and reflection of the thinking, the ideas, the conceptual structures which inform, shape and direct their observation and experiencing;
- Specific attention in pre-service and in-service programmes to the development of moral schemata and wider socio-political frameworks of thinking without which teachers will fall prey to the lowest forms of unquestioning pragmatism and lose that personal integrity without which they are scarcely entitled to invite the trust and confidence of their students.

None of this is incompatible with pre-service or in-service training which is substantially school-based (in the sense of being physically located within schools) but it does suggest, first, that practice alone cannot substitute for teaching and learning of the kinds described here and, second, that schools as they function institutionally at the moment and with the legitimate priorities they have in relation to their pupils' education may have some difficulty in providing the kind of adult learning environment described here.

But, of course, we do not have to assume that schools will stay as they are, as they take increasing responsibility for the initial as well as continuing professional development of teachers. The Oxford Internship Scheme has illustrated both some of the difficulties faced in turning the school into a proper learning environment for new teachers and some effective strategies developed through the partnership between schools and higher education; these strategies include giving articulation to teachers' craft knowledge; developing 'reflectivity' in both established and new teachers; investigating and examining the taken-for-granted aspects of schooling and teaching (see Benton 1990 and especially Judith Warren Little's overview).

CONCLUSION

This indeed is part of the exciting potential of the best forms of school-based teacher training run in partnership with higher education: the contribution which it can make to the invigoration of the professional and intellectual context of teachers' working lives. In the United States the location of teacher training in so-called 'professional practice schools', in which university staff work in collaboration with school staff and in which part of the initial socialisation of new teachers is into the process of educational change, has provided a dynamism which is reported as a successful if not trouble-free approach to educational reconstruction (Anderson *et al.* 1992, Grossman 1992, Whitford 1992, Miller and Silvernail 1992).

But, as Miller and Silvernail argue, with reference to their study of Wells Junior High, any success has clearly not been the result of rational linear planning. It rests on an approach which requires 'a map rather than itinerary, being long-range, being adaptive, and being value-based' (Miller and Silvernail 1992, p. 31). And these are the conditions which the development of school-based teacher education requires in England and Wales: the opportunity for universities and schools to establish new kinds of partnerships; the opportunity to experiment and to test approaches in practice; the opportunity to research and reflect upon experience; and freedom from incessant political interference so that the next stages in the development of teacher training can be based on the evidence of research and on reflection rather than contorted to satisfy the shrill but ignorant invective of politically unaccountable ideologues.

REFERENCES

Anderson, E.M., Stilwell, J.L. and Trevorrow, L.B. (1992) 'Educational reform: issues and answers in the Patrick Henry/University of Minnesota Professional Practice School', Paper presented to the Annual Meeting of the American Educational Research Association, San Francisco.

Benton, P. (1990) *The Oxford Internship Scheme*, London: Calouste Gulbenkian Foundation.

Bridges, D. (1981) *The Secondary School Curriculum: Theory into Practice: An evaluation of an extended school-based in-service programme at City of Ely College, Cambridge*, Mimeo, Cambridge: Homerton College.

Bridges, D. (1991) 'From teaching to learning', *Curriculum Journal* 2 (2): 137–51.

Department for Education (1992) *Initial Teacher Training (Secondary Phase)*, Circular 9/92, London: HMSO.

Department of Education and Science (1972) *Teacher Education and Training* (the James Report), London: HMSO.

Department of Education and Science (1984) *Initial Teacher Training: Approval of Courses*, Circular 3/84, London: HMSO.

Department of Education and Science (1989) *Initial Teacher Training: Approval of Courses*, Circular 24/89, London: HMSO.

Department of Education and Science (1991) *School-based Initial Teacher Training in England and Wales*, a report by HMI Inspectorate, London: HMSO.

Elliott, J. (1991) *Action Research for Educational Change*, Milton Keynes: Open University Press.

Elliott, J., Bridges, D., Ebbutt, D., Gibson, R. and Nias, J. (1981) *School Accountability*, London: Grant MacIntyre.

Froude, J.A. (1877) *Short Studies on Great Subjects: Party Politics*, London: Longman Green.

Furlong, V.J., Hirst, P.H., Pocklington, K. and Miles, S. (1988) *Initial Teacher Training and the Role of the School*, Milton Keynes: Open University Press.

Grossman, P.L. (1992) 'In pursuit of a duel agenda: creating a middle level professional development school', Paper presented to the Annual Meeting of the American Educational Research Association, San Francisco and to be published in L. Darling-Hammond (ed.) [provisional title] *Professional Development Schools: Schools for Developing a Profession*, New York: Teachers' College Press.

Hargreaves, D. (1989) 'Judge radicals by results', in *Times Educational Supplement*, 6 October.

Hoyle, E. (1974) 'Professionality, professionalism and control in teaching', *London Educational Review* 3 (2): 21–37.

Jamieson, I. (1992) 'Experiential learning in the context of teacher education', in G. Harvard and P. Hodkinson (eds) *Action and Reflection in Teacher Education*, Norwood, NJ: Ablex.

Kolb, D.A. (1984) *Experiential Learning: Experience as the Source of Learning and Development*, Englewood Cliffs, NJ: Prentice Hall.

Miller, L. and Silvernail, D.L. (1992) 'Wells Junior High School: evolution of a professional development school', Paper presented to the Annual Meeting of the American Educational Research Association, San Francisco.

Monck, L. (1992) 'A problematic partnership', in *Times Educational Supplement*, 21 February, p. 21.

Norfolk LEA (1991) *Making the Most of Curriculum Development Days*, Norwich: Norfolk LEA.

Rucker, D. (1969) *The Chicago Pragmatists*, Minneapolis, Minn: University of Minnesota Press.

Scheffler, I. (1974) *Four Pragmatists*, London: Routledge & Kegan Paul.

Schön, D.A. (1983) *The Reflective Practitioner*, New York: Basic Books and London: Temple Smith.

Snapper, B. and Charles, A. (1992) *Letter to Governors*, Cambridge: Netherhall School.

Whitford, B.L. (1992) 'Permission, persistence and resistance: the context of high school restructuring', Paper presented to the Annual Meeting of the American Educational Research Association, San Francisco and to be published in L. Darling-Hammond (ed.) [provisional title] *Professional Development Schools: Schools for Developing a Profession*, New York: Teachers' College Press.

Chapter 5

Teacher creativity and teacher education

Susan Halliwell

INTRODUCTION

'Are you creative enough to be a teacher?' challenged a DES recruitment advertisement in the national press last year.

It would seem that the idea of creativity as one of the characteristics of a good teacher still receives official recognition even though it has yet to find a place in official accounts of competences and even though the goals to which such creativity is directed are a matter of fierce debate. So how does this affect what we do in teacher education? This chapter offers ideas for discussion under two headings:

- It identifies certain aspects of creativity which are important for a teacher and for a beginner teacher in particular;
- It suggests how those aspects of creativity can be encouraged and developed in teacher education programmes.

These are issues of concern to anyone engaged in teacher development whether that development is taking place in school or in higher education.

Before going any further it is important to clarify what is under discussion here. The introduction of a National Curriculum and all the centrally controlled elements of education which accompany it have tended to focus our attention on the tension between creative teaching and imposed curriculum. However, to oppose creativity and control in this way can also be unhelpful. It tends to deflect our thinking from underlying issues that are present whether the curriculum is 'imposed' or not and whatever the source of that imposition, be it government, institution, department or course book.

In the same way that each act of speech is a creative act so too is each act of teaching. No two occasions in the classroom are identical. Whatever the common elements, the cognitive and social context of each teaching event is unique. A given lesson will not look exactly the same in the hands of two different teachers or in the hands of the same teacher with two different classes or indeed for the same class with the same teacher but on two different occasions. Teaching is an act of constantly adjusted mediation and those adjustments relate to the unique components of each event. If we overstress the opposition of creativity and control there is a risk that teachers will forget this underlying creativity and begin to believe that there is no role for creativity in a centrally imposed curriculum. Not only is this nonsense, it is also dangerously limiting as the following incident showed.

The lesson concerned was being taught by a PGCE history student. She settled the class competently, made sure they knew what to do and set them to work through the (perfectly reasonable) work-sheet provided by the department. During the lesson she kept an eye on behaviour and walked round commenting occasionally on what emerged as the learners worked. Eventually the bell went, the class stopped working and the student dismissed the class in an orderly fashion. When asked why she had run the lesson this way the student was puzzled. She said that she had been asked to use the work-sheet and she had. Once that decision had been made she did not see what else was expected of her. What was at issue here was not the fact that she had used someone else's materials – why should she not? – but that she had made no attempt to mediate what she had been given. It is, of course, possible to see such lessons as developing pupil autonomy, allowing scope for different rates of progress and as making efficient and economical use of material generated by others. Yet such lessons can equally well be regarded as an abdication of teacher responsibility. The teacher's role has been reduced to 'switching on' provided materials. This is an extremely limited view of teaching. Indeed it is hardly teaching. It is supervision. Such lessons could be conducted by almost anyone of reasonable intelligence and presence who might wander in from the street and find a note saying what the class should do. This might appeal to some of today's policy makers as a possible solution to recruitment problems but it does little for the learners. Beginner teachers often fall into this trap of underestimating their creative responsibility.

On the other hand if they are fully aware of the need for creativity but it is left as a generalised expectation, it can become a burden, a paralysing obligation, as a second example will show. One recent PGCE student became steadily worse, not better, at lesson planning as the year progressed. The more ideas he was encouraged to consider as alternatives the less he seemed capable of making any choices or having any ideas himself. In effect he became paralysed by his fear of not living up to the creativity he felt was expected of him. It was a very clear example of what Woods (1990) referred to in his chapter on teacher creativity as 'the reverse trend of emotion'. Ironically it was only when the tutor finally managed to get over to the student the apparently startling idea that he was not expected to create particularly innovative lessons that he found the confidence to explore his own ideas and create materials of his own.

Both these examples show that if those with responsibility for teacher training are to help beginner teachers we need to clarify with them and for ourselves what kind of creativity, what combination of qualities, we are looking for and we need to show how those qualities manifest themselves in better teaching. At the same time we need to identify as the basis for decisions about our own teacher training programmes the events and experiences which can encourage those qualities and support them.

WHAT ASPECTS OF CREATIVITY ARE IMPORTANT FOR TEACHERS?

One common perception of creativity is to accept with Parnes (1975) the fundamental notion of the 'aha', that is, 'the fresh and relevant association of thoughts, facts and ideas'. Even so, this apparent consensus conceals considerable differences of focus and emphasis in our everyday use of the term. It can signal, among other things, genius, innovation, aesthetic expression, self-realisation, imagination, productivity, and flexibility. In deciding which of these are most significant for teachers it will help to remind ourselves that we are looking for forms of teacher creativity which are at the service of the learner. If the whole point of teacher creativity is to stimulate and enhance learning then there are certain aspects of creativity which are less relevant in teaching, even less desirable. We can start by identifying three of these.

First, we are not talking about creativity as genius. We are talking about creativity as part of normality, as part of everyday actions and ideas. The kind of creativity which is essential for effective teaching comes into the same category as thinking of a way to distract or comfort a frightened child, planning an interesting holiday, choosing a good Christmas present, and finding simple ways to express complex feelings. This may seem obvious but it needs saying, as the man who struggled with his lesson plans showed. The creativity itself is not extraordinary though the context in which it has to operate is specific.

Nor are we concerned with what Irving Taylor (1975) summarised as the 'self actualisation' view of creativity, where the act of creation is above all an act of self-expression. Most of us have seen wall displays which say more about the teacher than the children or have watched pyrotechnic teaching performances which have dazzled and perhaps entertained a class without engaging the minds of the learners. Such self-centred creativity can even squeeze out the learners' own responses. If we as teachers cram too many of our own ideas and insights, our own reactions and activities into a lesson we leave our learners no space to develop their particular framework of understanding which is so vital to successful learning.

Perhaps more surprisingly we are also not really concerned with aesthetic and artistic creativity. It is an enviable talent and one which can undoubtedly contribute to the quality of the learning experience which a teacher offers. However, not even the most lovingly crafted worksheets, eye-catching displays or visually imaginative overhead transparencies are essential to good teaching. They may help through stimulus, entertainment and general motivation but they do not necessarily contribute to learning. This was shown clearly in the teaching of a recent PGCE modern languages student who built up an impressive file of teaching aids, in the form of visually most attractive and imaginative OHP transparencies, but sadly did not in the process generate anything like the language interaction prompted by the scruffy and spontaneous board sketches of a fellow student. This too needs saying because it is very easy for a beginner teacher with such talent to be seduced into artistic creativity as a substitute for real teaching and it is equally easy for those without much talent in this direction to perceive themselves as not very creative.

So what are we looking for? Obviously we are looking for inventiveness in some degree but not in the form of great innovations or constant novelty. There is nothing wrong with using your own ideas from previous occasions, using others' ideas, the textbook or departmental worksheets. The reason that the history lesson described earlier was such a poor experience for the learners was not because the student had failed to create novel materials of her own. In fact what she had been given to use was perfectly suitable. The problem was that there was no creative mediation on her part, as teacher, between the given materials and a particular group of learners on a particular occasion. Each class of learners is different. Each day or even time of day raises unpredicted issues. This is where inventiveness becomes essential. This kind of innovation is perhaps best described as inventive flexibility rather than as novelty.

Underpinning this quality of inventive flexibility are imagination and anticipation. At the same time they need to be backed by organisation and control of ideas. This is where the element of judgement comes into teacher creativity. Maadi (1975) credits Bruner with being among the first to introduce the idea of the creative act 'not just as novel but also as valuable and effective'. As Maadi says, 'once you add judgement to imaginativeness as the relevant abilities you already have a view of the creative person emerging, emphasising more discipline, planfulness and self criticality than would appear desirable in the actualising position' (Maadi 1975). Creativity is not just unsought, uncontrolled inspiration. Or, as Anouilh said in *Ornifle ou le courant d'air*: 'L'inspiration, c'est une invention des gens qui n'ont jamais creé'.

Woods (1990) also draws our attention to the essential combination of instinct and conscious organisation or, as he expresses it, holistic and algorithmic thinking.

> The teacher might have a profusion of ideas some of which work some of which do not, with a fair degree of unexpectancy [sic] and accident. The application of those ideas and certainly their evaluation will require more systematised working out and analysis.
>
> (Woods 1990)

To summarise the ideas in this first section, I am suggesting that we operate with a view of teacher creativity as inventiveness, which is a flexible response to the classroom context and which is subject to conscious monitoring. Where the word creativity is used from now on it will be referring to this form of responsive inventiveness.

The next section looks at ways in which teacher education can help new entrants to the profession to develop and sustain such responsive inventiveness.

STRATEGIES FOR DEVELOPING EFFECTIVE TEACHER CREATIVITY

Creativity is often not responsive to conscious efforts to instigate it or control it since it is highly unpredictable and resistant to scheduling. It is difficult to know whether developing creativity is like building a muscle or following a recipe.

(Taylor 1975)

On the other hand, as was clear in the earlier example of the PGCE student who struggled with planning, even when we have come to some agreement on what kind of creativity we are looking for we cannot simply exhort people to be creative. That is like telling them to be nice or, worse, telling them to be funny. So what can we do?

Responsive inventiveness depends primarily on

- A clear sense of need;
- The ability to read the situation;
- The willingness to take risks;
- The ability to monitor and evaluate events.

We are therefore looking for ways to develop such awareness, attitudes and abilities both implicitly and explicitly. We want to make sure that we know which elements of our existing programmes contribute to such development even when they are ostensibly focused on some other aspect of teaching. If we can identify them we have some chance of retaining them or finding new equivalents in more school-based work.

Feeling the need to be creative

I remember an enormous hand-out from Y [a tutor] and I remember that awful three-hour session in which he just churned through the whole thing, just a little more detailed, and I remember that I was never able to borrow anything from it actually – that wasn't mine.

(PGCE student taped interview)

This statement and the other quotations from PGCE students which follow come from an evaluation of one particular method course. The evaluation took the form of one-to-one conversations, lasting about an hour each, between each student in the group and the method tutor. The students' perspective on their essentially university-based experience of learning to teach (Maclennan 1985) is relevant to today's discussions of school-based training. The student quoted above was contrasting the experience of not being able to use one tutor's wealth of ideas with the experience of being given just a few ideas by another tutor, trying them out and working with fellow students to produce variations. Of this latter situation she said, 'I would never have felt I was borrowing from X [the tutor]. It was part of what we had done together . . . and became part of an experience in which we all shared.'

In general terms there is an important warning here for all of us in teacher education as we become more and more concerned to cover the required load of our courses, but in terms of this article the most important three words from the first quotation are the last three words: 'that wasn't mine'.

This is what Woods (1990) is talking about when he refers to 'ownership' as an essential part of creativity. There is already too much to do in classrooms which is in response to external demands and does not arise from a teacher's own insights, professional judgement and immediate circumstances. If creativity is another such external demand, albeit in the form of expectation rather than decree, it is unlikely to materialise. The urge to be creative must be part of a personal teacher culture. We each need to know and feel the need for and in ourselves. This is part of what Elliott (1990) is referring to when he says, 'practical understanding is insider knowledge and is grounded in an awareness of self as an active agent in the situation or experience'.

It is therefore important to identify those elements of our teacher training programmes which, whatever their main focus, help to develop a sense of creativity as a personal normality and as a necessary practical response to some of the daily challenges of the classroom. The following kinds of activities, which are at present part of many PGCE programmes, would come into this category of events which highlight the need for creativity:

- Watching a teacher or a fellow student teaching from a previously agreed plan and afterwards discussing the inevitable adjustments;
- Two student teachers preparing a lesson independently from the same unit or worksheet. One watches the other teach his or her own version and both discuss the nature of the differences and variations in the plans they have separately produced;
- A student teacher prepares a worksheet for an experienced teacher to use and watches how it is handled in the classroom;
- Watching a video of a lesson with the teacher's prepared lesson plan to hand and stopping for discussion at points of adjustment or suggesting where adjustment would have been helpful;
- Watching videos of the students' own lessons and discussing them in the same way;
- Teaching two classes on teaching practice which are working on the same materials but at different levels;

- Working as a support teacher in someone else's class with responsibility for adapting the materials for a particular learner;
- Analysing together with the tutor concerned the planning and realisation of a session in which the student teachers have themselves just been the learners.

The key elements that characterise these activities are the elements of collaboration, and the discussion of the experiences shared as observers and as active participants. In other words, these events combine to a greater or lesser degree Bruner's (1964) categories of iconic, enactive and symbolic knowledge. Whatever may be their prime purpose and focus, events of this kind also provide occasions for the need for inventive flexibility to be seen, discussed and put into action.

There is still a danger that the kinds of events listed are perceived by students simply as tasks set by the tutor. This is because in these examples the need for creativity may be highlighted but it does not arise as a personal need. There is, however, one particular area of a beginner teacher's work which more than any other generates an intensely felt personal need to 'think of something', namely the whole question of discipline and control.

This can provide a very fruitful starting point for building up creativity as a personal and realistic normality. In the teaching of modern foreign languages, for example, there is a constant tension between the importance of generating lively interaction and communication and the equally important need to maintain some calm and order in proceedings. Each student teacher, in order to survive and to promote language learning successfully, has to learn very rapidly how to find worthwhile but calm variations of activities which would be unsuitable if restlessness were on the increase and, on other occasions even within the same lesson, to find 'stirring' versions of the same activities when communication is getting bogged down. In this situation the focus of flexibility is clear, the need is clearly felt, and the situation is personal. This kind of simple but pressing need establishes right from the start that flexibility and inventiveness in prior planning and in spontaneous response are necessary, normal and within the grasp of each of us.

However, being persuaded of the need to respond flexibly is not enough on its own. To respond, the teacher has to be able to 'read' the situation.

Reading the situation

It's me sitting at the back of the class watching myself or putting myself in the kids' shoes thinking 'God, how boring'.

(PGCE taped interview)

Or, as Elliott (1990) said, 'situational knowledge is knowledge based on direct experience which gets stored in memory not as a set of propositions but as a repertoire of case narrative.'

Even when new entrants to the profession bring with them an instinct for flexibility and a readiness to be inventive, creativity as a professional characteristic is context specific. A teacher needs to be able to read the classroom and make specialist choices appropriate to it. Take, for example, human interaction in the peculiar circumstances of classrooms. All the understanding in the world about cognitive processes involved in learning will not help a teacher who cannot read the mood and responses of a class. Just as we had to learn to read print so too we have to learn to read new professional situations. The iconic element of knowing is particularly strong here. As Bruner (1966) said, 'it is still true that a thousand words scarcely exhaust the richness of a single image' or, as a PGCE student said, 'I cannot imagine how I would be in a class not having seen someone else's teaching and yet be able to see myself teaching' (taped interview).

But sitting looking at events is not enough, as the emptiness of some students' pre-course observation notes show. The iconic elements of understanding must be backed up by discussion and personal action. So here too we can try to identify those elements in our existing programmes which will contribute to the ability to read the situation, for example:

- Discussing 'frozen moments' from videos of the student teacher's own class;
- Discussing 'frozen moments' from videos of others' teaching (the bar coding of sections of a film in an interactive video system is one effective way of doing this, slide sets are another);
- Teaching in situations where teachers and observers can comment together as events take place (language teachers have the advantage here as they have the privacy of a foreign language in which to comment on what is happening as it happens);
- Peer teaching with immediate commentary.

Another major source of insights and skills in reading classroom situations comes from the students' own experiences as learners on the PGCE course: 'Being in the position of learner makes you aware of what goes on in learning and makes you aware of how you can get your pupils to learn' (taped PGCE interview). Some courses ask students to keep learning diaries, for example. Sometimes it is a matter of discussing the session that the tutor has just run for the students: 'I suppose to a degree you [the tutor] act as a kind of video, reflecting everything that happens because we cannot see ourselves' (PGCE taped interview).

It will be clear from these examples that, contrary to what one might expect, the 'direct experience' that John Elliott was talking about does not have to be in school. In fact, as one PGCE tutor group found (Maclennan and Seadon 1989), this can in certain crucial respects be less not more effective in school. This is because the experience needs to be processed by the student teacher in some way, not just survived. In school there is often little time for anything other than survival. Lessons do not stop for a replay. In school new teachers are beginners, operating all the time for real. In the training institution, on the other hand, they can temporarily step out of the teacher role and become real learners with all that implies of expectation of mistakes and the encouragement to take risks.

Confidence to take risks

> We became willing to blunder, to embarrass ourselves, because the group was supportive.
>
> (PGCE taped interview)

It is not possible to be creative without taking risks. Risk-taking depends on confidence. Confidence does not mean the belief that everything will go right, but is the knowledge that getting it wrong is a normal part of learning and improving and can be survived, however, uncomfortable it may feel temporarily. Such confidence to take risks can in turn generate a shared climate of inventiveness on PGCE courses which later becomes part of the personal teacher culture of each individual. So, on what is such confidence founded? What will sustain and develop it? The remark from the PGCE student quoted above makes it clear that the group plays a key role in this. It does so in two ways. First, 'most of us can work better creatively when teamed up with the right partner because collaboration tends to induce effort and also to spur our automatic power of association' (Osborn 1953) or, in the words of a PGCE student, 'with a dozen in the group each person is going to react differently to different things but by working them out together and then sharing them it makes you think of other things' (taped interview). Such inventiveness seems later to become part of the personal culture of individuals.

There is more to it, however, than just being spurred on by the presence of others. This is again one of the areas where being out of the classroom can in certain respects be of much more practical help than being in it. This showed clearly in the reaction of one school-based group who, during half-term, returned to the university base for a workshop identical in all but location to those they had been experiencing in school. They proceeded to conduct the whole day with more verve and freshness and light-hearted inventiveness than they had ever shown in school (Maclennan and Seadon 1989). One of their number even referred to this out-of-school session as 'the best session we ever had' (PGCE taped interview).

The second way in which the group plays an important part in the development of confidence and risk-taking is in the shared experience of 'failure'. If difficulties and failures are private they can assume exaggerated significance. As many PGCE students know, it can be a matter of enormous relief and a great confidence-boost to be observed struggling with your worst class by someone you trust. The trust is an important factor. As one student teacher reported, part of the reason why we all felt we could do things and didn't feel embarrassed when we got things wrong was because we did all laugh at each other and with each other and if we hadn't all laughed at each other it wouldn't have worked.

(PGCE taped interview)

If others are party to the difficulties, and student teachers are themselves party to the difficulties of others, then the problems stay in proportion. That is surely why teachers frequently swap horror stories in the staffroom.

So we come to the question of which elements of an initial training course develop and sustain the necessary confidence and trust. Some of these begin to look familiar, for example:

- Peer teaching;
- Any events which build up the techniques for peer criticism;
- Active workshops as well as verbal brain-storming;
- Paired teaching practice placings;
- Team teaching;
- Supervision by someone who knows the student well and with whom the student already has a relationship of trusting criticism and shared laughter.

Indeed we are looking for any events or schemes which allow for the collaborative generation and the shared experience of trying out ideas.

But even if we can help new teachers to develop the confidence to take risks and even if we can provide situations which encourage the generation of ideas, the teachers still need to be able to monitor and evaluate the outcomes of those risks and ideas.

The ability to monitor and evaluate events

I like to do something. That's what I can remember because I can remember what went wrong. I can [also] remember what went right and I can figure out how to do it again.

(PGCE taped interview)

Evaluation is often discussed as a rather cerebral activity. The student quoted above reminds us that it is actually a very active affair and in its most common form is actually a private event. Most of us do not have the luxury of constant company in the classroom. The development of personal evaluation skills is an essential part of the development of creativity. To become an effective self evaluator demands honesty.

I've become aware of my good qualities and more importantly am willing and able to confront my failures and in some cases surmount them. I have learnt an honesty I did not know before.

(PGCE taped interview)

Part of learning that honesty is learning how to formulate self-criticism which includes self-approval without delusion and which offers sharp self-criticism in such a way that one does not retreat from it or undermine oneself. The student quoted above went on to say, 'the ideas that criticism here was not punitive gradually dawned on me' (PGCE taped interview).

The best forum for 'learning to criticise each other in order to be able to criticise oneself in the same way' is provided by the kinds of events which are very similar to or identical to those previously listed as highlighting the need to be creative or developing the ability to read the situation; for example, peer teaching workshops with public commentary, shared experience as the basis for criticism, criticism of the tutor's teaching which they have experienced as learners. As the group learns to criticise effectively but positively, not only does it provide each individual with a possible model for self-criticism but also, as we have seen, by making public mistakes manageable it becomes the basis for confidence and risk-taking.

But evaluation is part of creativity in its own right. Parnes (1957) identifies five procedures for creative problem solving: fact finding, problem finding, idea finding, solution finding and acceptance finding. It is interesting to see that these relate closely to an action research cycle.

We have been talking so far of self-evaluation but such a process will also be promoted or undermined by the kind of public procedures for appraisal and assessment which are in operation in a school. It must be clear by now that creativity (the skills, instincts and characteristics which develop it and sustain it) does not fit within the NCVQ behaviourist model, since it will not manifest itself in predictable outcomes. By definition creativity operates in the field of the unpredictable, doubly so in that it encompasses an unpredictable response to unpredictable circumstances. We need to find a different competency model which is more in tune with the higher order competences that Klemp (1988) identifies as being displayed by successful professionals and which is along the lines proposed by Elliott (1991). This is one of several consequences if we wish to pay more than lip service to creativity. The final section summarises those consequences briefly.

SUMMARY AND CONCLUSIONS

By common consent, schools and their learners need teachers who can respond flexibly and inventively to the specific situations, people and materials of their individual classrooms. That flexibility cannot be taken for granted nor can it be left to chance.

In discussing the kind of events which will help us to generate and sustain such inventive flexibility, the intention has been to highlight certain features in the process of learning to teach which we can ill afford to lose if we seriously maintain that creativity is at the heart of good teaching. Those features include:

- Plenty of repeated opportunity to share experiences as they happen, not just to talk about them afterwards with someone who, however interested, was not there;
- Extensive collaborative work;
- Frequent peer teaching in stable groups;
- The deliberate development of constructive peer criticism;
- A competency model which moves away from a behaviourist outcomes approach;
- Above all, the opportunity temporarily to suspend responsibility and to become a true learner instead of a beginner teacher.

These are precisely the kinds of experience which are less likely to feature in school-based work unless we go out of our way to make them do so.

REFERENCES

Bruner, J.S. (1966) *Towards a Theory of Instruction*, Cambridge, Mass: Harvard University Press.

Elliott, J. (1990) 'Educational research in crisis: performance indicators and the decline in excellence', in *British Educational Research Journal* 16 (1): 3–18.

Elliott, J. (1991) 'Competency-based training and the education of the professions: is a happy marriage possible?', in J. Elliott *Action Research for Educational Change*, Milton Keynes: Open University Press, pp. 118–35

Klemp, G.O. (1988) *Three Factors of Success in the World of Work: Implications for Curriculum in Higher Education*, Boston, Mass: McBer.

Maadi, S.R. (1975) 'The strenuousness of creative life', in I.A. Taylor and J.W. Getzels (eds) *Perspectives in Creativity*, Chicago, Ill: Aldine, pp. 173–90.

Maclennan, S. (1985) 'The role of the PGCE tutor', *Cambridge Journal of Education* 15 (1): 8–16.

Maclennan, S. and Seadon, T. (1988) 'What price school-based work?', *Cambridge Journal of Education* 18 (3): 387–403.

Osborn, A.F. (1953) *Applied Imagination: Principles and Procedures of Creative Problem Solving*, New York: Scribners.

Parnes, S. (1975) 'Aha', in I.A. Taylor and J.W. Getzels (eds) *Perspectives in Creativity* Chicago, Ill: Aldine, pp. 224–48.

Taylor, I.A. (1975) 'A retrospective view of creative investigation', in I.A. Taylor and J.W. Getzels (eds) *Perspectives in Creativity*, Chicago, Ill: Aldine, pp. 297–326.

Woods, P. (1990) *Teacher Skills and Strategies*, Lewes: Falmer.

Chapter 6

The first year of teaching as a learning experience

Les Tickle

The recent past has seen a revival of concerns, and action, to provide professional development support for teachers in their first year as a 'bridge' between initial training and later, sustained INSET (DES 1982, 1988). The introduction and monitoring of induction programmes in individual schools and local regions has taken hold, though it is clearly not universal. Certainly there has been a failure to realise the aspirations for a sustained, continuous programme of learning for all new teachers, which stretches across initial training and induction and which continues into teachers' careers in some coherent form, as was expressed in different ways in the McNair Report (1944), the James Report (DES 1972), and the government White Paper *Teaching Quality* (DES 1985), to take just three examples. Making initial training substantially more school-based is one recent, controversial, policy change in these moves toward 'progression' and 'continuity' in teacher education curriculum. Another is a series of proposals by the Department for Education for the induction of newly qualified teachers, associated with the abolition of probation. Among these proposals is the inclusion of new teachers in Teacher Appraisal regulations, and the provision of specific training grants to some local education authorities to provide induction support (DFE 1992).

Whether new teachers participate in a formal induction programme or not, it is evident that most of their learning is and will continue to be gained from direct, 'hands on' experience in the classroom. This 'learning by doing' is a period when practical experience is built perhaps more rapidly and more critically than at any other stage in a teacher's career, because of the frenetic activity and learning which is required in meeting the full demands of teaching for the first time. It is also a period in which that learning occurs mostly in isolation from colleagues (Lortie 1975). It can be seen not only as a crucial period of learning how to teach but also as a formative period in teachers' perspectives on what their learning is or should be about, and how it is or might be gained.

So, while learning by doing is not the only means of professional development available at this or any other career stage, it is an important and,

I would claim, major element in the education of new entrants. Yet there is little evidence available about that element which might help new teachers themselves, and those who would wish to support and enhance their development.

In this chapter I want to outline an image of that learning, drawn from research with a group of new teachers with whom I worked in the late 1980s. The research derived from the need to elucidate and understand the nature of first-year teachers' thinking and learning, in order to improve induction arrangements in one local education authority. The research also contributed to the introduction of the University of East Anglia's B. Phil. (Teaching) Degree for teachers who have completed their first year of teaching. What is reported here is a small part of an extensive study associated with those developments, focusing on different aspects of the education of new entrants to teaching (see Tickle 1989a, b; 1990; 1991; 1992a, b, c; in press). The present report is based on the perspectives of a group of five teachers who met regularly throughout their first year. Their experiences of the learning world which they inhabited were discussed, and recorded, in a total of sixteen meetings. The recordings were transcribed, and transcripts given to each teacher at the latest by the next meeting. That permitted immediate checking, amendment or elaboration of reports, and longer-term cross-references among ideas expressed over the months. The research resulted in the accumulation of a comprehensive account of the teachers' reported experiences, among which were many references to the ways in which they learned.

'GOING THROUGH IT'

Their worlds consisted of largely lonesome routes to the range of knowledge required for teaching and to improved means of utilising and developing their knowledge. Given that lonesome and even private world, the conversation in the group was much less about how the teachers learned from colleagues, and more about how they learned alone, by 'going through it'.

DEB: Is that something somebody can actually tell you, or is it one of those things that infiltrates through osmosis and that, eventually, through seeing a year's lot of work, you actually get an in-built knowledge? (18 November)

SUE: I've been left on my own and if I've learnt I've learnt on my own terms and not on somebody else imposing ideas and strategies and everything upon me. (2 December)

The circumstances of that learning had a number of notable features. In particular, the unpredictability of events made direct experience perpetually problematic, since the combination of variables affecting any specific circumstance was complex. The information needed to predict and manage events was often elusive. Even the teachers' own ideas were sometimes unclear and uncertain. It was these factors which made 'second-hand' learning either irrelevant or at best subject to testing and first-hand experience. But, given the instability of situations and volatility of personal responses to events, what were the guiding procedures for gaining experience? Initially it was to treat events as a practice-ground, and to store them in memory.

SUE: The make-up of a particular group is different every year, so problems with one particular exam group are different every year, so experience is there for you to draw on and say, in a couple of years' time, when you have the same kind of problems, 'oh, yes, I remember that group, I did this with them'. (18 November)

This confirms the notion that it was important to construct a repertoire of such experience, to provide first-hand knowledge (Schön 1983). That, in Dave's terms, meant maintaining a healthy distrust of knowledge from all sources, while on the road to becoming experienced:

DAVE: I think it's important to distrust what you're doing. I think it's building up a body of experience that is your experience rather than second-hand information, and once you start doing that then perhaps you become, with a capital T, 'Teacher'. (18 November)

The notion of the capital T teacher (see Tickle, in press) as someone imbued with a body of practical experience was shared by each of the teachers. However, the acquisition of that body was not something which simply happened or which could be gained by the practice of specific classroom techniques. Such techniques, namely speaking clearly, asking questions, distribution of resources, preparation of worksheets, marking of homework, and so on, were largely taken for granted as 'those things learnt at college', and 'the kind of thing your supervisor told you about on teaching practice'. The teachers' concern now in gaining first-hand experience was much broader, and was seen as achievable only through the development of perceptiveness during classroom events, and through self-conscious reflection about the decisions made and actions taken. That involved a search for evidence, by monitoring the responses of pupils to one's teaching; by seeking impressions of what was actually done in specific situations, as against what might have been done; or simply by observing events as they occurred. These were some of the means of evaluation, adopted in striving towards the most effective teaching and learning. They amounted to constant surveillance and reflection, especially in the immediate post-action situation, and required rapid processing of data:

DEB: You've still got to be watching out the whole time for their eyes and for their attitude and for the way they are or what they are doing, as to whether they are lapsing or not. (2 December)

'Going through it' by testing out initial judgements made in planning, and implementation of those plans in teaching against pupils' responses, incorporated such reflection as the central feature of formative evaluation. Those evaluations were perceived with the same 'distrust' as were actions, when it came to considering their value for future events:

DEB: I think this year is for very much trying out these things, and then next year looking back and thinking, 'well, that one worked reasonably well but I would improve it in this way, and that way and another way to make it a little bit more slick, and it will actually work a little bit better, and it was a bit hit or miss in that place or that place'. (2 December)

In the practice-ground for now, however, it was largely a case of hit or miss, especially in the immediate and medium term. Recognising the pupils' immediate responses meant that the teachers also reflected on practice in the less immediate afterwards. The process certainly included immediate responses to the implementation of their own planning decisions, judgements, and performance. They selected information to feed the reflections in the immediate term, and responded to situations or adjusted their teaching on the spot on the basis of that information. On-the-spot reflections, responses, and adjustments to teaching were also remembered, and fed later thoughts in the process of reflecting back on events. These in turn were seen as feeding the capacity to predict and anticipate future events, in a way which the teachers saw as meeting their aspiration to improve teaching. At this stage the lack of experience was a self-conscious phenomenon which left most judgements and actions to be 'distrusted'. The teachers were self-conscious about their own inability to make sound, dependable judgements or to take assured action. These considerations were not about teaching technique, but about making 'effective' judgements. Developing such judgements was for them an important element of practical proficiency which was coupled closely with growing independence and self-sufficiency. The way in which this capacity could be realised was thought to be through self-criticism, again in private:

LIZ: Having to learn to be able to judge my lessons for myself, being self-critical, to work out 'Am I going along the right roads? Why am I teaching this lesson – is it leading to anything?' Having to do that the whole time. (2 December)

The immediate, on-the-spot judgements raised questions for the teachers about how to gauge a situation when immediate action was required so as to know how to act appropriately for the circumstances. Dave identified clearly the dilemmas involved in making judgements on the spot, and located recurrent examples of his practice when different judgements over superficially similar events were needed. For example, treating different children's social behaviour differently, in what might appear to be similar situations, in order to achieve the best results from action for each particular child, was crucial to the development of good relationships with pupils – a major priority for each teacher. In any case, some information was not available until after action had been taken. But it was not clear from the teachers' deliberations whether, for example, Liz could gain and sustain opportunities to address such questions as 'why am I teaching this lesson – is it leading to anything?'. Such deeper problematics appeared to be submerged by concerns about information processing in the more immediate context of classroom interactions and the rigours of the route to experience.

EXPLORATORY RIGOUR

What was the nature of these rigours? Was the pace of events such that they submerged any view of the reason for being on the route in the first place? Let me consider these in relation to just one element of teaching. The problem of judgement had to incorporate appropriate means of relating 'well' to individuals, within appropriate ways of responding to the corporate body of a group or class. And the solution needed to offer both short-term and long-term 'benefit', in the context of the aim to achieve the best learning for all pupils, when each of these may also require different responses. This was a feature of the route to be trodden with caution, yet which had to be crossed quickly, to establish the right combination of good rapport, high motivation and workrates, disciplinary approaches, and effective means of communicating concepts or instructing in skills. The combination did not constitute a recipe mix suitable for all events or people. For instance, judging the language appropriate for explaining concepts to different children, or particular teaching tactics appropriate to individuals, was clearly exemplified. How could that be achieved when getting to know individual pupils was exceptionally difficult in the first place? So the need to conduct teaching in a way which was perceptive and also receptive to the 'messages' of classroom events was part of the trial and error of experience. Yet the elusiveness of information was a feature of events which heightened the need for perceptual acuity, but maintained a sense of groping and grappling with uncertainty. This was discussed with regard to pupils' academic achievements. Dave had undertaken a prediction of exam scores for a class, which he compared with actual scores, as an investigation. Reporting it led Debbie to reflect on the problematic nature of information handling:

DEB: Well, all of us as teachers are making value judgements about the children, the work that they are capable of and able to do, based on certain aspects that we have seen of them. When you actually analyse it, we don't really know and that can be dangerous. (8 March)

The combination of searching, selecting, assimilating or rejecting information through this kind of monitoring and then modifying teaching in response engaged the teachers constantly. The management of individual 'cases' for these teachers was a search for 'appropriate' action, in the sense of action which solved problems and was 'effective', within the values which underlay their aims for the best possible learning for every child. Debbie described the deliberations as 'constantly turning situations over in my mind'. That occurred in anticipation prior to events, during the conduct of events, and in reflection after them.

Perhaps the most difficult pieces of the puzzles of classroom life which the teachers tried to solve were those with blurred images or no picture at all, where a lack of information or its inaccessibility formed a puzzle in itself. Difficulty in diagnosis led in such instances to uncertainty in trying out solutions. This was described as 'playing it by ear', for example, in talking 'maturely' with the children, testing their reactions, and proceeding step by step to balance motivation, good relationships, and effective learning. The notion of 'playing it by ear' seemed to form a central response to the acknowledgement that 'you can't say that that [i.e. any particular action] will work'.

Nevertheless, within this insecurity, this healthy 'distrust' of one's judgements, decisions were made, had to be made, and actions taken. So, what strategies were invoked in this gathering of experience? 'Playing it by ear' (and eye, of course) represented part of the exploratory process, the eliciting and receiving of impressions and information; the selection and interpretation of it; the formation of plans; and taking action based upon it. But the elusiveness of the information, its complexity, its lack of dependability, meant taking action on the basis of 'playing the hunch'. Playing the hunch with regard to choice of curriculum topic was also a recurrent feature of planning and practice. Debbie, for example, had introduced ecology as a concept in humanities, without knowing how the children would respond, in terms of interest or handling concepts. Sue introduced role play as a means of teaching about the Incas. The others had many different examples. Playing it by ear and playing the hunch (or vice versa) combined elements of underlying educational aims and ideals with managerial judgement.

Achieving motivation, good relationships, and the most effective learning for every individual pupil were common referents when the teachers discussed their aspirations for developing the quality of their teaching. Those aspirations were pursued, however, within the context of the uncertainties of situations, which meant that the teachers depended on 'intuition' for determining action. Other purposes and judgements were also evident in the conversations. Among these, gaining and maintaining credibility as a teacher, especially by being consistent in one's actions, was important. Being able to plan and prepare alternative courses of action rapidly if 'error' of judgement was detected was also a paramount concern. Sometimes such considerations were not easy to reconcile, and learning to play the hunch meant learning to manage inconsistency, tension and conflict as a persistent feature of the route to 'experience'. Handling that conflict and improving on the judgements seemed to depend on the frequency of hunch-playing and the intuitive handling of evaluative 'evidence' – the evidence of what 'worked', in specific teaching episodes and particular circumstances.

HONING EXPERIENCE

Evaluative judgements were made difficult because of the complexity of information-processing. Achieving their aspirations depended on the teachers' ability to manage multiple elements of information and events at one time:

DEB: It is so difficult when you've got the classroom management, the organisation, the marking, the problems, you're dealing with everything from SMP level 2 to SMP level 6 in my class and you all know that is a . . . so wide ranging from very remedial right to high-flying stuff, and its mental gymnastics. And then trying to talk to the children and deal with them as people – plus interruptions. (2 December)

There was a possibility of learning particular sequences, of routinisation, of becoming 'honed in', as Debbie put it, to particular tactics and strategies in teaching, especially where particular kinds of problems were recurrent and solutions tested to a point of removing the problematic. This certainly occurred with what Liz described as those 'hundreds of little things, nothing very big, nothing I can't really cope with', such as organisational arrangements. However, while this was regarded as a desirable state of 'certainty' in respect of such matters as organisation, it was also seen as an undesirable removal of thrill and challenge within the realm of teaching strategies. There was a desire to remove risk by mastery and achieve proficiency through practice in some areas, yet when that was done it was supplemented consciously by introducing new ventures, which were known to entail risk and the same sort of uncertainty in learning. During the first term most aspects of teaching carried risk of failure as well as promise of success until it had been demonstrated that they 'worked'. Not all, however; some carried such promise of success that they offered little stimulus or opportunity to learn. Teaching some lessons repeatedly, for example, led to a search for stimulus during that term as 'boredom' was experienced:

DAVE: [I] woke up one day [thought to myself] 'These lessons have been boring, they've just become boring because you are just doing the routine.' After a while you have to start inventing your own challenges. (4 November)

SUE: My main thing is that . . . it [level of subject knowledge] is just not very intellectually challenging. (4 November)

Both the search for and the willingness to initiate and undertake intellectually challenging ventures in the classroom ran in parallel with responding to the very many ready-made challenges, and the 'honing' and routinising of solutions. This can be explained by Dave's concern to identify not just 'what works?' but 'what is best?'. In the everyday demands for decisions, judgement and action, in the information-processing through perceptiveness and in the receptivity to ideas and possibilities which accompanied practice, the skills of mental gymnastics seemed essential. As for the physical gymnast, they entailed a range of routines (in the sense of movements and sequences) from the mastery of 'basic' actions, through tried and tested repertoire elements, to new developments. However, there were considerable differences from the world of physical gymnasts. Even some 'basic' elements confounded mastery because of the elusiveness of information, the unpredictability of events, and the relative anarchy of human responses and interactions. Others were mastered. Certainly there was a sense of mastery and confidence in the technical 'skills' of teaching, with some minor exceptions.

UNDERLYING EDUCATIONAL VALUES

What was problematic, and also deliberately problematised (I use 'deliberate' in terms of conscious intention and thoughtful action), were teaching strategies which would enable the aims of teaching to be realised. There was persistent discussion about those matters. However, those aims themselves, and the underlying values of education which were held by the teachers, were not the subject of deliberation among them. Their thoughts, provided through detailed descriptions of their teaching, were centred around the means of realising pre-determined goals which in themselves seemed to be treated as unproblematic in discussions. It was the conduct of the instructional role, rather than its purposes, which provided the substance of conversations.

Perhaps the volatility of events surrounding the teachers' instructional role was in some respects responsible for this focus of attention because of their very unpredictability. Dave raised the issue of dealing with the sudden, unexpected event of a faint child, and the tension between providing for the child and managing the rest of the class. Kathy had children in her reception class who wet themselves, let alone the many other features of young children's behaviour and thoughts which simply 'happened'. Examples were legion, and by no means easy to classify: a sudden, unanticipated 'break-through' in a child's achievements; information from parents about a child; an unannounced visit by the priest.

Gaining insight and experience in such instances and events, especially those which occurred in interaction with pupils, depended, it seemed, on 'picking up on' concerns or issues, or information, which was often gained from 'a sort of feeling' and which helped to 'fill in some of the gaps' in knowledge which might have been critical for making sound judgements and taking effective action. The elusiveness of information made the topography around the route to experience very uneven and rather precarious.

What the teachers' reports indicated was that the lack of control over events and the unavailability of data, even to the perceptive teacher engaged in constant surveillance, ensured that proceeding *en route* was intrinsically problematic. Handling such events could not be achieved through an apprenticeship in skills training, in the view of these teachers, nor did the events themselves constitute a body of knowledge to be transmitted by experts and applied by novices. In that respect, 'going through it' was a rational description of what was seen as necessary for the acquisition of practical experience. 'Playing it by ear' and 'playing the hunch' could be regarded as creative strategies in that acquisition, using mental gymnastics in that playing to try to ensure 'satisfactory' practice in the face of inherent instability and unpredictability in situations.

For the teachers the call upon that mental agility continued beyond the immediacy of events. The need to interpret data, whether it was flimsy like Dave's 'feeling' or substantive like Debbie's contacts with parents, succeeded the acquisition of the data itself. The implementation of teaching plans and the making of on-the-spot judgements, applied in trial and error, led to further reflective evaluation on the events which ensued. Judgement, action and outcome were considered, providing the basis of experience for future reference. This involved questions such as 'did I do the right thing in that situation?' It was an evaluation of role performance, as well as further reflection on the circumstances surrounding that performance, and it was another form of deliberative thinking, conducted in less immediate circumstances.

As I suggested earlier, the aims and values which guided actions seemed themselves to be largely taken for granted, and appeared in discussions at a subliminal level, by inference or implication, in the description of problems and practice. For example, the treatment of all pupils as individual persons of equal worth, especially irrespective of gender, was a matter about which Liz minded deeply. A realisation that she had apparently not translated these values into practice caused her considerable anguish. She acknowledged that 'drifting along generally accepting things' in a period of quiet and calm characterised her disposition. Turbulence which led her back to questioning everything was sparked by recognition that her practice in this instance was not consistent with her values. But it seemed at this point that what mattered was to review the practice, to ensure that 'effective' strategies were invoked to realise her aims in practice. There was no discussion about the aims or about the personal theories which underlay teaching; these were only inferred in the discussions within the group, and only in relation to 'critical incidents' which in some way challenged the implied aims and values.

At such times 'minding' about the quality of practice was characteristic of the teachers' thoughts. 'Minding' focused on the acquisition of subject knowledge by the pupils (mathematical and scientific concepts, historical events, the rules and skills of sport, communication skills in language were cited examples), teaching strategies for effecting this acquisition, and the motivational and ethical questions which might ensure success for the strategies.

It led to a search for indications of success, in constantly turning things over mentally, but also in the longer term accumulation of 'indicators'. In particular the latter part of the year offered some indicators of the successes or otherwise of teaching. Earlier anticipations could now be checked against events – if only impressionistically or on the basis of restricted evidence. As well as seeking the evidence of pupils' learning achievements from the pupils themselves, the teachers reflected on just what those achievements should be, or were. The ways in which they learned criteria by which to judge the effectiveness of teaching was another experience of soliciting, assimilating and managing the largely intangible. The importance of this 'monitoring' was in part to ensure that colleagues, especially those who taught the same children, or soon would do so, would recognise the quality of teaching which had occurred. It was a matter of achieving professional credibility and respect. But it was also a matter of minding deeply about that quality on the pupils' behalf, as it were, as well as on their own behalf through the sense of professional satisfaction in realising their aims in practice.

The notion of mirroring such aims in practice was apparent at points in the discussions, especially in the later part of the year. 'Technical competence', in the sense of basic classroom skills, was still on the agenda, but was very clearly relegated. The way in which it became relegated seemed to be partly through routinisation; partly through being overshadowed by more problematic aspects of teaching, especially in the realm of making difficult judgements. Perhaps, too, the search for challenge led the teachers to other creative considerations, some of which reflected the problematics of teaching being considered at national level. Debbie, for instance, was wrestling with records of achievement. In an attempt to describe how such challenges had become more complex, Dave identified the shift from assumed technical competence to problem-awareness and self-evaluation as he broke out of a 'confidence of ignorance'. And Debbie highlighted how that state of awareness was born of the passage of time and looking back on events which had fermented and matured with experience and reflection. Once again these concerns rested predominantly within the realm of instructional strategies, where perceptiveness appeared to increase, as basic teaching skills were 'deproblematised':

DAVE: People have said my lessons are better now than they used to be. I think, because of things I've learnt, they are worse because I know I now can see the mistakes I was making and the mistakes I am making. I'm now beginning to see the problem, so instead of me appreciating that there has been an improvement it's almost as if my self-evaluation is beyond my improvement, so I can turn round and say, 'well, they [lessons] could be better', whereas I think sometimes you are in a position when you are first starting off of 'I don't know how anybody can do this better' – almost the sort of confidence of ignorance. (5 July)

SUMMARY

Most of the forms of deliberation which the teachers recorded were part of the process of determining future classroom action. Using the experience of events as perceived in reflection, potential action was constructed in that constant mental turning-things-over. The development of practice appeared to be dependent on the development of the capacity to gauge situations and to apply professional judgement, in specific circumstances, and through their own professional enterprise. Throughout the discussions the major theme of uncertainty and unpredictability was paramount. It was the sustenance of learning; in the problematic elements lay the potential for discovering not just what worked but what worked best, as Dave put it. At the same time, teaching day-to-day brought repetition of myriad minor experiences, which led to the routinisation of some things – administration, resource storage and distribution, aspects of classroom management, and so on. Other 'one off' events were 'stored' for future reference, but remained a feature of the unpredictable and were the topics of conversation throughout the year. The data confirmed and consolidated the notions of being *en route*: of going through it, playing it by ear, playing the hunch, and conducting mental gymnastics. The experiences *en route* were often unforeseen, but the focus of attention was guided by minding about the quality of judgements and actions. That disposition led to surveillance and monitoring, through whatever means possible, as a feature of learning teaching, in those worlds of often intangible evidence and anarchic information handling.

The teachers confirmed the view of beginning teaching which was described by Lortie (1975), in relation to a different group, as a time of atomised, individualistic, and 'self-made' professional experience in which:

> to an astonishing degree the beginner in teaching must start afresh, largely uninformed about prior solutions and alternative approaches to recurring practical problems . . . teachers are portrayed as an aggregate of persons each assembling practices consistent with his (or her) experience and peculiar personality. It is not what 'we the colleagues' know and share which is paramount, but rather what I have learnt through experience . . . one's personal predispositions are not only relevant but in fact stand at the core of becoming a teacher.
>
> (Lortie 1975, pp. 70, 79)

Here, personal expertise and experience which are often the currency of teacher discourse were having their foundations laid. The way in which their learning occurred was largely through the perception of, and reflection upon, phenomena and events along the road to experience. Schön's (1983) notion of a reflective practice 'cycle' of appreciation, action, reappreciation, further action, seemed to be illustrated here, though not necessarily neatly. Action occurred sometimes in the 'confidence of ignorance', sometimes through routine, or sometimes as risk where there was insufficient evidence to appreciate. Sometimes evidence was exposed after action, at times resulting in surprise, shock or even guilt. In short, not all action was 'researched', and that which was was researched in different amounts of prediction, hypothesising, immediate responsiveness and deliberative contemplation. Perhaps most important of all, actions were, as Schön's view of practitioner research allows, steered towards intended results which were judged according to 'what works for me'. That criterion confirmed that the focus of attention was not technical classroom skills, about which there is broad consensus and little room for idiosyncrasy, but 'clinical competences', that is, judgements based on practical reasoning and problem solving which underlay actions (Zimpher and Howey 1987).

The criterion, and those judgements, are inevitably conditioned by the underlying aims and values which the teachers brought to their situations. Those aims and values were much less apparent in their deliberations. They were mainly implicit, and the teachers' search seemed to be to realise them in practice, rather than to discuss, question, and perhaps develop them. That is not surprising, but is significant as a feature of their learning. It has implications for the way in which 'experience' is construed, and the way in which it is used later as a referent. What seems especially significant is that the teachers showed how repertoires of experience came to belong to them, and how that ownership was crucial in building their individual world-views of teaching, at the level of understanding their practice. This also has implications for the kinds of knowledge which they come to see as 'useful' and 'relevant' to their teaching, and their receptiveness and responsiveness to other ideas and proposals about teaching, which might arise in other forms of INSET activities.

It further has implications for whether such in-service teaching is, or should be, concerned with the professional development of teachers, in the educative sense of developing their understanding of educational events, and of their own educational aims and values, or whether it is, or might be, concerned with the long-term accretion of skills and strategies. Such potential differences in orientation towards the purposes of teacher education and the conduct of advising and tutoring, and the significance of those differences for the educational experiences of teachers, have been analysed by Zimpher and Howey (1987). I want to propose that the span of the 'bridge' which stretches from induction into sustained INSET should be built of components which take account of the significance for the teachers of learning through research, and the development of practical judgements based on perceptual acuity, as well as the need for the clarification and development of underlying educational aims and values. The latter constitute what Zimpher and Howey have called 'personal competence'.

These two kinds of components have formed the curriculum structure of the B. Phil. (Teaching) Degree at the University of East Anglia (see Tickle 1989b). This is not to suppose that classroom skills are or should be abandoned or hidden from view. They are, after all, the instruments which are brought into play in order to put judgements into effect, and to realise aims, but they can be subsumed within considerations of effectiveness in decision-making and the achievement of aims. However, it is the shift into consciousness about and development of aims and educational values which potentially is much more difficult to achieve. Values are often deep seated and hard to uncover. Yet it is through reflection on underlying educational values that the idea of 'what works for me?' could be transformed into professional debate and understanding about 'what is educationally most worthwhile?' – while practice is simultaneously modified in order more fully to express those values.

REFERENCES

Department for Education (1992) *Induction of Newly Qualified Teachers*, Administrative Memorandum 2/92, London: HMSO.

Department of Education and Science (1972) *Teacher Education and Training*, London: HMSO.

Department of Education and Science (1982) *The New Teacher in School*, London: HMSO.

Department of Education and Science (1985) *Teaching Quality*, London: HMSO.

Department of Education and Science (1988) *The New Teacher in School*, London: HMSO.

Lortie, D. (1975) *School Teacher*, Chicago, Ill: University of Chicago Press.

McNair Report (1944) *Teachers and Youth Leaders*, London: HMSO.

Schön, D. (1983) *The Reflective Practitioner*, New York: Basic Books and London: Temple Smith.

Tickle, L. (1989a) *Norfolk Probationary Teachers Project; A Report*, Norwich: School of Education, University of East Anglia.

Tickle, L. (1989b) 'New Teachers and the Development of Professionalism', in M.L. Holly and C.S. McLoughlin (eds) *Perspectives on Teachers' Professional Development*, Lewes: Falmer.

Tickle, L. (1990) 'The reflective practitioner in the first year of teaching', Paper presented to the annual conference of the British Educational Research Association, London: August.

Tickle, L. (1991) 'New teachers and the emotions of learning teaching', in *Cambridge Journal of Education* 21 (3): 319–29.

Tickle, L. (1992a) 'The assessment of professional classroom skills', in *Cambridge Journal of Education* 22 (1): 91–103.

Tickle, L. (1992b) 'The wish of Odysseus: new teachers' receptiveness to mentoring', in D. McIntyre, H. Haggar and M. Wilkin (eds) *Issues in Mentoring*, London: Kogan Page.

Tickle, L. (1992c) 'The education of new entrants to teaching', Unpublished Ph.D. thesis, School of Education, University of East Anglia.

Tickle, L. (in press) 'Capital T Teaching', in J. Elliott (ed.) *Reconstructing Teacher Education*, Lewes: Falmer.

Zimpher, N. and Howey, K. (1987) 'Adapting supervisory practices to different orientations of teaching competence', in *Journal of Curriculum and Supervision* 2 (2): 101–27.

Chapter 7

Newly qualified teacher training
A model for progress in a time of change

Michael Ransby

The future for newly qualified teachers (NQTs) is uncertain as the Secretary for State shifts the emphasis for induction training towards schools and colleges (DES 1991c).

This chapter aims to:

- Provide an overview of induction training based on experiences in Norfolk Local Education Authority (and realise the opportunity to raise some relevant questions for a wider audience);
- Offer a strategy to develop competency profiles based on guidelines from the National Curriculum Council and the Norfolk Curriculum Policy Statement (NCPS);
- Draw on changes taking place in local education authorities (LEAs) with reference to corporate planning and the role of inspectors and advisers;
- Propose a model of continuous professional development – initial teacher training (ITT) → induction → in-service education and training (INSET) – which incorporates a record of professional development (RoPD).

Induction is defined as the process by which newly qualified teachers receive developmental support in order to demonstrate competence during their first year of teaching. The term developmental support is used synonymously with induction training but this semantic convenience is discussed later in the chapter. A number of inter-related themes are considered which refer to student, articled and licensed teachers as well as teacher-tutors and curricular and professional mentors. The chapter makes reference to issues and implications arising from the 1988 Education Reform Act; in particular local management of schools (LMS) and the National Curriculum (DES 1988b). It is intended that the chapter should be perceived as contentious, exploratory, and developmental in the light of changing circumstances at national and local level (Calderhead 1992, HMI 1992, Lambert 1992). Those familiar with theories of change will detect influences from the fields of educational research, the Department for Education and business management.

The account which follows is an attempt to describe a high quality induction programme which will have credibility in the new world. It is based on an evolving pattern of training, development, support and consultancy in Norfolk Local Education Authority; its specific features are highlighted in the description; its shape and format are offered as a contribution to the continuing need to provide high quality induction – and about the form this might take.

A MODEL FOR INDUCTION

Norfolk Local Education Authority's induction development programme (IDP) was conceptualised during the spring and summer terms, 1991. It evolved out of discussions between members of the inspectorate and advisory service (IAS), representatives from ITT and higher education institutions (HEIs), teachers' centres' co-ordinators, teacher-tutors and newly qualified teachers. The Local Education Authority personnel responsible for the induction development programme are a project co-ordinator and project assistant based at the County INSET Centre.

Their roles include responsibilities for:

• Strategic planning;
• Budget management;
• Liaison with schools and colleges;
• Project evaluation;
• Product marketing.

The above responsibilities are administered alongside others associated with a primary management team although the project co-ordinator is responsible for both primary and secondary phase newly qualified teachers. There are four area consultation teams which provide additional developmental support for newly qualified teachers and teacher-tutors across the Local Education Authority. Each area consultation team is composed of a senior adviser, a teachers' centre co-ordinator, and a primary and secondary phase teacher-tutor and meets at a teachers' centre. One role of the area consultation teams is to offer advice on areas relating to key stage, phase and cross phase when this is not available in a school or college; as well as guidance on curricular, professional and managerial matters which are not resolvable in a school or college.

The induction development programme caters for approximately 150 primary and secondary phase newly qualified teachers per year. In 1991/92 there were 57 primary phase (33 permanent and 24 temporary) appointments and 67 secondary phase (48 permanent and 19 temporary) appointments of newly qualified teachers. The principal aim of the induction development programme is 'to enhance the curricular, professional and managerial development of newly qualified teachers through a cohesive model of developmental support' (in 'Vision Statement': internal report to senior

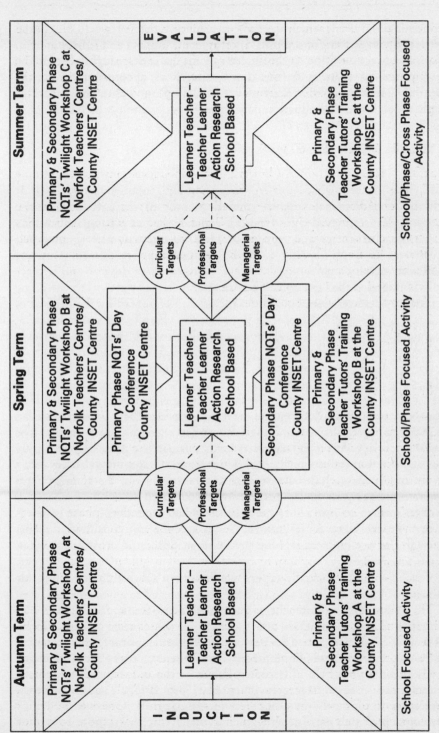

Figure 7.1 Induction development programme: Conceptual map

M. Ransby/LL/September 1992 ©

adviser [INSET/FE] from project co-ordinator, March 1991, p. 1). It operates in the light of requirements of the Department for Education's Administrative Memorandum 2/92 (DFE 1992b) and the principles and procedures embodied in *A Statement of Policy for the Curriculum, 5–16*, often referred to as the Norfolk Curriculum Policy Statement (NCC Ed. Com. 1989). There are three prime elements to the induction development programme which attempt to ease the transition between ITT and employment in schools and colleges:

- In-school developmental support for NQTs;
- An area programme based at five teachers' centres;
- A central programme based at the County INSET Centre.

All the developmental support offered as part of the area and central programmes is achieved within modest expenditure but is based on a policy of equality of access and opportunity. A conceptual map (Figure 7.1) illustrates the overall model of developmental support offered to newly qualified teachers.

It is intended that the conceptual map should be read horizontally and vertically; in-school developmental support is represented by the process of learner/teacher–teacher/learner action research which focuses on curricular, professional and managerial experiences. In the model, readers can observe that the primary focus for developmental support is the classroom in a school or college during the autumn term. Newly qualified teachers spend this term addressing the demands of the National Curriculum and being socialised into the cultures of schools and colleges. In the spring term newly qualified teachers are encouraged to explore other schools or colleges in similar phases so as to appreciate alternative approaches and to reflect on their practice. The Local Education Authority supports visits through the provision of supply teacher cover but expects newly qualified teachers to report their observations in writing or through discussion with teacher-tutors. In the summer term opportunities exist for newly qualified teachers to visit other phase schools or colleges so as to acquire a 5–16 perspective and consider cross phase issues. It is the responsibility of teacher-tutors to guide newly qualified teachers through the varying stages of development according to shared patterns of experiential learning.

Teacher-tutors are usually experienced teachers who are able to act as role models for newly qualified teachers; they are expected to enjoy the respect of pupils or students, headteachers, governors and parents. Their ability to articulate views about classroom practice in the context of a personal, philosophical or conceptual framework is deemed a desirable characteristic. In recent years school development (management) plans have provided teacher-tutors with helpful frameworks for action which relate to specific schools and colleges (Hargreaves *et al.* 1989, 1991). The fundamental principles and procedures embodied in the Norfolk Curriculum Policy Statement provide a more general guide to which teacher-tutors are expected to relate. These innovations are important as they underpin moves towards more cohesive approaches at school, college and Local Education Authority level; they mirror similar developments at national level. In a number of schools and colleges the role of teacher-tutor is officially recognised as part of the senior management team's responsibility with documentation on role descriptions and person specifications. There are many schools and colleges where the role of teacher-tutor is undertaken without the benefit of role descriptions and person specifications. All schools and colleges receive detailed notes on 'actions to be taken' and 'support to be communicated' by the teacher-tutor which begin from the time of the newly qualified teacher's appointment.

There are plans to enhance the status of teacher-tutors based on a new qualification which will focus on classrooms in schools and colleges. A credit accumulation and transfer scheme has been negotiated with City College, Norwich which will offer teacher-tutors an Advanced Diploma in Professional Development (ADPD). The ADPD will necessitate submission of a portfolio of action research which will equate with a module of study of approximately one hundred and fifty hours. It will be possible for teacher-tutors and newly qualified teachers to engage on shared approaches to classroom-based problems with accreditation for collaborative action research. The ADPD will allow teacher-tutors to develop their knowledge, skills and understanding of the role of teacher-tutor from September 1992. It is unknown whether the ADPD will inspire teachers to become teacher-tutors but much interest has been expressed by those currently in post. Those teacher-tutors who complete the ADPD will have an opportunity to upgrade their qualifications for a higher degree from any eastern region HEI consortium – in this case Anglia Polytechnic University. Norfolk Local Education Authority views the ADPD as a way of improving the quality of developmental support available to newly qualified teachers; it may, incidentally, lead to increases in incentive allowances paid to teacher-tutors.

All newly qualified teachers receive a Norfolk Local Education Authority fact pack during the autumn term (end of September). The fact packs provide comprehensive information which is designed to supplement that supplied by schools and colleges as recommended by the Local Education Authority and includes:

- A diary (with Local Education Authority telephone contacts);
- Details of the induction development programme;
- Guidelines on the role of the teacher-tutor;
- A copy of the Department for Education's Administrative Memorandum 2/92;
- A copy of the Local Education Authority's Networks (INSET) magazine;
- A copy of the NCPS;
- Documentation on the County INSET Centre and Norfolk's teachers' centres;

- A synopsis of employment conditions;
- A Local Education Authority procedural paper on the role of the adviser involved with the observation of NQTs together with a self-assessment checklist;
- A list of the area consultation teams with helpline telephone contacts.

The fact packs are distributed at a series of area induction meetings (held at twilight time) at the five Norfolk teachers' centres over one week. A small number of representatives from the inspectorate and advisory service, personnel branch and policy and planning branch attend the meetings. Newly qualified teachers are offered opportunities to raise items of interest or concern in small groups which are carefully structured but informal in style. They have the chance to listen to the experiences of newly qualified teachers who successfully completed their induction the previous year.

The developmental support available to newly qualified teachers as part of the area programme at Norfolk's teachers' centres is all workshop based (Figure 7.1). Newly qualified teachers elect in advance which teachers' centre to attend according to their school or college location or distance from home. These workshops are always jointly led by personnel with primary and secondary phase experience who adopt a collaborative approach to planning, presentation and evaluation. The workshop leaders respond to areas of perceived need which are identified by newly qualified teachers and communicated via teacher-tutors, directly to the project co-ordinator or (occasionally) through the area consultation teams. This year, topics have included:

- Classroom management;
- Teaching skills;
- Information technology;
- Flexible learning;
- Career guidance;
- Interview techniques.

The workshops during the autumn term are all run by practising teachers or headteachers many of whom hold full-time classroom responsibilities (in some cases they are also teacher-tutors). All workshops in the spring term are jointly led by advisory teachers from the County INSET Centre who often work alongside newly qualified teachers in schools and colleges. Those workshops in the summer term are jointly led by advisers based at County Hall who provide guidance from the Local Education Authority beyond the induction year.

Two newly qualified teachers' conferences are held during the spring term and are based at the County INSET Centre (Figure 7.1). All themes for the newly qualified teachers' conferences arise out of current needs or from needs identified in the previous end-of-year evaluations. These are often shaped by interests and concerns derived from the National Curriculum; in essence they focus on teaching skills and pedagogic processes. The themes for the newly qualified teachers' conferences in 1993 are classroom observation and pupil assessment (primary phase) and teaching style and pupil behaviour (secondary phase). These newly qualified teachers' conferences provide the principal opportunity for sharing perceptions, heightening understanding and reflecting on practice as a Local Education Authority group. Primary and secondary phase newly qualified teachers work in key stage, phase and area groups so as to facilitate networking, challenge in-school attitudes and promote wider understanding. The newly qualified teachers' day conferences are planned with the assistance of the inspectorate and advisory service, external consultants and newly qualified teachers. Those principles and procedures embodied in the Norfolk Curriculum Policy Statement are recurring points of reference for personnel with responsibility for leading the newly qualified teachers' conferences.

Newly qualified teachers and teacher-tutors have frequent opportunities to evaluate the induction development programme. Evaluations may comprise individual or collaborative verbal reactive evaluations throughout the programme; also individual or collaborative written reflective evaluations during the programme. At the end of the induction year there are face-to-face meetings, based at teachers' centres, between newly qualified teachers, teacher-tutors and the project co-ordinator in order to complete summative evaluations. These area evaluation meetings (held over a week) cover evaluations on in-school, area and the central programmes and involve questionnaire responses. The written evaluations from these meetings are read by the senior adviser (INSET/FE) and an adviser (primary) as well as the project co-ordinator (IDP). Members of the area consultation teams further communicate areas of general concern to the project co-ordinator throughout the year whilst respecting the confidentiality of newly qualified teachers. Her Majesty's Inspectorate also report from time to time on aspects of the induction development programme to the project co-ordinator as part of their role. All internal and external evaluations are used to improve the quality of developmental support available to newly qualified teachers for the following year.

Teacher-tutors receive a similar fact pack of materials to newly qualified teachers in order to assist them with their role in schools and colleges. These are discussed at a series of teacher-tutor training workshops held at the County INSET Centre (Figure 7.1). It is policy for primary and secondary phase teacher-tutors to attend the same workshops which exemplify collaborative working principles embodied in the Norfolk Curriculum Policy Statement. At the time of writing six supplementary papers are being prepared by external consultants for inclusion in the 1992/93 fact packs. These will underpin teacher-tutor training workshops on the following:

- Action research;
- Classroom observation;
- Questioning techniques;
- Report writing;
- Target setting;
- Co-counselling approaches.

The fact packs also include materials from outside agencies on associated topics (such as the Teacher Education Project) compiled by the senior adviser (INSET/FE). These materials are being revised at present to include procedures for setting up distance learning modules for newly qualified teachers and teacher-tutors. It is anticipated that these new resources will be available soon for use with teacher-tutors and the curricular and professional mentors with the licensed teacher development programme.

A copy of the Norfolk Curriculum Policy Statement is included in the fact pack for both the newly qualified teachers and the teacher-tutors. The Norfolk Curriculum Policy Statement outlines the principles and procedures which should guide teaching, learning and assessment for all teachers in Norfolk Local Education Authority (accepted by all governing bodies in 1989). Norfolk's inspectorate and advisory service uses the Norfolk Curriculum Policy Statement as an evaluative framework as part of its rolling programme of inspections, reviews and surveys of schools and colleges. A senior adviser has suggested that 'The National Curriculum tells you what, but the NCPS tells you how'; as such it represents a continuum of expectations which transcend age, stage and phase. It is not expected that all newly qualified teachers will meet the high expectations outlined in the Norfolk Curriculum Policy Statement; it is hoped that they will aspire towards them as part of their continuous professional development in Norfolk Local Education Authority. The Norfolk Curriculum Policy Statement is an important reference point for newly qualified teachers and teacher-tutors to share curricular, professional and managerial development. It is used as an evaluative framework for newly qualified teachers and teacher-tutors to agree targets, outline tasks and detail success criteria on specified time scales. The Norfolk Curriculum Policy Statement represents a unique focus to help to integrate the disparate programmes offering developmental support for student, newly qualified, articled and licensed teachers.

NATIONAL POLICY

It is still unclear as to how induction training for student, newly qualified, licensed and articled teachers will be organised in the future but it is certain to be set against a background of government policy. Some attempt to examine that policy is a useful starting point.

A number of the ground rules for securing Grants for Educational Support and Training (GEST) to support induction training in 1992/93 have changed from previous years (DES 1991a). For the first time GEST funding was the subject of a competitive bid from amongst 116 LEAs in England and Wales. This move raises issues about the concept of induction and has implications for management training as a priority for LEAs in future years. In 1992/93 approximately £2.5 million was made available for induction training, which was shared between approximately forty LEAs. One reason for the change was revealed at an HMI conference on induction and probation where it was declared that 'The DES is no longer intending to support indifferent practice' (Parliamentary Private Secretary; Coventry, July 1991). The intention behind this change of policy was to encourage induction training which is conceived as cohesive, cost effective and imaginative. GEST funding is to be made available for up to three years only, with annual monitoring of the performances of LEAs so as to access funding for years two and three. The performance indicators relate to newly qualified teacher profiling, recruitment and retention and teacher-tutor training in observation, guidance and assessment. This approach is aimed at securing models of sound practice which can be disseminated to LEAs, supported by distance learning materials for schools and colleges. These developments cannot be ignored by schools, colleges and LEAs – especially those who have appointed articled and licensed teachers in efforts to overcome difficulties with recruitment.

Indeed the move to establish articled teachers' and licensed teachers' schemes is the outcome of government policy; schools, colleges and LEAs have had little option but to comply. At present Norfolk Local Education Authority has ten licensed teachers engaged in its licensed teacher development programme. A principal education officer and an adviser (INSET) designed this new start, two-year programme which is open only to those with graduate status. There are three main elements to the licensed teacher development programme:

- In-school developmental support provided by curricular and professional mentors;
- A fortnightly developmental support programme based at a teachers' centre;
- A funded three-term Open University course on 'Frameworks of Education'.

Licensed teachers have opportunities to access parts of the induction development programme including the two conferences in the spring term. The programme for licensed teachers is being monitored, with changes considered to integrate their experiences with those of newly qualified teachers. Three possibilities exist:

- Access to a local part-time, post-graduate certificate in education course;
- Use of materials from the Distance Education for Teaching Project based

at the South Bank University and Westminster College, Oxford (Kerry *et al.* 1992);
• Use of a new induction training programme produced by the National Curriculum Council.

Some need for a differentiated programme of training, development, support and consultancy is acknowledged but it is thought possible to achieve this within a cohesive, flexible and relevant induction framework.

The integration of licensed and newly qualified teachers' training has immediate appeal but is not without some difficulty. At present licensed and newly qualified teachers are recruited from national sources with limited comparable evidence to inform LEAs about suitable induction training. There appears marked variation in the ITT in which newly qualified teachers engage – despite the influence of the Council for the Accreditation of Teacher Education (DES 1989); and there is a wide range of experiences which licensed teachers have enjoyed prior to seeking qualified teacher status. In Norfolk the difficulty of providing shared induction training is compounded by the number of short-term and part-time contracts. The main concern surrounding the integration of induction training programmes is one which Her Majesty's Inspectorate recognised in 1987; namely, the need for agreed statements on the competences that newly qualified teachers are expected to achieve (DES 1988a). There have been preliminary discussions with local ITT and HEIs with a view to producing competency profiles for newly qualified teachers which will be trialled within the European Community. It is intended to pursue developments with the National Curriculum Council so as to secure a continuity of approach model at national level; with an eastern region ITT and HEI consortium so as to ensure a competency profile which relates to Norfolk Local Education Authority.

A 1991 publication of non-statutory guidance by the National Curriculum Council on initial teacher training offers a framework for supporting collaborative work on newly qualified teachers' competences (NCC 1991). This document signposts the knowledge, understanding and skills 'which might reasonably be expected of all newly trained teachers in relation to the National Curriculum' (NCC 1991, p. 2). These are detailed as:

• Awareness of the statutory framework in which the National Curriculum functions;
• Knowledge of subject content and teaching methods;
• Skills in assessment, recording and reporting achievement;
• A view of the whole curriculum; understanding of curriculum continuity; information technology capability;
• Skills in curriculum planning and review.

(NCC 1991, p. 3)

Each of the above is expanded to include detailed reference to the opportunities and experiences deemed appropriate to ITT and licensed teacher training – a menu for planning, presenting and evaluating training. The identification of a set of national expectations offers the prospect of:

- Securing a cohesive pattern of training amongst ITT and HEIs;
- Promoting developmental progression from ITT through induction and INSET.

This document paves the way for schools, colleges and LEAs to record achievements as part of a standard professional development profile for use throughout the state sector.

The development of competency profiles is currently the subject of much debate at national and local level (see Husbands' chapter in this volume). These discussions have served to highlight the issues and implications associated with accrediting curricular, professional and managerial development – which are not unproblematic; in some cases they have centred on the difficulties of reconciling philosophical perspectives with educational practice (see Elliott's chapter in this volume, and Elliott 1991).

It is advanced that any competency profile should be sensitive to an LEA's principles and procedures which influence the education in its schools and colleges. This suggests that the Norfolk Curriculum Policy Statement should be a central feature of any Norfolk Local Education Authority model which attempts to quantify or standardise newly qualified teachers' competences. There are a number of advantages to basing a competency profile around the Norfolk Curriculum Policy Statement which include:

- Its relationship to the National Curriculum;
- Its formative assessment framework relevant to primary and secondary phase and HEIs;
- Its summative assessment framework relevant to student teachers, NQTs, licensed teachers and articled teachers;
- Its acceptance by all governing bodies in Norfolk LEA.

It would be possible to expand the twelve key aspects of 'Teaching, Learning and Assessment: the best of current practice' (Figure 7.2) to include the competences proffered by the National Curriculum Council. This modification would be timely in view of the recognition that 'the accreditation criteria for ITT courses should require HEIs, schools and students to focus on the competences of teaching' (DFE 1992a, p. 1). Such a development would be compatible with Norfolk Local Education Authority's policy that all schools and colleges should contain a 'set of staff development profiles ... [which] ... take account of the needs of the individual, the school and the service as a whole' (NCC Ed. Com. 1989, p. 12). The presence of competency profiles would serve as uniform performance indicators which would be advantageous to governing bodies and new-style HMI or local authority inspectorate teams. All moves towards the development of Norfolk Local

Figure 7.2 Teaching, learning and assessment: the best of current practice

1   Active learning which provides opportunities for pupils to pose their own questions, to investigate issues, and to take increasing responsibility for what they do, rather than to depend exclusively on teacher 'input' and direction. Such learning makes full use of libraries and other resources to sustain enquiry and initiative.
2   Discussion between pupils and their teachers about learning programmes, and about expectations, choices and decisions within them, as part of the curriculum.
3   Continuity of learning so as to ensure progression, especially at transition between schools.
4   A variety of learning experiences, of teaching styles, and of appropriate assessment methods that the pupil can understand. These should take place in a well-ordered environment and a clear curricular framework.
5   Working contexts which offer a range of opportunities for participation individually and cooperatively in groups of various sizes.
6   Knowledge which is relevant to each pupil's needs, interests and abilities, giving emphasis to its practical application and to its future use in adult and working life.
7   Cross-curricular work which draws on knowledge, experience, understanding and skills from a variety of curricular areas.
8   Community involvement, and experiences which enable pupils to contribute to the community, to understand it and use it as a resource for learning.
9   Involvement of pupils' families in supporting the school's objectives and the pupils' learning.
10   Opportunities for pupils to reflect upon and to appraise their own work, to identify goals for further progress, and to make appropriate choices.
11   Guidance and counselling, involving the parents wherever practicable, to help pupils to recognise and assess their particular strengths and potential.
12   The assessment and recording of attainment as an integral part of the learning process at various stages through a course, involving pupils in assessing and recording their own progress.

Source: NCC Ed. Com. (1989).

Education Authority competency profiles would need to be consistent with other relevant developments.

LOCAL POLICY

It is difficult to see as yet how many schools and colleges will access opportunities to acquire grant-maintained status (GMS). The evidence at national level suggests an increasing number of schools and colleges will opt for this route but this pattern may not materialise in Norfolk. National policies, however, will have to be reflected in schools and colleges or in the new-style LEAs which remain, so there is an urgency to develop local policy.

Reports from HMI suggest that changes emanating from the 1988

Education Reform Act are becoming embedded (HMI 1991). Improvements in the range and quality of the National Curriculum; growth in whole school approaches to assessment, recording and reporting; concern for continuity, progression and moderation of 5–16 initiatives are examples of the new order of education. These moves have been mirrored in Norfolk which has been keen to establish a corporate image with shared understandings about the nature of sound educational practice. All recent Local Education Authority developments in Norfolk have placed emphasis on raising standards through a systematic 5–16 process based on regard for equal opportunities. A number of developments reflect the approach towards greater cohesion at Local Education Authority level:

- The reorganisation of Norfolk LEA into four areas;
- The requisitioning of school development (management) plans to inform schools' and LEA planning cycles;
- The utilisation of cross phase cluster groups as a basis for key stages one and two assessment training and assessment moderation;
- The implementation of appraisal training for teachers, headteachers and the IAS;
- The introduction of information technology training to support LMS.

These major initiatives have been planned to meet national directives and the priorities of the education department of Norfolk County Council.

The role of new-style LEAs in the future is far from clear; but one likely role is that of corporate planning. Norfolk County Council produced a corporate plan in 1990 to provide information on the role of the education department (NCC 1990). In the mission statement the general aim is described as 'within the resources available, to promote the full development of the individual by making available high quality educational provision and opportunities for young people and adults, maintaining responsiveness to the needs of the community in the County' (Figure 7.3). The corporate plan, which is typical of such plans emerging in the new world, contains eleven objectives which place emphasis on corporate values, collaborative working and cross branch activity on an unprecedented scale. There is already evidence of cross branch activity driven by the inspectorate and advisory service, personnel branch and policy and planning branch which draws on the methodology of management teams in business settings (Hastings *et al.* 1986). Some examples of cross branch developments which have applied team building techniques to educational contexts include:

- Induction training for NQTs and licensed teachers;
- Management training for deputy headteachers and headteachers;
- Continuous professional development for vice principals and principals in HEIs (Belbin 1981, 1991).

A need for the education department to promote a range of high quality

Figure 7.3 The corporate plan: the role of the Education Department

Aim
Within the resources available, to promote the full development of the individual by making available high quallity educational provision and opportunities for young people and adults, maintaining responsiveness to the needs of the community in the County.

Objectives
1   To define and review the LEA's Curriculum Policy statements and secure their effective delivery (including the National Curriculum) for all pupils and students, including those with special educational needs.
2   To monitor, evaluate and support the progress of all establishments.
3   To identify, and then distribute, approved levels of resourcing through the efficient administration, review and development of the County's Local Management Schemes.
4   To provide efficient and cost effective services in accordance with legislative requirements.
5   To promote a more effective awareness of the needs of pre-school children.
6   To improve the range and quality of opportunities available to students beyond 16 years of age and to increase the number of such students in appropriate full and part-time education and training.
7   To plan and reorganise accommodation and sites in the light of the level of need and demographic and curricular change.
8   To promote collaborative working throughout the service and to establish and maintain effective relationships through good communications with parents, employers and all external agencies.
9   To plan staff requirements, recruitment and retention, and to promote the development and morale of all staff through appropriate appraisal procedures and in-service education and training.
10 To provide an efficient professional service to the elected members of the County Council and make appropriate contributions to the County Council's corporate strategies.
11 To promote a positive image of the Department through good practice and effective public relations.

Source: NCC (1990).

products and services for its customers through a team approach is recognised as instrumental to the principal aim.

The use of language borrowed from business management to accompany major changes in education has received mixed reviews. It is acknowledged that language empowers or disenfranchises its users in a constant situation – a pattern which is accentuated during times of rapid change; witness the evolution of computerspeak alongside information technology. In this example (as with the National Curriculum) 'putting a handle on it' represents a means of control over a changing environment. The choice of the terms 'developmental support' and 'training in education' cannot be dismissed as inconsequential to the above train of thought. There have been semantic changes in the terminology used to describe INSET activities which reflect real and philosophical shifts at national and local level. Patterns of INSET in Norfolk Local Education Authority have changed in the last five years from relatively 'bottom up' to relatively 'top down' – and they are predicted to change again with financial devolution to schools and colleges. During this timescale, individual action strategies for managing change have given way to whole school approaches driven by national agencies backed by statutory requirements. One consequence of this has been to place emphasis on the quality of training (product) as opposed to the development (process): away from 'do it yourself INSET' towards so-called 'designer INSET'. The Department for Education's policy to focus GEST funding on management training for 1992/93 suggests that LEAs will need to follow this route towards improved quality in training (see Kerry's chapter in this volume).

SOME IMPLICATIONS OF CHANGING POLICY

It is maintained that the concept of induction entitlement fits into the national and local conditions prevailing at this time. One possibility is that an eastern region ITT and HEI consortium (including Norfolk Local Education Authority) should endorse induction training as a continuous professional development model. This would mean that induction training would become an entitlement at key stages for teachers (and others) beginning with student, newly qualified, licensed and articled teachers through to headteachers and beyond. The resourcing for induction training would be placed in the province of management training which is currently GEST funded. Norfolk Local Education Authority's commitment to a continuum of induction training would not be impossible to achieve but it would call for a radical rethink of present arrangements. It is suggested that induction training be planned by cross branch management teams to meet needs identified in school development (management) plans. The summer term of each year would be devoted to cross branch management planning to assist with in-school, area or centrally based induction training in the autumn and spring terms. It is predicted that the time devoted to planning would lead to higher quality training at the delivery stage, supported by higher quality resources. This is of major importance as Norfolk Local Education Authority moves towards substantial devolution of the education budget by 1995; other LEAs will be facing similar situations.

THE ROLE OF THE INSPECTOR/ADVISER IN THE INDUCTION PROCESS

Any review of induction training would be remiss without reference to other developments likely to affect the ways in which LEAs discharge their future responsibilities. The Audit Commission's report on the role of the local authority inspectorate pointed to serious concerns and discrepancies in operating practices amongst LEAs (Audit Commission 1989). Since 1989 many LEAs have placed greater emphasis on the role of inspection as well as continuing to provide evaluation and support for schools and colleges. This trend has been concomitant with the government's philosophy regarding:

- Subjecting schools and colleges to market forces;
- The introduction of pupil assessments;
- The publication of standard attainment task and examination results;
- The introduction of compulsory teacher and headteacher appraisal;
- The spread of LMS into primary as well as secondary phase.

All these innovative demands place more responsibility for quality control of curricular, professional and managerial matters on schools and colleges. It is maintained that any increase in GMS will accelerate the demand for a new-style HMI or local authority inspectorate (with a shared quality assurance role) to monitor the quality of such developments. Schools and colleges with newly qualified, licensed and articled teachers will need to ensure that their training programmes can stand up to examination by any new-style regulatory HMI or local authority inspectorate teams.

The responsibilities of LEAs towards newly qualified and licensed teachers have not yet been totally delegated to all schools or colleges (August 1992). Administrative Memorandum 2/92 makes it clear that newly qualified teachers – and surely by inference articled and licensed teachers – should 'have some of their teaching observed by experienced colleagues and/or LEA advisers . . . receive prompt written as well as oral feedback on the teaching observed' and further that 'LEAs should have monitoring and reporting procedures which seek to ensure that all NQTs in schools maintained by them are known and adequately supported' (DFE 1992b, Annex A, 9v, 11). In Norfolk, Local Education Authority advisers help teacher-tutors to assess the performance of newly qualified and licensed teachers against success criteria devised by members of the inspectorate and advisory service, representatives from ITT and teacher-tutors from schools and colleges. Three copies of the notes of visit (based on classroom observations) are provided for the newly qualified or licensed teacher; for the headteacher and governors; for the adviser and Local Education Authority. This approach has the benefit of drawing on advisers' understanding of the contexts and cultures in which competence is assessed. It is possible that financial devolution may threaten the advantages of this approach, especially where first time provision for newly qualified or licensed teachers is the rule. A means of safeguarding against this happening would be through the use of cross branch inspection teams operating in partnership with those engaged in management training. In this model an LEA such as Norfolk (or its specified teams which might include a new-style HMI or local authority inspectorate) would evaluate, monitor and support its schools and colleges – from a service which would be bought in.

An introduction of a record of professional development (RoPD) would help to foster quality assurance across schools and colleges in the new-style LEAs. It would not be difficult to extend the competency profiles associated with newly qualified teachers to include those in middle and senior management posts; substantial work has already been accomplished in the field of school management competences (Earley 1992b). This type of information (in rudimentary form) is available in most schools and colleges as role descriptions which already inform discussions during teacher and headteacher appraisal conferences. The facility of a Norfolk Local Education Authority RoPD would provide accreditation of management training at in-school, area and LEA level on a model with five levels (e.g. novice → advanced beginner → competent → proficient → expert). This proposal to accredit continuous professional development would have its genesis in the National Curriculum Council but would operate in the context of an LEA's curriculum policy statement and its corporate plan and would be LEA driven. An RoPD would be the final element in this new view of induction entitlement and management training applied to schools and colleges as a corporate initiative. It is maintained that the adoption of an RoPD by LEAs would fit into a national system as envisaged by the Department for Education in their review of ITT and licensed teacher training. The development of a national system based on an RoPD would offer ease of recruitment, retention and development of teachers throughout the European Community post-1992. Figure 7.4 shows a possible model.

The last few years have witnessed attempts to apply management training strategies, which are common to successful multi-national organisations, in schools and colleges (Peters 1989). Some headteachers recognised early on the move towards education becoming a people management business; they welcomed the opportunities of LMS and GMS; they were quick to dispense with the dependency cultures of LEAs (Beare *et al.* 1989). It should be apparent now that the future of new style LEAs is going to depend on their ability to market a range of high quality products and services which relate to customers' needs at reasonable cost. One consequence of this will be that newly qualified, licensed and articled teachers will be attracted to LEAs that offer high quality continuous professional development opportunities. The prospect of enhancing the quality of teachers by improving the quality of available training is consistent with principles enshrined in the Parent's Charter (DES 1991b). It is anticipated that the demand for high quality training, development, support and consultancy will lead LEAs to strive towards 'kitemark' (BS 5750) status for their products and services post-1993 (Stebbing 1990).

This chapter has reviewed induction training (including teacher-tutor, curricular and professional mentor training) in Norfolk Local Education Authority with a view to generalising its positive elements. The discussion on related issues offered some observations on integrating induction for student,

Figure 7.4 Continuous professional development model

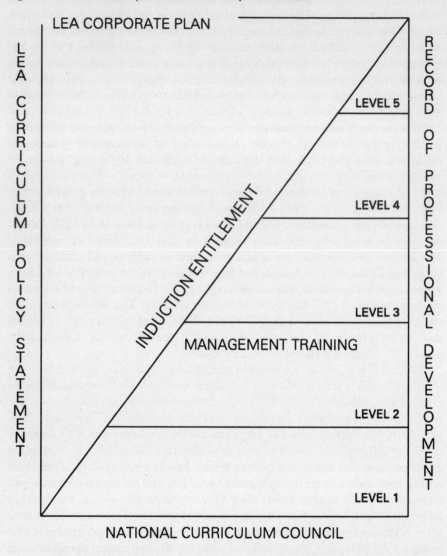

M. Ransby/LL/September 1992 ©

newly qualified, licensed and articled teachers. A case was made to develop competency profiles for newly qualified teachers which incorporated the National Curriculum Council's recommendations and the Norfolk Curriculum Policy Statement. The proposal to place an entitlement for induction training in the context of Norfolk Local Education Authority's management training was argued with reference to the role of a new-style

HMI or Local Authority Inspectorate. An innovative model which linked a Norfolk Local Education Authority RoPD with in-school, area and LEA development planning and the corporate plan was outlined. It was stated that Norfolk Local Education Authority is about to embark on a four-year programme to devolve most of its education budget, with buy-back conditions attached to the first three years. The evidence suggested that cross branch teams would be the best means for Norfolk Local Education Authority to evaluate, monitor and support its schools and colleges. If Norfolk Local Education Authority wants to deliver a high quality service to its customers it must be prepared to risk 'hands on, value driven' approaches to meet the objectives of its corporate plan (Peters and Waterman 1982, pp. 279–91).

CONCLUSIONS

The radical changes affecting education – driven by national and local policies – are transforming relationships between schools and colleges, ITT and HEIs and LEAs (Earley 1992a). A number of the views expressed in this chapter infer that LEAs keen to prosper in the new world should offer the following from a range of products and services:

- High quality induction training which meets the curricular, professional and managerial needs of student teachers, NQTs, licensed and articled teachers within a 5–16 perspective;
- High quality development, training, support and consultancy for teacher-tutors, curricular and professional mentors which is accompanied by accreditation and associated with high quality resources;
- High quality inspectors and advisers (or Officers for Standards in Education as the former are now known) able to help to evaluate, monitor and support student teachers, NQTs, licensed and articled teachers.

It is predicted that the government's interest in the three Is – ITT, Induction and INSET – and the three Cs – coherence, consistency and competency – will increase (Alexander et al. 1992). LEAs are well placed to establish models of continuous professional development within any newly formed educational partnerships. The provision of high quality 'cradle to grave' products and services should prove attractive for all concerned in the new business that is now education.

REFERENCES

Alexander, R., Rose, J. and Woodhead C. (1992) *Curriculum Organisation and Classroom Practice in Primary Schools: A Discussion Paper*, London: HMSO.

Audit Commission (1989) *Assuring Quality in Education: The Role of Local Education Authority Inspectors and Advisers*, London: HMSO.

Beare, H., Caldwell, B.J. and Millikan, R.H. (1989) *Creating an Excellent School: Some New Management Techniques*, London: Routledge.

Belbin, R.M. (1981) *Management Teams: Why They Succeed or Fail*, Oxford: Heinemann.

Belbin, R.M. (1991) *Building the Perfect Team*, training video plus briefcase booklets, Cambridge: Belbin Associates.

Calderhead, J. (1992) *Induction: A Research Perspective on the Professional Growth of the Newly Qualified Teacher*, London: General Teaching Council (England and Wales).

Department for Education (1992a) *Initial Teacher Training (Secondary Phase)*, Circular 9/92, London: HMSO.

Department for Education (1992b) *Induction of Newly Qualified Teachers*, Administrative Memorandum 2/92, London: HMSO.

Department of Education and Science (1988a) *The New Teacher in School: A Survey by H.M. Inspectors in England and Wales 1987*, London: HMSO.

Department of Education and Science (1988b) *Education Reform Act*, London: HMSO.

Department of Education and Science (1989) *Initial Teacher Training: Approval of Courses*, Circular 24/89, London: HMSO.

Department of Education and Science (1991a) *Grants for Educational Support and Training 1992/93*, Draft Circular, London: HMSO.

Department of Education and Science (1991b) *The Parent's Charter: You and Your Child's Education*, London: HMSO.

Department of Education and Science (1991c) *School-based Initial Teacher Training in England and Wales: A Report by H.M. Inspectorate*, London: HMSO.

Earley, P. (1992a) *Beyond Initial Teacher Training: Induction and the Role of the LEA*, Slough: National Foundation for Educational Research.

Earley, P. (1992b) *The School Management Competences Project: Executive Summary*, Crawley: School Management South.

Elliott, J. (1991) 'Three perspectives on coherence and continuity in teacher education' (Paper prepared for the Universities' Council for the Education of Teachers annual conference, Oxford), mimeo, Norwich: Centre for Applied Research in Education.

Hargreaves, D. *et al.* (1989) *1 Planning for School Development (Advice to Governors, Headteachers and Teachers)*, London: HMSO.

Hargreaves, D. *et al.* (1991) *2 Development Planning: A Practical Guide (Advice to Governors, Headteachers and Teachers)*, London: HMSO.

Hastings, C., Bixby, P. and Chaudhry-Lawton, R. (1986) *Superteams: A Blueprint for Organisational Success*, Glasgow: Fontana.

Her Majesty's Inspectorate (1991) *The Implementation of the Curricular Requirements of ERA: An Overview by H.M. Inspectorate on the First Year, 1989-90*, Education Observed series, London: HMSO.

Her Majesty's Inspectorate (1992) *The Induction and Probation of New Teachers 1988-1991*, Reference 62/92/NS, London: HMSO.

Kerry, T. *et al.* (1992) 'Distance education for teaching project', South Bank University and Westminster College, Oxford: (under negotiation).

Lambert, J. (1992) *Induction of Newly Trained and Appointed Teachers*, London: General Teaching Council (England and Wales).

National Curriculum Council (1991) *The National Curriculum and the Initial Training of Student, Articled and Licensed Teachers*, York: National Curriculum Council.

Norfolk County Council (1990) *Norfolk Education Department Corporate Plan: A Guide for Staff*, Norwich: Norfolk County Council.

Norfolk County Council Education Committee (1989) *A Statement of Policy for the Curriculum, 5-16*, Norwich: Norfolk County Council Education Department.

Peters, T. (1989) *Thriving on Chaos: Handbook for a Management Revolution*, London: Pan.

Peters, T.J. and Waterman Jun., R.H. (1982) *In Search of Excellence: Lessons from America's Best-run Companies*, New York: Harper & Row.

Stebbing, L. (1990) *Quality Management in the Service Industry*, Chichester: Ellis Horwood.

Chapter 8

Profiling of student teachers
Context, ownership and the beginnings of professional learning

Chris Husbands

Competency-based approaches to planning and assessment are common throughout education and training. Competency-based approaches tend to spawn profile-based assessment formats (see, e.g., Jessup 1991). Drawing on experience from both outside initial teacher education, in other vocationally related training and induction programmes, and developments within initial teacher education, a consensus appears to be emerging around the potential significance of the profiling of student teachers as a resource for their professional development in the early years of their work in schools. This paper sets out to explore some of the sources of the interest in profiling, and then distinguishes two broad lines of development within the consensus. It suggests that profiling, in spite of its acknowledged power as a tool in designing teacher education strategies and in planning for school-based induction, is a problematic strategy.

THE CONTEXT OF PROFILING INITIATIVES

The context for the developing interest in profiling can be traced to a number of sources. Amongst these, the most pervasive seems to be the development of interest in competency-based, outcomes-led professional training (Jessup 1991), perhaps seen as an alternative to incompetency-based training. The Training Agency and the National Council for Vocational Qualifications framework share perspectives within this context. At a policy level, the concept of an outcomes-based model for teacher education commands widespread support. Thus, in the Secretary of State's speech to the North of England Education Conference at the beginning of 1992, an outcomes-based model is explicitly advocated:

> The government considers that more emphasis [should be placed] on the achievement of professional competence and the achievement of defined levels of professional competence . . . The required competences should be

realistic in terms of what can be expected of newly qualified as distinct from experienced teachers.

(Clarke 1992, para. 25)

At the same time, Labour's policy document on teacher education called for

specification of standards of competence in such areas as teaching techniques, the teaching of key skills such as reading, writing and numeracy, classroom management, curriculum organisation, assessment, working with parents, record-keeping and special needs.

(Labour Party 1991)

The rapid growth of interest in competency-based models of professional learning has been paralleled by developments within teacher education (see, e.g., Pring 1991, Zimpher and Howey 1987) and by an attempt to define in detail the nature of competences which might be required of beginning teachers. It is a complex area. Writing specifically about the teaching of history, Peter Limm (1991) has recently outlined three distinct competence domains in teaching. He describes these as ideological, knowledge and action domains (Figure 8.1). The ideological domain is concerned with addressing the values and beliefs which underlie individual practice. The knowledge domain is made up of five strands: subject knowledge, pedagogical content knowledge, institutional knowledge, wider knowledge of education and knowledge of how children learn. The action domain is concerned with planning, teaching and evaluating performance. Limm's domains reflect a concern not only to specify in detail pedagogical content knowledge (see also Wineburg and Wilson 1991) but also, more generally, to isolate strands of professional competence as a basis for the generation of competency-type statements.

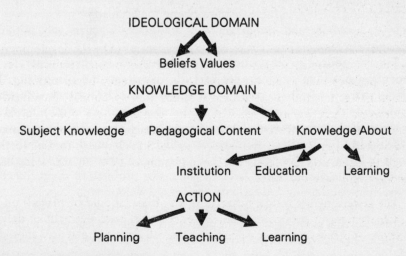

Figure 8.1 Domains of teaching
Source: Adapted from Limm (1991).

A second source for the interest in profiling is an increasing and overt concern with the application of quality control indicators in educational contexts (see, e.g., DES 1992a, CIPFA 1987); against this background, the development of interest in competency-based models for initial teacher education reflects the development of interest in appraisal as a quality control mechanism for serving teachers, through the development of criteria for the assessment and comparison of 'quality teaching'. It is in this area that there may be strong connections with discussions on teacher appraisal, since the assumption is that the constituent elements of effective practice can be isolated and defined quite separately, and can then be assessed and aggregated (Elliott 1989). The reports of the government's Interim Advisory Committee on Teachers' Pay (DES 1992b), which determined teachers' salaries between 1989 and 1992, indicate a concern to isolate generic performance indicators against which performance and, by extension, performance-related pay might be set.

Both these sources have their origins outside teacher education. However, the initiative towards profiling in initial teacher education comes also from within. Considerable information about student teachers' classroom performance is accumulated by schools, training institutions and students themselves in the period of training. This information is potentially a powerful resource for the detailed planning of school-based induction and professional development in the early years of teaching, but this information is frequently 'lost' once a student moves into employment. Profiling reflects a concern to present and make usable this information. At the same time, it reflects a concern that the award of qualified teacher status at the end of any period of training represents only a partial statement about a student's competences and achievements at a time when the professional culture of teaching is being changed rapidly. Indeed, the creation of an increasing number of entry points into teaching is likely to increase the demand for detailed information on the abilities, aptitudes and competences of beginning teachers which school management requires.

Teacher education institutions have responded to these demands by producing profiling schemes that vary in their form and complexity, but which share a common concern to increase the amount of structured information about a student which is produced in the course of training. Many of these developments were brought together in the 1990 conference on profiling in ITT. Its title, 'Building the Bridge', probably homes in on what seems to be the key issue: the idea that a professional profile which begins in the training institution can overcome the major problem of the disjunction between initial training and early professional development.

A fourth source is rather different, and is provided by the general assumption that profiling offers the possibility to involve learners, in this case beginning practitioners, in their own learning in a way which encourages them to take increasing responsibility for their own development. The introduction of profiling and records of achievement in schools has tended to be accompanied by an increased concern with the processes of teaching and learning which underpin outcomes recorded in summative profiles. Seen in this way, profiling offers an opportunity to shift the emphasis in teacher education from teaching, as represented in the models of the Council for the Accreditation of Teacher Education (DES 1984, 1989), to learning. Profiling opens the way to focus on the skills and prior learning which individual trainers bring into training, and, thereby, to identify what additional learning experiences the individual needs to undergo in the course of training. However, as David Bridges has indicated elsewhere, this is a more problematic notion than many have allowed (Bridges 1991). It can become minimalist in its definitions of education and narrowing in terms of the curriculum, reducing teaching to the 'delivery' of those experiences which are to be recorded on summative profiles.

SHAPING PROFILING

Against this background, there have been two general lines of development. The first, which draws extensively on the competency-based approach to teacher education, depends on the isolation and definition of specific-skill strands with competency descriptors. This was the model adopted in 1989 for a pilot profile at Cambridge University, and since abandoned (Reiss and Beardon 1990). The difficulties relating to such an approach seem to be quite considerable. The Cambridge model rests on similar assumptions to those outlined in the revised CATE model for teacher competence which will operationalise the government's reforms to initial teacher education: specific competences are isolated and identified and performance against these competences is then separately measured. It constitutes what might be described as a laboratory model of teacher-competence and it rests on a number of assumptions.

In the first place, the demonstration of competency descriptors in this approach is assumed to be context-free: that adequate performance in a particular skill area can be assessed irrespective of context. 'Classroom control', whilst it can be defined as a competence descriptor ('is able to control a class') is far from being either discrete or measurable in any context-free way: the ability to control Class X does not of itself generalise to the ability to control Class Y; the ability to control classes will depend on the class, the setting, the content being taught. And, in this case, classroom control is not a direct performance indicator of effective teaching; it does not measure the effectiveness of what is taught nor the ways in which teacher activity links to what is learned. At best it is an indirect indicator of classroom relationships. Finally, control in school A will differ from what counts as control in school B. Thus, a competency-descriptor approach is of little use: it does not seem to be the way in which teaching works. Context is all important, and the descriptor is too general, defining a cluster of skills rather than just one.

Second, effective performance in this approach is seen as being defined by effective performance against discrete descriptors. Thus, for example, the Cambridge UDE pilot project on profiling identified fifteen different classroom skills, including:

- To understand the different ways in which pupils develop and learn and the ways in which pupils' work can be planned to secure clear progression;
- To establish good working relationships with classes and individual pupils.

In addition, it identified twelve separate 'Wider professional skills', including:

- To understand the structure and legal framework of the educational system;
- To contribute to the pastoral aspects of the school.

Each of these was assessed on a four-point scale. It is not that any of these is an undesirable feature or quality, but that effective teaching is probably defined by some combination of them rather than discretely in each of them. As John Elliott has suggested, effective professional performance can be alternatively defined by effective performance across a range of indicators in a particular context: the ability to act intelligently in context (Elliott 1991).

The third general difficulty relates to the possibility of defining performance descriptors which are valid across disciplines, contexts and age-phases and which will provide a simple and usable map of professional learning; in other words, to the issues raised by the values which underpin the descriptor statements. The Cambridge example is again appropriate: the criterion on 'establishing good working relationships with classes and individuals' is clearly value-laden. What constitutes effective working relationships in, say, science will be different from that in drama, and the tactics and strategies by which effective relationships are established will differ. In fact, though it would be difficult to argue the point without detailed case study research, it may well be that it is only possible to show where the negative situation pertains: where, in this instance, effective working relationships are absent. It is difficult to construct positive profiles in such cases.

For these reasons there is a second approach to the issue of teacher profiling, which depends on the designation of broad, generic areas of performance. If there is a consensus in policy terms that a competency-based generic approach to the assessment of student and beginning teacher is needed, there is also a broad consensus in policy terms on the sorts of generic competences which might be required. The government's competence-based proposals for the reform of initial teacher education (DES 1992c) are construed on this model, based on pedagogical content knowledge, subject application, classroom management, assessment of and recording pupil progress and wider/further professional development. Generic approaches underpin practice in a number of PGCE profiles. For example, the profile used at the University of East Anglia identifies the following as the constituent elements of student teacher performance:

- Preparation;
- Teaching skills;
- Classroom manner;
- Relationships with pupils;
- Analysis of teaching;
- Professional attitudes.

However, the generic approach, which at its most basic reflects a rather gruff common sense 'man on the Clapham omnibus' approach to what constitutes effective teaching, is none the less problematic in a number of important respects.

In the first place, the policy basis for the assertions reflects empiricist assumptions about the definition of teaching competence, in which teaching is a technical and procedural activity. The assumptions are starkly different from those made by HMI in defining the 'qualities of good teachers in 1985':

> it goes without saying that the minimum expected of teachers is that they should be reliable, punctual and co-operative and willing to take on essential tasks which relate to the care and safety of those in their charge ... It should also be expected that they are of such a personality and character that they are able to command the respect of their pupils not only by their knowledge of what they teach and their ability to make it interesting but by the respect which they show for their pupils, their genuine interest and curiosity about what pupils say and the quality of their professional concern for pupils.
>
> (HMI 1985, pp. 2–3)

The descriptors here are in no way technical indicators; rather they are descriptions of personal qualities and a cast of mind. HMI shy away from the description of technical competences.

A second area of difficulty relates to different definitions of what constitutes adequacy in performance. Norris has cast doubt on competency-based approaches to teacher assessment (Norris 1991). However, competency debates themselves are frequently confused, eliding teacher competency (any single knowledge, skill or value position relevant to the successful practice of teaching) with teacher competence (the repertoires of competences a teacher possesses) and both of these with teacher performance (what a teacher does in a specific classroom as opposed to what she or he is able to do). It would, for example, be possible for a teacher described as exceptionally competent to perform none the less in a merely mediocre way in some settings. As Richard Pring notes, 'professional development cannot be analysed out into a list of competences, even though to be a professional requires, amongst other things, being competent at a range of identifiable tasks' (Pring 1991, p. 2).

Finally, all of these presuppositions focus on teacher-inputs only and fail to consider the critical issue of teacher-effectiveness (the effect that a teacher has on pupils) which depends not only on competence and performance but also on pupil performance. Meryl Thompson has suggested (Thompson 1991) that policy-definitions of competence in NVQ and Training Agency formulations draw incoherently on these definitions, ranging from 'the ability to perform work activities to the standards required in employment' to 'competence characterised as ... encompassing intellectual, cognitive and attitudinal dimensions, as well as performance' (CNAA 1990).

Furthermore, both current and proposed models of teacher education produce problematic issues for the development of profiling. There is a dichotomy between a training programme leading to the award of QTS and one culminating in the production of a profile. In the one, a straight pass/fail judgement is made; competent performers are deemed to receive qualified teacher status (QTS), and their career begins with, so to speak, a *tabula rasa*. Professional induction may, but need not, build on strengths and weaknesses already defined, and much current induction work is based on 'administrative-learning': adapting to the demands of a new institutional setting. In the latter, the profile indicates broad areas of weakness and strengths which are addressed in the first years of teaching. In this model, the award of QTS at the end of training may or may not be justified and, in many cases, a more qualified judgement may be appropriate. The evidence of the HMI report on 'The New Teacher in School' (HMI 1987) is that many schools expect too much of newly qualified teachers: 'The expectations of many [schools] were excessive and a small number of secondary schools were unrealistic in expecting ... [NQTs] ... to function as fully fledged practitioners' (p. 6).

CONCLUSIONS

The development of profiling in schools has been most apparent as an alternative to more traditional models of assessment, with some evidence of cynicism amongst students about its long-term utility for them as opposed to traditional 'pass/fail' assessment. Students who achieve QTS move on to schools as fully fledged teachers. The reality is more complex: formative profiles reveal a whole host of issues which they need to address. But there is, at the moment, every incentive against making this information public to employers. Since the profile is student-owned, it is difficult to unlock its information.

Finally, both generic-competency and individual competency-based models cast teaching as a practical activity: teacher performance and teacher competence are elided. Darling-Hammond describes this as a 'bureaucratic' model of teaching in which 'teachers do not plan, conduct and evaluate their work; they merely perform it' (Darling-Hammond et al. 1983, Darling-Hammond 1986). Elliott concludes that competency-based models effectively collapse theory on to practice (Elliott 1991). Darling-Hammond's alternative model of teaching, which she articulates as a 'professional' model, emphasises the importance of reflection and evaluation, and approaches the models of professional education that are derived from the Home Office Project on police training in which effective performance is defined in terms of deriving from 'competence in assessing the total situation' 'self-monitoring one's own conduct', 'empathising accurately with the concerns of others' and 'exercising power and authority in a manner consistent with organisational goals and professional ethics' (Elliott 1989, pp. 96–7, MacDonald *et al.* 1987).

It is possible to envisage a scenario in which profiling-based approaches to the assessment of teachers in initial training could be workable in administrative and management terms; indeed, we may well be moving into such a scenario. It would be based on a 'National Curriculum' for initial teacher education, in which the coherence of training is provided not through the institutional location of training but through the common core experiences offered to trainers, and models of such training are now available (NCC 1991). Against this background, profiling appears to offer a mechanism for the tighter management and assessment of entrants to the profession. There is a need for debate on the extent to which such a prospect is desirable. As Fennell (1989) observes, competence profiling 'is the area in which the industry itself stamps its ownership and exercises a decisive influence on the validity of its future qualifications'.

However, profiling as a basis for the assessment of new entrants will remain chimeric. There is an important distinction between the definition of minimal competence and competency-based outcomes in professional training. Competency-led profiles re-define the nature of teaching. They direct attention to technical and managerial components of teacher performance and away from more important issues of teacher effectiveness. They assume a consensus on teaching style and input which is rarely in evidence. The technical and value issues which underpin profiling approaches in teacher education cannot be avoided; as Ashworth and Sexton (1990) note, 'not all human activity – even directly work-related human activity – fits the competence model'. With Pring (1991) we might note that competency and profiling-based approaches are unable to record the internalising of certain values: 'those which determine the quality of the relationship between teacher and learner . . . being introduced into a professional community defined by social and ethical purposes, not merely a range of competences' (p. 3).

REFERENCES

Ashworth, J. and Sexton, E. (1990) 'On competence', *Journal of Further and Higher Education* 14 (2): 15–27.
Bridges, D. (1991) 'From teaching to learning', *Curriculum Journal* 2 (2): 137–51.
Certified Institute of Public Finance Accountants (1987), *Performance Indicators in Schools: A Contribution to the Debate*, London: CIPFA.

Clarke, K. (1992) Speech delivered to North of England Education Conference, January, London: HMSO.

Council for National Academic Awards (1990) *Competence-based Approaches to Teacher Education: Viewpoints and Issues*, London: CNAA.

Darling-Hammond, L. (1986) 'A proposal for evaluation in the teaching profession', *Elementary School Journal* 86 (4): 61–84.

Darling-Hammond, L. *et al.* (1983) 'Teacher evaluation in the organisational context: a review of the literature', *Review of Educational Research* 53 (3): 161–75.

Department of Education and Science (1984) *Initial Teacher Training: Approval of Courses* [established Council for Accreditation of Teacher Education], Circular 3/84, London: HMSO.

Department of Education and Science (1989) *Initial Teacher Training: Approval of Courses*, Circular 24/89, London: HMSO.

Department of Education and Science (1992a) *Reform of Initial Teacher Training: Consultation Paper*, London: HMSO.

Department of Education and Science (1992b) *Report of the Review Body of Teachers' Pay and Conditions*, London: HMSO.

Department of Education and Science (1992c) *Criteria for the Accreditation of Initial Teacher Training*, London: HMSO.

Elliott, J. (1989) 'Appraisal of performance or appraisal of persons', in H. Simons and J. Elliott (eds) *Rethinking Appraisal and Assessment*, Milton Keynes: Open University Press.

Elliott, J. (1991) 'Three perspectives on coherence and continuity in teacher education' (Paper prepared for the Universities' Council for the Education of Teachers annual conference, Oxford), mimeo, Norwich: Centre for Applied Research in Education.

Fennell, E. (1989) 'The analysis of competence: an overview', *Competence and Assessment*, 1 December, pp. 1–17.

Her Majesty's Inspectorate (1985) *Good Teachers*, London: HMSO.

Her Majesty's Inspectorate (1988) *The New Teacher in School*, London: HMSO.

Jessup, Q. (1991), *Outcomes: NVQs and the Emerging Model of Education and Training*, London: Falmer.

Labour Party (1991) *Teacher Education and Training*, London: Labour Party.

Limm, P. (1991) 'The professional craft knowledge of the history teacher', *Teaching History*, July.

MacDonald, B., Argent, M.J., Elliott, J., May, N.H., Miller, P.J.G., Taylor, J.T. and Norris, N.F.J. (1987) *Police Probationer Training: The Final Report of the Stage II Review*, London: HMSO.

National Curriculum Council (1991) *The National Curriculum and the Initial Training of Student, Articled and Licensed Teachers*, York: National Curriculum Council.

Norris, N. (1991) 'The trouble with competence', *Cambridge Journal of Education* 21 (3): 331–41.

Pring, R. (1991) 'On being competent', Paper presented to the Universities' Council for the Education of Teachers annual conference, Oxford.

Reiss, M. and Beardon, T. (1990) 'Profiling in initial teacher education: a pilot study', *Science Teacher Education*, April.

Thompson, M. (1991) 'Competences: the implications for training courses', Paper presented to the Universities' Council for the Education of Teachers annual conference, Oxford.

Wineburg, S. and Wilson, S. (1991) 'Subject content knowledge and the teaching of history', *Advances in Research on Teaching* 2: 304–47.

Zimpher, N. and Howey, K. (1987) 'Adapting supervisory practices to different orientations of teaching competence', *Journal of Curriculum and Supervision* 2: 101–27.

Chapter 9

Can 'professional development' de-professionalise the teaching profession?

David R. Wright

Scene 1: Teachers in a lecture room in a university

Wisdom pours forth. Japan's nineteenth-century industrialisation progresses intensely, enthusiastically, in magnificent detail. Three questions, and it's time for coffee. Wisdom pours forth again. Indonesia is developed, exploited, devastated, redeveloped. Four questions, and it's time for lunch. Job's question 'where shall wisdom be found?', has been answered. Wisdom is found in universities, and it flows forth like a mighty flood. We are overwhelmed. The days of boring monotones are gone. These lectures cannot be faulted for their presentation. And yet, is not something missing?

Scene 2: Teachers in a teachers' centre, in a circle

Enthusiasm pours forth. A deputy head enthuses about loving his pupils, especially the bottom-stream ones. A young teacher seeks more interaction. An older teacher enthusiastically suggests that immigrants would be happier if they went home, but this jarring note is quickly glossed over. We all agree that examinations are a problem, but we will work at it. Coffee and biscuits do not interrupt the flow, and we all agree to meet again as the meeting ends at 10 p.m. And yet, is not something missing?

These two accounts of teachers' in-service meetings are not fictional. Even though they may be extreme examples, they are both representative of familiar types of in-service work. Both seem to have very little effect on classrooms.

When I was a classroom teacher in the USA, Scene 1 was enacted frequently during in-service days. No matter who I sat next to, the whispered comment during the opening applause was always the same: 'D'ya know the definition of an expert? Someone who's travelled a hundred miles with a briefcase.' A well-known in-service teacher had made a similar point many years earlier: 'A prophet is not without honour, save in his own country.'

So the 'experts' come from afar and then go. Do they leave any trace behind them? We all know that this jug-method of teaching has limited success and effectiveness with pupils. Yet Scene 1 persists in so many in-service courses for teachers. If the course is pure 'content', we make some hasty notes. Am I a particularly difficult case – a particularly lazy and disillusioned teacher? A quick survey of the glazed faces in the audience suggests that this is not so. At least I try to make notes; it seems that many of my neighbours do not even have a piece of paper available.

There may be a short evaluation-sheet to fill in at the end of the conference, but it is difficult to write what one feels. There is a numbness at the sheer amount of wisdom imparted. I return feeling more ignorant and less confident than at the start.

One therefore turns with some relief to Scene 2. If Scene 1 could be dubbed the university model, Scene 2 can perhaps be called the teachers' centre model. The scene has positive points. Teachers are participating rather than merely receiving. Each member can influence the structure. Real classroom situations can be discussed. Problems can be shared. At the end of the meeting there can be a feeling of encouragement.

And yet, one has doubts. The main weakness would seem to be the introverted nature of the meeting. Although Scene 1 is so diametrically opposed to Scene 2, it is possible to find one major similarity. Neither 'Scene' offers more than one type of expertise. In Scene 1 the expertise is entirely external to classrooms; the teachers are mere receivers. In Scene 2, expertise is almost entirely from within classrooms. What seems to be needed is a Scene 3, where there is a recognition that there are two types of expertise, and the two types of experts need to meet and explore a topic together. The 'content experts' (from universities etc.) would need to emphasise that they recognise that teachers have major expertise in understanding young minds – and unique expertise in knowing and understanding the particular needs of their own pupils. (Prior exposure to Scene 1 events means that deliberate morale-boosting for teachers would be needed.) Scene 3 could have far more effect on classrooms than either Scene 1 or Scene 2.

Sadly, it seems unlikely that Scene 3 would often succeed. There are too few university lecturers who have sufficient interest, patience, and time to interact in this way.

So, if Scenes 1 and 2 are unsuccessful, and Scene 3 usually fails, we need Scene 4: an 'experts-and-mediators' model. The recognition of two types of experts must remain. But between the two groups of experts are 'mediators', with some familiarity with both types of expertise. The mediators could be classroom teachers who have recently been seconded for curriculum development work or for study for a higher degree; they could be 'teacher-fellows', or advisers, or inspectors, or education lecturers.

Scene 4 sounds excellent, but it usually fails. If it does not fail on grounds of misunderstandings, it fails on financial grounds: the costs are far too great. Not only are there two people whose employers, in these cost-conscious days, need to be paid for each session; there are also substantial pre-course commitments in terms of time and energy. In the past, I have enjoyed 'Scene 4' as a teacher, as a 'mediator', and as an 'expert'. But in practice it works only if money is plentiful or if money is irrelevant, as in a voluntary conference. Scene 4 cannot be seen as a normal or regular pattern for professional development.

Thus, there are problems with all the types of INSET work described. There is, in fact, plenty of positive work happening – despite the problems. But a recognition of problems is necessary in order to see why new styles were assumed to be necessary, to deal with the big changes caused by the introduction first of GCSE and then of the National Curriculum.

There was much to welcome in the advent of GCSE. But the style of INSET provision had some alarming features. This is what I wrote at the time. My original intention was to rewrite the article for this book, with the advantage of hindsight, but in fact the point it makes comes across more strongly if the tense remains unchanged.

The coming of GCSE has been widely welcomed. Although the INSET funding for the introduction of GCSE is condemned as 'not enough', it is nevertheless by far the biggest ever allocation of INSET funds for a single topic. Complaints are concerned mainly with the inadequate time for INSET courses, and the lack of information on syllabuses.

I would argue that there are much more serious questions raised by the nature and style of the INSET provision. Parts of this provision appear to break long-established and fundamental conventions of the teaching profession. These conventions are so much a part of the basic assumptions of the teaching profession that they are rarely mentioned.

The three basic assumptions to which I refer are that:

- Teachers are responsible individuals;
- Teachers are committed to honesty and integrity in their own work, and expect honesty and integrity from INSET providers;
- Teachers are intelligent individuals, and they expect and deserve to be treated as intelligent individuals.

The presence of such assumptions is difficult to prove. Indeed, I only became aware of them when, in a year's teaching overseas, I found myself at times treated as potentially delinquent and of very low intelligence, subject to instructions such as 'Where it says Name, write your name' and frequent injunctions 'Teachers are not to . . .'.

However, it is the unspoken and unwritten nature of these assumptions that renders them vulnerable, when a very large INSET scheme is developed very quickly. In the rush to get things done for GCSE, these basic assumptions have apparently been forgotten.

Most teachers of GCSE classes teach only one subject, and will be involved only with INSET work in that subject. The examples in this paper are therefore drawn from one subject: geography. The quotations are from 'GCSE INSET: Group Leaders' Notes; Geography' (SEC 1986).

'When preparing for your sessions, it would be useful to make a few notes about each activity'

Group Leaders here are treated in an arrogant and condescending manner. The concern of the anonymous author is presumably to ensure that INSET sessions are worthwhile, and this is a laudable aim. But to assume that one can achieve good leadership by 'teaching one's grandmother to suck eggs' is contrary to the spirit of INSET as being 'professional' development. This approach appears to de-professionalise professionals. The teachers, too, are treated similarly: on page 7 of their booklet (SEC/OU 1986) they will read, 'underline all the key phrases'. Once instructions of this type are used, it is not far to 'teachers are not to . . .'.

'Discussion could drift into time-consuming debate on matters which are not negotiable . . . [this] could detract from the main purpose of the training programme'

Notice the phrase 'the training programme'; the 'Group Leaders' are not really group leaders; they are trainers. A Group Leader would welcome debate; these 'trainers' are told to avoid debate on topics that might be controversial. The concept of a debate being a positive form of developing understanding of each other's viewpoint – a concept that is surely at the heart of a democratic society – is rejected here, in favour of training. Training is clearly designed to encourage conformity.

'Objective: to encourage the participants to take a positive attitude towards differentiated forms of assessment [video]'

'Differentiation' is one of the most controversial aspects of GCSE. Open discussion might lead to the wrong answers; once again, real debate is too subversive for this new-style INSET. In this case, the video will perhaps succeed in lulling teachers into conformity. After the video comes the following extraordinary instruction.

'15 Minutes: General discussion on the video and outcomes of Activity to clarify the terminology used and positive reasons for differentiated schemes of assessment, referring to Working Paper 1'

The tortuous syntax and lack of punctuation almost obscure the serious implications of this statement. But the objectives are incredibly low-level: merely 'to clarify the terminology used', not to understand or reason. And then teachers are invited to discuss only one side of the argument for and against differentiation. This is a pseudo-discussion, not a discussion. Who is manipulating teachers, and why?

'Course-work assessment is therefore not open to question. However, it is important that participants are conversant with the argument in favour of course-work'

Group Leaders here seem once again to be invited to manipulate a discussion. Questioning might result in the wrong answers; so might looking at both sides of an issue. So, the Group Leader's role is once again to lead a pseudo-discussion, to get the right answers. The teachers are not told that it is a pseudo-discussion; this dishonesty is one of the most worrying aspects of the whole project.

'Experience suggests, however, that discussion about the lack of resources can be unproductive'

Once again, Group Leaders are asked to manipulate a discussion. The booklet that the teachers receive asks: 'what additional resources would you require to implement such approaches?' (p. 42).

Only the Group Leaders are warned that the discussion can be 'unproductive'. Once again, we see the Group Leader placed in the role of controlling answers rather than leading discussion.

My own conclusion from the 'Group Leaders' Notes' is that teachers are not treated as intelligent people, as people open to reason, but instead are not to be trusted. Furthermore, the notes advocate manipulation of discussion in ways that are not ethical.

The implications of these approaches are very grave indeed. It is not simply that they ignore established conventions, although this is serious. Nor is the problem principally that they ignore all the good work of the past decade in developing constructive approaches to INSET, and in using group sessions constructively. Nor do I fear that teachers will be crushed by these approaches; I have every confidence that they have the intelligence, resilience and responsibility to resist manipulation.

My main concern is about the lack of outcry, or even complaints, about the assumptions in the notes and the techniques they advocate. If we 'de-professionalise' teachers, we lose infinitely more than we gain. And if we reject ethical principles, we have little left that merits the term 'education'.

And so we come to INSET for the National Curriculum. Inevitably we encounter examples of Scene 1 and Scene 2. In the early stages, the Scene 2 events were particularly impressive. For example, over 200 geography teachers in East Anglia gave up two Saturdays, and many teachers made journeys of one hundred miles or more, for Scene 2 meetings. Here was INSET in which teachers' enthusiasm, creativity, intelligence and professionalism were maximised, rather than minimised, as in Scene 1, or destroyed, as in the GCSE INSET system. And in the brief 'MacGregor era' teachers even felt that their expertise might be listened to, and their enthusiasm appreciated.

The advent of Kenneth Clarke and his red (blue?) pencil on the National Curriculum documents soon moved us back to Scene 1. We obediently sat through mass lectures, in which Kenneth Clarke *et al.* told us how wonderful it all will be, once we obey the instructions. This is a new, and much nastier, type of Scene 1; in the older format, we could take it or leave it, but we retained our professional self-respect.

Not everyone can attend the 'big meeting', so the provision of books for teachers is a necessary next step for National Curriculum INSET. The long-established conventions of writing and publishing books have been abandoned by the National Curriculum Council: they are into the world of competitive tendering. Schools are familiar with this approach for cleaning; it is now the chosen approach for INSET books as well. In fact, the National Curriculum Council is becoming as efficient as Mulbarton Parish Council. From first-hand experience of my parish council, I find I can grasp the way the National Curriculum Council works.

First, councillors decide that something is needed; for example, some litter-bins on Mulbarton Common, or some books on how to teach National Curriculum geography. Second, we spend a few months talking about the project. Should the bins/books be:

• Big or little?
• Posh or basic?
• Green or white on the outside?

For a moment, we wonder whether the electors/teachers should be consulted first, but we decide it is simpler to decide for ourselves. After all, the councillors were chosen by the electors/government, so we are sure we make the right decisions.

Third, we have some more meetings and make the key decisions: the bins/books will be Big, Posh, and Green. Fourth, the Clerk (salary £1200 p. a. for MPC; unknown for the National Curriculum Council but probably 20 times more) eventually draws up the specification and produces an 'Invitation to Tender' for the bins/books. The NCC letter is sent out by the 'Accommodation and Supplies Officer'; our £1200 clerk has to do everything for MPC.

By now, we have spent a good few months talking about bins/books, so in stage five we give less than a month for people to tender. The National Curriculum Council adds fifteen pages of incomprehensible but fierce-sounding 'Terms and Conditions'. It should take tenderers only a few days to work out the cost of a litter-bin, and probably books are much the same really. Then, sign the form: 'We offer to supply the Council with the above goods/works/services.' Remember: quotes for bins to MPC; quotes for books to the National Curriculum Council (seven copies).

After this, both councils are extremely efficient. Tenders in by the twelfth instant; contracts awarded by the twentieth. The Parish Council is really good at taking-away sums and does not need long to sort out the cheapest and most cost-effective tender. The National Curriculum Council has discovered how to do the job equally smoothly.

The councils allow exactly ten weeks before the bin has to be installed, and the draft manuscript has to be received. That should be ample time to collect the bin, dig a hole and put it in the hole, and/or to collect the words, put them through a word-processor and into a letter-box.

It is all so clear and so foolproof. Why not undertake all litter-disposal and Curriculum Development through this perfect system? All we need now is for the clerks of the two councils to meet and shake hands, while press photographers record the happy day.

Perhaps the Director of the National Curriculum Council could be invited to the formal opening of the new litter-bin on Mulbarton common? Better still, the Director could be invited to place the first item in the big, posh, green bin. We do not even need competitive tendering to choose the most cost-effective and appropriate item for the Director to place in the bin. I would suggest that the chosen item should be a big, posh, green book on the teaching of geography, written in ten weeks.

However, I hope that one sentence from the book might be preserved. It is apparently concerned with urban geography. It reads:

'Rome wasn't built in a day – either.'

CONCLUSION

In the olden days of the 1970s, long before this age of the Tender Approach to the Curriculum, there was Curriculum Development, and there were Schools Council Projects. It was another age, impossibly difficult to envisage unless one lived through it. I would love to tell people the exciting stories from that long-gone age – an age when the curriculum was developed, not imposed; an age when teachers were consulted, not shouted at; an age when pupils were involved in trialling the new ideas and the new resources. But this was another age, and I would doubtless seem as old-fashioned and as irrelevant as an old soldier with his interminable stories of great victories of long ago. Instead, let us try to rejoice at the advent of the Tender Approach to the National Curriculum.

That paragraph would have been a good final flourish; the chapter would have gone out with a bang. But I do not want the chapter to finish on this negative note. Schools – and the Nation – are very fortunate to have many established and new teachers of outstanding dedication, intellect and character. Every day, hundreds of inspiring lessons occur and, even at worst, thousands of everyday miracles occur: pupils behave and learn. If there is a moral to this chapter, it is not that everything is a disaster. It is that, despite the inherent problems of INSET, and despite the follies and errors of national policy, teachers deserve more respect, and better treatment, than they have received in recent years, and are receiving at present.

REFERENCES

Secondary Examinations Council (1986) *GCSE INSET: Group Leaders' Notes; Geography*, London: Secondary Examinations Council.
Secondary Examinations Council/Open University (1986) *Geography GCSE: A Guide for Teachers*, Milton Keynes: Open University Press.

Chapter 10

Supporting the professionals who support professional development in schools

Terry Cook

THE CHANGING CONTEXT OF THE WORK OF ADVISORY TEACHERS

At this time of change in education, the role and function of advisory teachers is in a state of flux. The traditional relationship between the LEA Inspectorate and Advisory Services and schools is changing and with it comes a 'new look in-service, support and training' system. Traditionally, advisory teachers on one or two-year secondment or even permanent contracts have been crucial in the delivery of any LEA Inspectorate and Advisory Service INSET programme. Although a number of these posts will continue to survive, this model looks increasingly under threat in the 'new world'. More and more short-term secondments (perhaps lasting a term or less) will need to be negotiated, temporary or fixed-term contracts will become the norm or, even more radically, in the 'new world' the very existence of LEAs is in doubt. LEA Inspectorate and Advisory Services may exist in a modified form, or as self-financing business units within an LEA provision, or as independent agencies providing advisory services.

What is certain, however, is that the new organisations, whatever their format, will need trainers to provide the services required by schools. To meet the requirements of this new situation there is a need to look at the relationship between the new organisations and schools and between advisory teachers and schools, and the in-service training of advisory teachers will need to be reviewed. For the purposes of this chapter these 'new' organisations will be referred to as 'in-service support and training agencies'.

A crucial factor in the ability of 'in-service support and training agencies' to provide advisory teacher support is the willingness of schools to release experienced and talented staff for a period of secondment as an advisory teacher. Within the area of 'recruitment and career development' several issues need to be addressed, including uncertainty surrounding future career prospects after completion of the role (is it career suspension or career development?), views/knowledge/understanding of headteachers and governors in relation to benefits of secondment for both the school and the individual, problems the school faces when a teacher is seconded. The reluctance of some schools to allow staff to apply for secondment means that more fixed-term contracts are being offered. However, how many teachers will want to move into the uncertain world of the advisory teacher if future employment prospects are hindered by being 'out of school' for any length of time?

If headteachers and governors are to be persuaded to release staff on secondment they must be able to see some benefit for the school. Therefore, an 'in-service support and training agency' should have a policy on the 'Role and Professional Development of Advisory Teachers' and a fully co-ordinated system for their management and deployment. In this way schools will be able to see that the period of secondment will be beneficial not only for the 'in-service support and training agency' but also, personally and professionally, for the teacher involved and thus that the school will benefit when the teacher returns with enhanced skills. How this will be accommodated into the cost-cutting world of business units will require very careful consideration and negotiation.

Also, the whole question of advisory teacher 'working patterns and practices' needs to be assessed. Here the issues to be addressed include: different functions and purposes (working with individual teachers or presenting whole school workshops, duration of time spent in schools, schools' motives for inviting in advisory teachers etc.); broad working patterns; division of labour (system required for recording allocation to phase, area, etc.); selecting and entering schools; modes of working with teachers; 'people skills' essential for advisory teachers; relationship with the Inspectorate and Advisory Service (if they exist in any area); 'in-service support and training agencies'; their line-manager; freelance education consultants who may well be working full time in this role; Teachers' Centres/ Professional Development Centres and the support they receive. What will be their role in following up and supporting the four-yearly inspection cycle for schools?

Taking into account these issues, I have been assessing the current situation concerning advisory teachers, both within Norfolk and nationwide, identifying needs for both the immediate and long term, preparing and implementing a professional development programme for Norfolk Advisory Teachers, and undertaking negotiations with local, regional and national training organisations. As a result of my findings from formal and informal discussions and written responses to my papers, I have come to the following conclusions regarding in-service training for advisory teachers.

THE ISSUES WHICH A TRAINING PROGRAMME FOR ADVISORY TEACHERS NEEDS TO ADDRESS

My findings raise both issues and questions which need to be addressed by 'in-service training and support agencies' if they are to meet current and future needs of the advisory teachers and take into account changes in funding arrangements and the political situation. Whilst formulating these I had very much in mind the findings of Dr John Harland (1990), who carried out a study for the National Foundation for Educational Research and published 'The work and impact of advisory teachers'. He warned that the recent progress made by advisory teachers in effectively delivering in-service training and support within schools would be severely disrupted if the career development and status of advisory teachers seconded from the classroom were not put on a firmer footing. If an 'in-service training and support agency' does not have an accepted and adopted policy and management plan for advisory teachers, the considerable potential of advisory teachers to contribute to an improvement in the quality of teaching and learning in schools will not be realised.

This leads on to the whole area of support and development given to the advisory teachers during their period of secondment. This needs to be looked at in terms not only of formal occasions, but also informal sessions. There is a great deal of benefit to be gained from regular, informal meetings with colleagues from a wide range of teams, though the heavy schedule of advisory teachers may make this difficult at times. There is also the question of balance between in and out-of-county contacts, as there are great benefits to be obtained from meeting with colleagues from other 'in-service support and training agencies'.

Whatever programme is organised, it should be developmental and responsive to the changing needs of advisory teachers and it must also involve the work of all teams, without exception. By making the programme developmental, I see that the stages in the 'cycle' of advisory teacher development have very different requirements (Figure 10.1).

It is necessary for any 'in-service support and training agency' to maximise the effectiveness of advisory teachers if they are to be cost efficient. John Harland identifies four areas which require attention if the long-term effects of the advisory teacher's work are to be worthwhile:

- The need to provide follow-up or aftercare in-service support;
- The need to provide continuity of advisory teacher contacts and developments;
- The need to ensure that the impact of an advisory teacher input is spread and embedded across several staff;
- The need to sequence and co-ordinate participation in in-service activities in order that teachers can experience them as a coherent provision.

From my experience, both in schools and talking to staff, and from published texts such as Harland (1990), and McLaughlin and Rouse (1992), there is much evidence to support the effective role that advisory teachers perform. This evidence shows that advisory teachers are accepted as key personnel in initiating and sustaining developments in classroom practice, in affirming and recognising 'good practice', and that they are successful in in-service activities which are appreciated by the teachers concerned. However, much of their

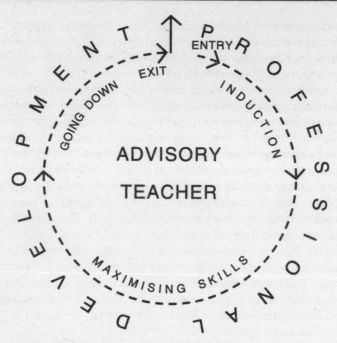

Figure 10.1 **The 'cycle' of advisory teacher** development

credibility comes from their expertise as classroom practitioners and few of them have had any training in support and advice prior to their appointment. This has an effect on their confidence and can lead to 'entry problems'. There is therefore a need for a firm policy on the role of induction and an adequate induction programme. Without this, the effectiveness of advisory teachers is likely to be reduced because of the following 'entry problems':

- Time is wasted and anxiety levels are raised because of uncertainties about office space, administrative support, administrative regulations, county/business unit structures;
- They become suddenly aware of the 'magnitude of their task', problems of time, etc., at which point there can be a feeling of isolation – 'who can I talk to?'; such general lack of security is heightened by the absence of a lack of routine, time management, setting priorities, etc.;
- They experience a sudden transformation, without any training, from being a teacher at the end of one term to being an advisory teacher at the beginning of the next, which can be quite traumatic if there is no transitional stage;
- They are uncertain how to approach schools: what are the procedures and protocols, how is entry negotiated, what are the expectations of an advisory teacher?

- They lack knowledge/understanding of who other advisory teachers/teams are, of their function, role, method of operation and time and place of operation; of who/what are the other services offered by the 'in-service support and training agencies' to schools and colleges;
- In the rapidly changing world of educational support services, what are the links between advisory teachers and consultants? Do they complement or rival each other? Certainly consultants will have a longer 'life span' in their support role. However, this can have both advantages and disadvantages. The main advantage is that they are longer in post and so can maximise their potential, and the main disadvantage is that the longer they are out of schools the more they can lose touch with the workings of the classroom.
- If the time allocated to advisory teacher induction/INSET is not carefully calculated, serious problems occur within the system. There must be a balance struck between the time spent on induction and time spent performing the task. Too much time spent on induction can be as bad as too little. This is particularly the case if the advisory teacher is on a one-year fixed-term contract or secondment, because the relationship between training and delivery for this time period is critical. This point is even more relevant in the present political climate if an advisory teacher is operating within a business unit and the financial implications of induction and INSET need to be costed into the unit fees.

It must be stressed at this early stage that it is not an easy task to develop a fully co-ordinated INSET programme for advisory teachers. The reason for this is that there is not one typical model of an advisory teacher on which to base planning. Very few 'in-service support and training agencies' will operate with the same system and a distinction needs to be made between types of advisory teacher by virtue of their contract. Are they seconded, on a fixed-term contract, or a full-time contract; are they appointed for a short or long term, full or part time, on APT/C or school teacher pay and conditions? Is the advisory teacher part of a large, medium, small or even one person team? Advisory teachers will also be employed in a wide range of roles and this will greatly affect the support/training required during any INSET programme. Each and every one of these points needs to be borne in mind when constructing individual INSET plans.

Although advisory teachers will all have very different needs according to contract differences they will also have a great many common needs and concerns. Therefore, there will be certain threads which can run through each INSET plan and so to a degree a common and co-ordinated programme can, and must, be developed.

Once this induction period is complete and the advisory teachers have become competent by 'doing', there is a need to maximise on their potential, particularly at a time when they are at the top of their own learning curve. There is also a need to provide some counselling at this stage on possible future strategies for the advisory teachers' own personal and professional development.

When the 'moving on' stage is reached this can be a time of worry and concern for advisory teachers. Some of the issues here include: when to start applying for post-secondment or post-fixed term contract jobs – if an application is made too early it can seriously hit the project but there again it cannot be left too late; how 'marketable' is an advisory teacher – if returning to a previous position, the issue of readjustment/re-entry needs to be addressed.

A POLICY FRAMEWORK FOR ADVISORY TEACHER TRAINING

When addressing the initial 'training and in-service' of advisory teachers, the following points should be taken into account when policy is formulated by employers of staff who will fulfil this role and function.

1   To enable the work of the advisory teacher to be efficiently and effectively carried out there is a need for an advisory teacher management plan and for a formal advisory teacher INSET budget, in both financial and time terms, which must be built into the costings/charges of the 'in-service support and training agency'.

2   An advisory teachers' handbook should be produced each academic year and given to all advisory teachers. This document must be clearly structured and laid out, must provide all the administrative procedures in an easily usable format and must be regularly revised. The reason for stressing this point so strongly is because the very nature of advisory teachers' work means that they are away from the centre for considerable amounts of time and so require administrative detail without having to constantly refer to the centre.

3   An 'Advisory Teachers' Support Group' should be developed which would act as the forum to enable advisory teachers to meet colleagues to discuss/exchange ideas on matters of interest and concern. There should be negotiated release for advisory teachers to participate in its activities and dates negotiated at the start of any secondment/fixed-term contract.

4   It is desirable to have as compulsory for all new advisory teachers a well organised, officially recognised and externally accredited induction programme which is timetabled to start in the first week of the secondment/fixed-term contract and to be continued at relevant stages throughout the first year. The advantages of such a programme would include:

- Overcoming the anxieties of advisory teachers and helping them to come to terms with basic organisational and administrative procedures;
- Assisting advisory teachers to adjust quickly and effectively from the classroom role to the advisory role;

- Being seen as part of a professional development programme which would be a positive component in career development;
- Being an important stage in the development of team building, not only as part of advisory teachers' own particular projects but also as part of a wider 'advisory teacher' team;
- Coping with issues of 'people skills', working with adults, as this will be new to many advisory teachers;
- Addressing the issues of role related learning – as change agents, as INSET providers;
- Knowing how to approach schools, procedures and protocols;
- Being the first stage in a co-ordinated programme which would add continuity and coherence to a period of secondment/fixed-term contract; in some instances this would also be the first stage in a modular course which could be used in further external courses/qualifications;
- Affording credibility and status in the longer term for the participant if the programme were externally accredited via an HE institution.

5   Ideally all advisory teachers should have built into their programme, before the start of the academic year, at least five days (on a pro rata basis) of professional development time. This would be based on an identification of needs jointly negotiated between the advisory teacher and the line manager. The programme would be developmental and would build on the 'induction programme' to meet the 'learning curve' requirements of the advisory teachers. It would be helpful to have these days included in the in-service support and training agencies' time allocation for tasks and to have priority for this purpose.

6   There should be recognition of the differing needs of advisory teachers according to length and type of secondment/fixed-term contract. An on-going INSET programme needs to be developed which builds on the foundations laid during the induction period. Therefore, no one overall professional development programme can meet all needs; instead, a constant theme running throughout a general programme needs to be supplemented by developing individually negotiated programmes.

7   Because of the changes in role and working patterns and environments, advisory teachers require INSET on 'time management'. Also, policy is required on time managing advisory teachers, as there is a clear need to monitor and control workload and to guard against overcommitment. This is particularly important in the primary phase where there can be several demands from various initiatives. This can be achieved by:

- Effectively preplanning and 'critical path scheduling';
- Formally logging time and using this as a basis for discussion with the 'line manager' when planning future activities;
- Effectively using support systems.

8   Advisory teachers require INSET on how they can be effectively involved in the support of 'newly qualified teachers' and 'licensed teachers'. A policy statement is necessary so that they are clear about their role, since they should not be involved with monitoring or assessment but with classroom support, advice, INSET, etc.

9   Advisory teachers need INSET and support on a co-ordinated approach to the in-service support and training agencies' own INSET activities. Therefore, this INSET really needs to be undertaken with the organisation as a whole. Advisory teachers need to be clear on the business units policy and they should be used to prepare teachers/schools for INSET and to follow up activity within the unit's programme. The use of advisory teachers to follow up INSET is a cost effective method of extending value and the initial impact made by 'one off' conferences or short courses. Also, they are invaluable support for INSET course participants wishing to disseminate information to their own staff.

10   At the time of appointment a decision needs to be made on a commitment to enable seconded advisory teachers, if they require, to take part in their own schools' curriculum development days. This would be necessary for secondees if their future return to school were hampered by missing out on planning for the next academic year.

11   There should be a commitment to use past advisory teachers in INSET. This would have many advantages including:

   • Allowing current advisory teachers to share the experiences/information/skills obtained by past advisory teachers;
   • Being a cost effective use of the expertise of experienced past advisory teachers;
   • Being a morale boosting exercise for ex-advisory teachers at a time when often they are feeling under-used and neglected;
   • Being a source of potential income for the ex-advisory teacher's school.

12   Links should be developed with other 'in-service support and training agencies'; even joint programmes should be investigated at times. These could be fostered through joint attendance at award-bearing induction programmes/courses via HE institutions.

13   Close liaison should be maintained with FE and HE to provide award-bearing courses, tailor made for the advisory teachers and their needs.

14   A service for re-entry counselling should be provided for all secondees and fixed-term contract advisory teachers. For secondees a system could be established whereby they would be enabled to negotiate a regular release back to their school in the term prior to returning to school.

AMPLIFICATION OF THE ISSUES AND QUESTIONS ARISING FROM THE ADVISORY TEACHER POLICY FRAMEWORK

At the present time much government money is spent on advisory teachers through the GEST scheme and, if the effectiveness of advisory teachers is be maximised, a number of issues within the policy need to be addressed and a detailed policy formulated.

Headteachers, governors and teachers are looking closely at the support services available from the 'in-service support and training agencies' and are assessing the value of each to their own particular institution. Therefore we must ensure that our advisory teachers are delivering a product which is required, effective, cost efficient, professional, and of value to schools. Quality advisory teachers and support staff are being appointed to enable this to be achieved, but we must ensure that their training provides them with the skills to be fully effective. Thus, a complete review of training methods and needs is necessary and the following issues are amongst the main points to be addressed when formulating an advisory teacher policy.

Advisory teacher management plan

If there is to be an efficiently run advisory teacher service then an 'in-service support and training agency advisory teacher management plan' is required. It is desirable that advisory teacher INSET is included in this plan and that each and every advisory teacher plays a part in the construction of the plan. If this does not happen, decisions will be made in relative isolation from each other and the service will lack coherence.

Induction

The strategy of 'shadowing' an experienced colleague by a new advisory teacher when first taking up post is a most effective element in an induction programme. This I have discovered from personal experience and from discussing the issue with numerous advisory teacher teams. An experienced colleague is able to help to develop the effectiveness of the new advisory teacher by (i) introducing him or her to 'known schools and staffs' and thus helping to create confidence and trust; (ii) acting as a facilitator and thus easing initial entry into schools; (iii) helping him or her to surmount the problems of schools not understanding or using the 'in-service support and training agency'. However, is there time to spend on this when an advisory teacher is in post for only one year? This issue needs to be resolved by the in-service support and training agencies and a decision made in the light of the advantages obtained set against cost.

Depending on the type of contract on which the new advisory teachers are appointed, should those on APT/C conditions of service be maximising the school holiday periods, as a point of policy, for induction and INSET? Certainly this would be more cost effective as the income generation capabilities of business units are far less at this time than during term time. Alternatively, if appointed under the conditions of service relating to working time (para. 36) in the School Teachers' Pay and Conditions Act 1991, could regular release of the new advisory teacher in the term prior to taking up secondment be negotiated, in order to facilitate a period of training working in tandem with an experienced advisory teacher who has some time left on secondment, or could the previous advisory teacher continue as a 'teacher tutor', in a pastoral role, in the early stages for the new secondee?

Planning

Every advisory teacher needs INSET on planning strategies. It is desirable, if an 'in-service support and training agency' is to have a unified and co-ordinated service, for each advisory teacher team to provide a forward operations plan. The plan would include the type of support it intends to offer and its INSET delivery. This information would then enable central co-ordination to eliminate the danger of repetition, saturation, and overload for schools and the 'in-service support and training agency' alike. However, it should also be recognised that there must be an allowance for an element of flexibility to allow for response to real needs in individual cases.

Time in post

Is one year or less a cost effective period for an advisory teacher? A number of indicators show that short-term contracts/secondment are not effective. The main reason for this is, that by the time a new advisory teacher has come to terms with the role his or her period of tenure has come to an end. Often this is before the person has become fully effective and certainly before the benefits of the post can be maximised.

However, in the 'new world', longer terms in post may not be as common and so it is vitally important to have efficient structures in place to maximise the effectiveness of advisory teachers no matter how long they are in post.

Wherever and whenever, the recommendation must be made to employ advisory teachers on longer-term contracts in order to make the most effective use of their time in post.

Appraisal

The DES regulations published in 1991 and the 1991 Pay and Conditions Act have now placed the duty for teachers to participate in Appraisal in compliance with the regulations on teachers' pay and conditions of service (DES 1991a, sect. 35.4; DES 1991b, c). This has implications for advisory teachers, whether they are on secondment or fixed-term contract. To come to terms with the issues involved, I have worked closely with Michael Pennington, Norfolk LEA Appraisal Co-ordinator, and we have developed the following strategy to meet the requirements of advisory teachers.

As appraisal is designed to be an integral part of the management and support of teachers and not an isolated exercise, this implies that the process must continue during a period of secondment or fixed-term contract. For those advisory teachers on longer-term placements within in-service support and training agencies there will not be a problem, as they can participate in the agreed appraisal system for that particular agency.

However, there is an issue if the period of secondment or fixed-term contract is less than two years. Two years is the minimum operative period for effective data collection, the setting of targets and their achievement. Therefore, in the case of those advisory teachers on contracts of less than two years, it may be more realistic to incorporate some of the appraisal elements (e.g. negotiation of targets, drawing up of success criteria, support towards their achievement) in the induction and support programme. This means that the short period as an advisory teacher can act as contributory data towards the teacher's appraisal scheme which remains school-based. There would then be a requirement for the advisory teacher to retain contact or contacts at his or her school.

When negotiating with line managers it is important for the advisory teacher first to define clearly the advisory teacher job specification for the period of secondment/fixed-term contract. This would involve establishing:

- What is my job?
- Who is my line manager?
- With whom shall I be working?
- What targets will be realistic, worthwhile and measurable?
- What success criteria will be relevant?
- How and by when are these to be agreed?
- What support will be necessary for their achievement?

Second, after negotiation, it is best to be specific about tasks. It would be desirable at this stage to identify approximately six specific functions which the advisory teacher would be expected to perform. Then a table should be drawn up and against each function answers to the following should be plotted: when? with whom? for whom? where? expected outcomes?

Third, it is necessary to identify the possible focuses for advisory teacher appraisal. The following areas need to be investigated:

- Curriculum planning and development;
- Initiatives;
- School support;
- INSET delivery and management;

- Communications with schools;
- Dissemination of information;
- Time management.

Fourth, there is a need to draw up a timetable to ensure that the whole activity is undertaken within an agreed and achievable framework. This will include the process of self-appraisal. A possible model for a self-appraisal form for advisory teachers could be:

- Are you achieving what you set out to do?
- What are the main tasks of your present post?
- What have you done during the year?
- What learning has taken place?
- How worthwhile was it?
- What can be done to improve your working environment and to remove constraints and difficulties?
- In what area would you hope to develop your experience and strengthen your expertise in the coming year and in the long term?

Themes for advisory teacher INSET

Very early in the induction process some time needs to be spent with the new advisory teacher in clarifying his or her role. This is essential if a person newly in post is to be effective. Perhaps it is of relevance for an advisory teacher to spend some time investigating, discussing and analysing this question for several reasons. Each 'in-service support and training agency' has a different viewpoint on the question, there is not a definitive answer. This fact is complicated further by the number of different funding regulations which can govern advisory teachers, and by the different type of contract – full time, part time, fixed-term or secondment – which different individuals will hold. Add to this the varying perceptions of 'in-service support and training agencies', headteachers, governors and teachers of the role of advisory teachers and it soon becomes clear why it is vital to spend time coming to terms with this particular question.

This is especially the case given the kind of diversities and complexities of the role as identified by Harland (1990):

- Class trainer, work in classroom;
- Presenter, INSET;
- Researcher;
- Developer, supporting school developments;
- Co-ordinator leading team;
- Administrator.

Even this list fails to take into account the role of 'critical friend', of monitoring and evaluation, and the situation in which the advisory teacher finds him/herself when taking the 'in-service support and training agency' view into schools and when being a resource provider as a result of the needs of schools.

I feel that it is vitally important for all new advisory teachers, as well as clarifying their role, to come to terms with three other questions during the initial induction process. The first, 'what gains/benefits does the teacher expect to obtain from being an advisory teacher?', needs to be addressed and the views taken into account throughout the period in role so that personal professional development can be achieved. The second, 'what experience and expertise does the advisory teacher have to offer the post?', requires attention in order to give reassurance and confidence when nerves are playing a part at the very point when a new career is about to begin. The third, 'what are the issues in building relationships with schools?', is fundamental if the relationship between the advisory teacher and the school is to be positive and productive.

I have found that typical responses from advisory teachers to the question, 'what do you hope to gain from being an advisory teacher?', include:

- Professional/personal development;
- An opportunity to review/reflect;
- To gain a wider cross agency perspective;
- To be involved in cross curricular/cross phase work;
- To learn new skills;
- To be involved first hand in innovations;
- Involvement in INSET planning and delivery;
- A variation in role, working with whole school, senior management, and individual teachers.

Advisory teachers' responses to the question, 'what experience and expertise do I have to offer the advisory teacher post?', are many and varied but they include points such as:

- Having experience of senior management in schools or colleges;
- Development of teaching and learning strategies;
- Cross phase and/or cross curricular work;
- Specialist subject developments;
- Experience of INSET planning and delivery;
- Pilot project involvement as well as personal attributes and various professional qualifications.

Several issues arise when addressing the creation/building of relationships between advisory teachers and schools. The most fundamental concerns who it is who makes the initial contact. If the school contacts the advisory teacher, issues for the advisory teacher to address include:

- Who requested the support – the headteacher or teacher(s)?
- If it was the headteacher, the teachers may feel threatened, there might be

a clash of opinion, pressure may exist, it may be viewed as an imposition, prejudice and resistance may be experienced; this requires understanding on the part of the advisory teacher;

- Are the school's expectations realistic?
- Clarifying why the advisory teacher is there;
- Establishing priorities.

If the advisory teacher contacts the school, issues for the advisory teacher to address include:

- Introductory strategies;
- Practical communication;
- Link person;
- Etiquette – preparation;
- Time expectations;
- Establishing credibility.

General issues for the advisory teacher to address include:

- Identification of needs – school, teachers, pupils;
- Establishing negotiated contracts that are flexible and can be renewed;
- Totally professional attitude, covering confidentiality, establishing trust, health/safety issues, honesty on both sides, handling differing personalities;
- Negotiation of input – pace of delivery, by whom, when input is made and how input is delivered, timescale, personnel, differing perceptions of need, differing perceptions of role;
- Development of supportive techniques;
- Development of non-confrontational strategies;
- Reporting to schools – debriefing, formal and informal – and time implications for written reports; this whole area needs to be systematic and negotiated;
- Follow up and aftercare;
- Evaluation.

There are also two themes which need to be addressed initially during induction but which must be kept in mind by advisory teachers throughout their period in post. They will also be vital points to consider whenever the self-appraisal process is undertaken.

The first theme is: 'what are the individual needs of an advisory teacher?' Responses to this question will include:

- When first appointed, basic information must be supplied in relation to the schools they will need to service, e.g. maps of how to find the schools, timetables, site plans, staff lists/responsibilities, telephone numbers, school times;
- Clarification of the different nature/roles of consultants, advisers, advisory teachers, LEA advisory service, in-service support and training agencies;

- Establishment of the level and nature of the work and a definition of the term 'advisory teacher';
- Time management; a strategy for planning and working; a time to review, reflect and talk to others; opportunity to learn from others and to learn something new and assimilate it;
- The development of new and fresh methods of implementing INSET/working with individuals/teaching and learning styles (old ideas in a new guise!);
- Team building and support for professional development;
- Personal and professional development, to include:
  (a) How to make initial contacts with schools;
  (b) Communication skills;
  (c) Consultancy role and skills;
  (d) Negotiation skills;
  (e) Course delivery skills;
  (f) Management skills;
  (g) Stress awareness/management;
  (h) Induction;
  (i) Appraisal.

The second theme is: 'what are the challenges facing advisory teachers?' Responses to this question will vary according to the individual advisory teacher/team. However, some common topics will emerge, including:

- How the role of advisory teacher fits in with the person's career development structure;
- Definition of an 'advisory teacher'-defining role/multiplicity of role;
- Understanding the role of the advisory teacher, particularly in the context of the changing role of the 'in-service support and training agency';
- For advisory teachers working in business units, how to market themselves;
- For advisory teachers working in GEST /LEA units, how to cope with the effects of increased devolution within LMS, of reduced funding as a result of GMS, and of uncertainty over the future of advisory services;
- Awareness raising with both sections within the 'in-service support and training agency' and 'client groups' of the role of advisory teachers;
- How to build effective links with the inspectorate/advisory and other support services;
- Appraisal; system and implications;
- Developing different models for INSET, e.g. strategies for getting teachers out of the classroom, accessing teachers who are reluctant to develop;
- Developing skills of confidentiality, consultancy, diplomacy;
- Coming to terms with conflicts of loyalty (in-service support and training agency/LEA/teacher/school) and issues of confidentiality;
- Time management/problem of coverage within a large geographic area.

Evaluation

Evaluation of the work of advisory teachers needs to start being addressed at the earliest opportunity. It is an element which needs to be discussed, planned and implemented from the outset of any work. It cannot just be left to chance or tagged on at the end. Also, it is an area which needs to be constantly reviewed and updated.

In the 'new world', business units need to ask questions such as: 'How effective do schools see advisory teachers to be in delivering INSET?' 'What credibility do advisory teachers have in schools?' 'Is the investment in advisory teachers seen as cost effective/worthwhile?' 'What is the extent of the impact on teachers' classroom practice of advisory teacher inputs?' 'Are schools sufficiently aware of the identity of the advisory teachers, their roles, the services they can offer, and how to contact or access them effectively?' If schools can answer these questions in a positive way, they are likely to purchase the services of advisory teachers; however, if they are negative then services will not be purchased. Business units need to know the answers to these questions in order to evaluate if the services offered by advisory teachers are cost efficient in business terms within the self financing in-service support and training agencies.

This is an interesting exercise to undertake; as well as providing hard data on the effectiveness of advisory teachers and their work, it helps to establish, with other data available from monitoring processes, why some schools/areas/phases/faculties, etc. do not use advisory teachers. It also enables a system of 'targeting' schools to be established in order to ensure 'equality of opportunity and parity of access'.

However, the timing of any evaluation process is very important. This whole area needs very careful consideration and a variety of strategies needs to be employed. One effective method is to carry out a structured programme involving an evaluator who is not a member of the immediate advisory teacher team. The evaluator must:

- Visit the 'client' of the advisory teacher immediately prior to the first contact with the advisory teacher and ask questions about preparations made by the 'client', expectations of the 'client', whether the 'client' had requested contact with the advisory teacher or whether it had been imposed;
- Undertake a follow-up visit immediately after the contact with the advisory teacher is complete and make a detailed evaluation of the client's opinions on the effectiveness of the advisory teacher/team;
- Make a follow-up visit at a later date, preferably 6–12 months later, and ask the client the same questions as previously.

By using this method of evaluation a more accurate picture of the effectiveness of advisory teachers can be obtained. At the same time hard data is collected which will be an invaluable aid in any advisory teacher INSET programme and forward planning by a self-financing business unit.

ISSUES REMAINING

In recent times within the world of education we have had to come to terms with the fact that 'the only certainty is change'. The 1980s, as a result of central government legislation, saw a major redefinition of the roles and powers of the LEAs. This has continued at an even faster rate in the 1990s and, coupled with the increased delegation by the LEAs themselves, we have seen a complete revolution in the organisation and management of our in-service provision. In the brave 'new world' of GMS, delegated budgets and services, there will be numerous agencies offering to schools and colleges a wide range of in-service and professional development opportunities. These will include the business units created by the LEAs, the independent educational consultancy businesses, increased INSET services being provided by FE and HE institutions, and even enterprising schools or clusters of schools.

Whatever the structural or funding changes which have affected, or will affect, education, one thing is certain and that is the continuing need to develop teachers professionally. This point is emphasised by Tyrrell (1991):

> teachers are the most effective vehicles for change and development in schools ... they are the most valuable resource available to headteachers, governors and parents for the effective teaching to children in a variety of learning environments ... Consequently, the continuing professional development of heads and teachers is to be a fundamental part of any strategy designed to meet the consequences and the challenges presented by change.
>
> (Tyrrell 1991, p. 10)

However, where will these new agencies obtain the professionally qualified and 'expert' staff required to deliver or support in-service training? Certainly there will not be the finance available to maintain the sufficient numbers of staff required on a permanent full-time basis. Therefore, in the future, I would predict that the INSET agencies will still be generating a significant level of demand for seconded or fixed-term advisory teachers. I outlined in my introductory paragraph of this chapter that I feel that many of these posts will be on a short-term basis. This means that the 'training of the trainers' becomes a crucial element in the provision of effective in-service education and training in the future.

Headteachers and governors in schools need to keep in touch with the advantages of the provision of well qualified and trained advisory teachers and must also be aware of the potential 'knock-on effects' for their schools and for the professional development of their staff. These include:

- The advisory teacher who is on secondment to or is employed on fixed-term contract by an in-service support and training agency will, if provided with a fully co-ordinated programme of training, return to teaching in school and will

  (a) have enhanced skills;
  (b) have developed personally and professionally;
  (c) be able to contribute to the school's own professional development programme;
  (d) stimulate and sustain developments in classroom practice;
  (e) have developed administration, management and time management expertise;
  (f) have enhanced team building skills;
  (g) have a wider vision/knowledge of the education world and innovations taking place;

- All schools will have the opportunity to access advisory teachers offering an effective, cost efficient and professional service in a wide range of areas;
- Individual schools, or clusters of schools, which have ex-advisory teachers on their staff who can provide the necessary knowledge, expertise and organisational skills, may wish to offer on a commercial basis in-service opportunities to other schools.

The 'new world' offers a different perspective on the provision of in-service training and realistic business principles will have to be adopted. When approaching the issue of the professional development of advisory teachers the first question that any business unit will ask is 'is the programme of training affordable, cost efficient and does it enhance the business prospects of the unit?' As outlined in this chapter, I firmly believe that a fully co-ordinated system, clearly defining the role, management, deployment and professional development of advisory teachers, will enhance the effectiveness of any in-service support and training agency. I am certain that advisory teachers have a crucial role to play in the emerging in-service agencies and that it is vital to provide a co-ordinated programme of training for these support staff so that high quality, professional INSET is provided for our schools. Also, it is vital schools are fully aware of the training and support given to advisory teachers so that they can understand and appreciate their role and function, use them efficiently and appreciate the need to release experienced and talented staff for a period of secondment.

REFERENCES

Department of Education and Science (1991a) *Education (School Teacher Appraisal) Regulations*, London: HMSO.
Department of Education and Science (1991b) *School Teacher Appraisal*, Circular 12/91, London: HMSO.

Department of Education and Science (1991c) *School Teachers' Pay and Conditions Act*, London: HMSO.

Harland, J. (1990) *The Work and Impact of Advisory Teachers*, Slough: National Foundation for Educational Research.

McLaughlin, C. and Rouse, M. (1992) *Supporting Schools*, London: David Fulton.

Tyrrell, H. (1991) 'Professional, teacher and school development', *Networks* 2 (3): 10, County INSET Centre, Norfolk County Council.

Chapter 11

Management development for further education staff

Joni Cunningham

INTRODUCTION

> Effective management development will enable everyone in the Education
> Service to face the challenge of the 1990s with increased confidence.
> (Leicestershire Management Development Project 1990)

The Norfolk Management Development Programme grew from a review of
existing management training practices and opportunities within the County
and the need to develop a coherent policy and strategy for the future. The
impetus for this review was threefold. First, the recognition by the DES of
management as a National Priority Area for INSET under the LEATGS and
now GEST schemes, and second, the recent Education Acts (DES 1988, DFE
1992). The latter are bringing about significant and major changes in
post-sixteen education which are affecting management practices at all levels
within the organisation. Lastly, management development practice has
changed radically in recent years. Indeed the scheme has proved quite
prophetic in that, with colleges becoming incorporated from 1 April 1993, the
impetus for all-round effective management by the college itself could not be
stronger or more opportune.

Management training had been supported centrally by the LEA with a
series of residential events, conferences and workshops for college managers.
In addition, a small proportion of college staff participated in the Diploma of
Management Studies (DMS) course offered by one of the County's colleges.

There are obviously strengths in this approach which include its cost
effectiveness, the participation in shared activities with colleagues from other
colleges, and responsiveness to areas of identified management need.
However, there are also some serious weaknesses in this approach. Individual
events provided in this manner tend to lack coherence and meet short-term
need rather than long-term strategic goals. There are constraints on colleges
targeting and releasing appropriate staff for attendance. Opportunities to put
new skills into practice may often be lost by lack of follow-up in a college
manager's own institution after completion of a training course.

The Norfolk Management INSET programme was formulated as an attempt to build on the strengths of the then current practice and to address these areas of identified weakness. Like the Leicestershire Management Development Project its aim was the establishment of an INSET programme which would 'enhance the quality of learning by increasing the effectiveness of all those engaged in the service', and see management development as an essential part of the process of organisational development.

The School Management Task Group argues cogently in its report on Developing School Management (DES 1990) that management training must be delivered as an integral part of the management role rather than taking place on external courses which are divorced from the workplace. The course-driven model of management training is seen as restricting access. A need is identified to provide development opportunities which include regular professional review and the creation of a better balance between on-the-job support and top-up training. This is in line with the major shift in management development from the attendance on external courses which emphasise the acquisition and practice of specific skills towards the recognition of the value of experiential learning which meets individual professional needs within a specific organisational context. The School Management Task Group notes the movement in many leading organisations towards an integrated corporate approach to management development which recognises that the development of the organisation is closely related to the development of its managers.

To quote Drucker (1983), 'we need management development precisely because tomorrow's jobs and tomorrow's organisations are going to be different from today's jobs and today's organisation' (p. 330).

A new approach to management development in Further Education had already been piloted in Cheshire as the Cheshire Education Management Programme (CEMP). It was a collaborative venture between Cheshire LEA, colleges and the adult education service (Quinlan 1991) and provided an invaluable model upon which to begin to develop a similar collaborative management development initiative in Norfolk.

THE NORFOLK MANAGEMENT DEVELOPMENT PROGRAMME

The job environment of the individual is the most important variable affecting his development. Unless this environment is conducive to his growth, none of the other things we do to him or for him will be effective. That is why the 'agricultural' approach to management development is preferable to the 'manufacturing' approach. The latter leads, amongst other things, to the unrealistic expectations that we can create and develop managers in the classroom.

(Douglas McGregor, quoted in Armstrong 1988, p. 129)

Drawing from the recommendations of the School Management Task Group, the starting points for the programme were the following principles:

- Management development should be co-ordinated into a single programme (irrespective of the various initiatives or their funding) and should provide access to accreditation for those desiring it;
- All those with management responsibilities in institutions need regular access to opportunities for development; entitlement to such access must recognise that the resources available are limited;
- Individual responsibility for professional development and review of performance is a core concept and development opportunities should be designed with this in mind;
- Development opportunities should serve the needs of both the individual and the organisation;
- Management development is about team-work and its purpose must therefore be enhanced team effectiveness;
- Management development programmes should place a strong emphasis on learning through real management tasks undertaken on-the-job;
- Management development is for all those who manage, at whatever level, within the organisation.

In designing a management programme based on these principles it was necessary first to establish a County Management Liaison Group, with senior management representation from each of the five Norfolk Further Education Colleges and Institutions and the two services, Adult Education and the Youth and Community Service. This group then tackled a range of issues, which are summarised in figure 11.1.

A FORMAT

At the heart of the issues is the belief stated by the School Management Task Group and very clearly articulated by Pedler *et al.* (1986) that formal management development has not been a 'significant force'. For example, in selecting for management posts, formal qualifications are often taken into account only as a minor factor. What really counts is not what has been formally taught but having visibly and successfully coped in difficult situations. The Norfolk Management Programme chose to adopt the premise that any 'effective system for management development must increase the managers' capacity and willingness to take control over and responsibility for events, and particularly for themselves and their own learning'.

Drucker (1983) states that development is always self-development with the responsibility resting with the individual. The Norfolk Management Programme is a self-development process operating within a particular framework. It is designed to give individual colleges/services the flexibility to provide management development, which is placed within the context of the

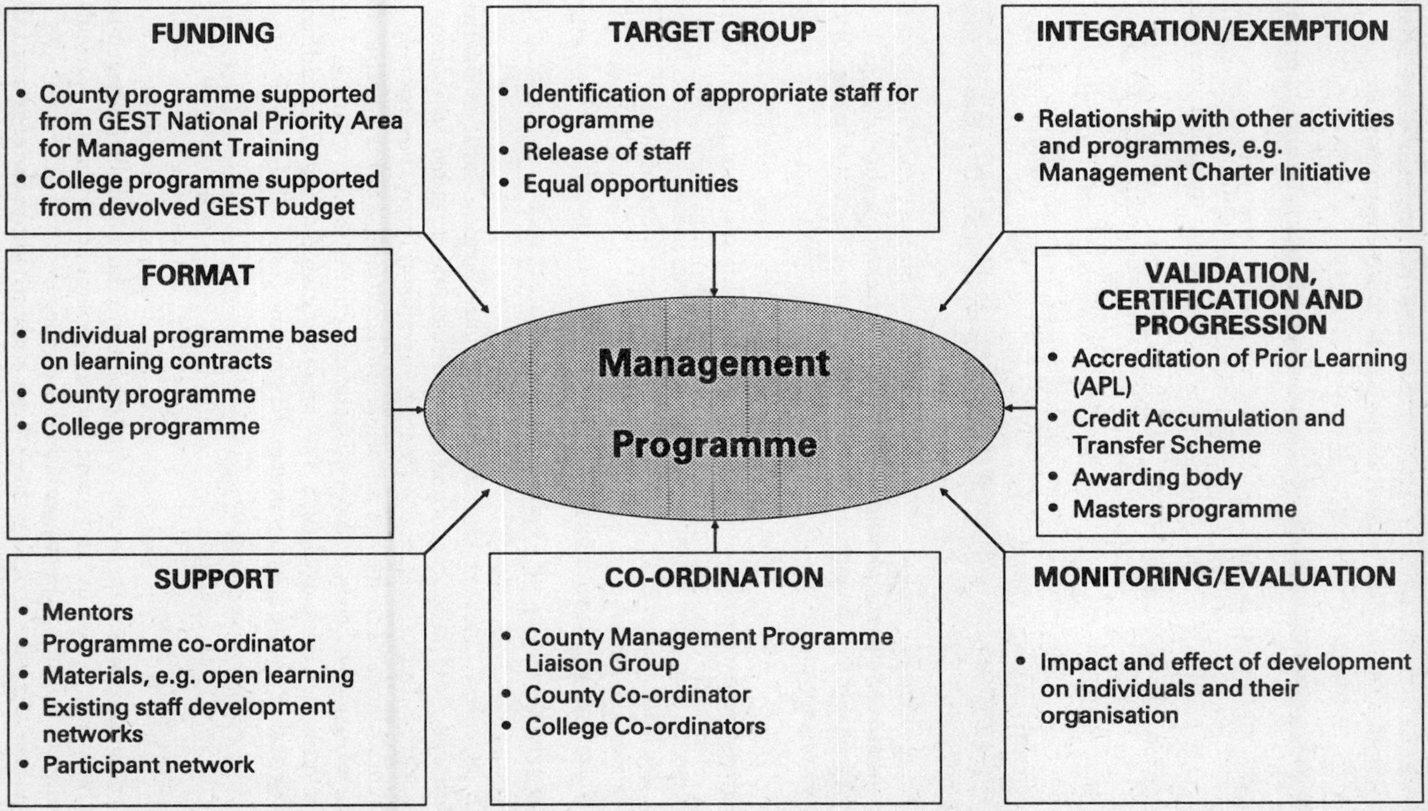

FUNDING

- County programme supported from GEST National Priority Area for Management Training
- College programme supported from devolved GEST budget

FORMAT

- Individual programme based on learning contracts
- County programme
- College programme

SUPPORT

- Mentors
- Programme co-ordinator
- Materials, e.g. open learning
- Existing staff development networks
- Participant network

TARGET GROUP

- Identification of appropriate staff for programme
- Release of staff
- Equal opportunities

Management Programme

CO-ORDINATION

- County Management Programme Liaison Group
- County Co-ordinator
- College Co-ordinators

INTEGRATION/EXEMPTION

- Relationship with other activities and programmes, e.g. Management Charter Initiative

VALIDATION, CERTIFICATION AND PROGRESSION

- Accreditation of Prior Learning (APL)
- Credit Accumulation and Transfer Scheme
- Awarding body
- Masters programme

MONITORING/EVALUATION

- Impact and effect of development on individuals and their organisation

Figure 11.1 Formulating a Management Programme: tackling the issues

organisation's goals and integrated as far as possible with the work of the organisation. The process will be based on an individual manager's analysis of his or her management development needs and the formulation of individual or team learning contracts documented in a management development plan. Like the CEMP system, the learning contract is a record of agreed targets, learning opportunities, specific learning outcomes, completion dates and evidence of outcomes. This approach is consistent with Mumford's (1989) conclusions that greater attention needs to be given to the learning process in management development. He suggests increasing the use of real problems, owned by the learner, as the means of developing effective managers. The learning contract(s) negotiated in the Norfolk Management Programme are based on major, real, management work projects which should therefore act as powerful learning experiences.

The framework for facilitating this process in the Norfolk Management Programme is as follows:

- The introductory unit;
- In-house and external development opportunities;
- The management development portfolio;
- Mentor support.

The introductory unit

Participants start the Norfolk Management Programme by attending a three-day Introductory Unit (Figure 11.2). It is intended that this should satisfy the 'psychology of beginning' and promote a bond between the participants as well as with mentors. The aims of the Introductory Unit are:

- To induct participants into the framework and process of the Norfolk Management Programme;
- To provide a common understanding of management skills in Further Education, Adult Education and the Youth and Community Service;
- To identify individual and team management development needs;
- To negotiate and formulate management development plans which meet the professional needs of the organisation;
- To discuss with participants the opportunities for accreditation and progression in management development.

Management development needs are assessed in the Introductory Unit using the approaches described by Jones and Woodcock (1985). These can be summarised as follows:

- Organisational analysis in which the College or Service Development Plan is the starting point for an assessment of present human resources and the design of learning programmes to fill the gaps;
- Job Analysis, where the emphasis is on studying the knowledge and skill

requirements of individual jobs, and the learning programme is then designed to ensure proficiency in these areas but does presuppose a current job description;

- Self-profiling exercises which allow individuals to determine their 'felt needs'.

Jones and Woodcock recommend that learning programmes are based on multiple assessments from a mixture of these approaches as it is important to balance felt needs with organisational and job analysis in the needs assessment. Participants on the Introductory Unit are introduced to a range of these assessment approaches, including the Team Role Self-perception Inventory (Belbin 1982), the Blockages Survey (Woodcock and Francis 1982) and the Manager Self-assessment Checklist (Jones and Woodcock 1985) as a basis for analysing, with their mentor, their current strengths and areas for development.

The Cheshire Management Abilities Profile (MAP), described by Quinlan (1991), is used to establish the shared understanding of management skills and knowledge. This is essential for a programme using this range of assessment approaches, and drawing participants from a range of organisations, each with its own management culture.

In-house and external development opportunities

The Norfolk Programme takes Drucker's view that courses are 'tools of management development' and hence (Figure 11.3) learning needs are met by:

- Carrying out individual or team tasks which may include using open learning materials, shadowing, observing, job sharing and carrying out planned management activities, all of which will have the support of a mentor;
- Attending in-house and external training programmes which may include workshops, courses and conferences, all of which will have the support of workshop and course leaders.

The learning contract forms a summary of how an individual's learning needs will be met. This is discussed and agreed with both the mentor and the assessor.

The management development portfolio

The individual portfolio is essentially a self-analysis tool to be maintained by each manager admitted to the programme. The Portfolio is divided into three parts and contains the following:

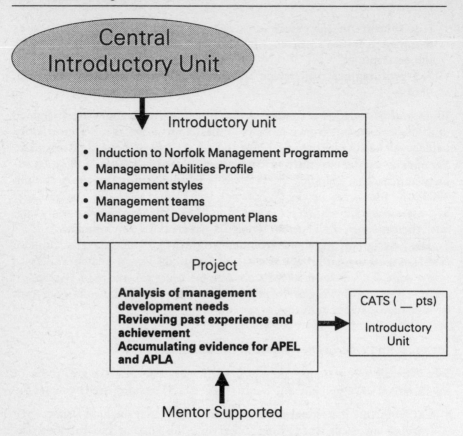

Figure 11.2 Norfolk Management Programme: Introductory Unit

Part 1   Background information

Consisting of:

- The manager's job description;
- Curriculum vitae;
- Reports on specific management activities already completed for submission for APL purposes;
- A pen sketch of how managers see themselves in relation to their present post and their future career;
- Relevant certification.

Part 2   Management development plan

This is presented on a standard pro-forma and is divided into five sections.

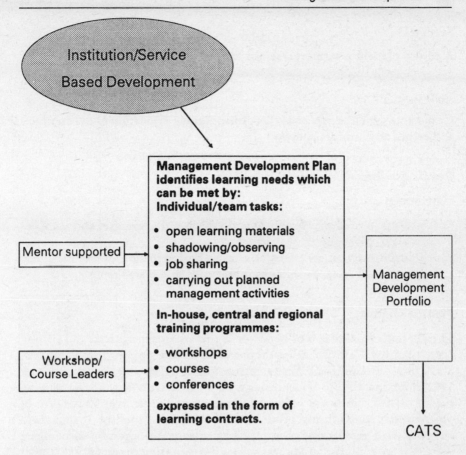

Figure 11.3   Norfolk Management Programme: in-house and external
            development opportunities

Section A

Summary of development needs which have been identified from diagnostic
tests, self-profiling and discussions with the mentor.

Section B

Summary of learning contracts and likely CATS rating, based on
identification of development need and agreed with the mentor and assessor.

Section C

An action plan for each contract, recording objectives, methodology,
resources, learning outcomes and target completion dates.

Section D

A record of mentor support received throughout the Programme.

Section E

Comments which review and reflect the on-going evaluation of the contracts and record any critical incidents.

Part 3   Evidence of learning

Containing:

- A process journal which records and evaluates the exercises and activities carried out throughout the Programme;
- All documentation generated as a result of completion of contracts, e.g. results of field research, minutes of meetings, completed reports.

Mentor support

The dictionary definition of a mentor is that of an experienced and trusted counsellor, and it is probable that the process of mentoring goes on in all organisations on an informal basis. A report on mentoring in *Personnel Today* (Falconer 1992) notes that the use of mentoring is on the increase with the latest training survey carried out by the Industrial Society finding that over 40 per cent of organisations have a formal programme of mentorship in place. It appears to be becoming a popular way of involving experienced managers by encouraging them to act as confidential advisers and guides in the training and development of their usually junior management colleagues. The growth of mentoring is attributed to the changing view that the real place for learning is the workplace.

Each Institution and Service participating in the Norfolk Management Programme is required to provide mentor support. This support may be for individuals or teams as appropriate. The role of the mentor is:

- To ensure that participants understand the opportunities provided by the Norfolk Management Programme;
- To help participants to identify their immediate and future management development needs and match these to corporate needs;
- To ensure that the individual learning programmes are agreed and outlined in management development plans which meet the needs of each participant;
- To facilitate access to college learning opportunities;
- To guide the development of the Portfolio and the production of the appropriate evidence;
- To provide a forum for discussion and decision-making concerning assessment and certification.

Mentors on the Norfolk Management Programme will be engaging in the four roles of coach, teacher, sponsor and devil's advocate as described by Armstrong (1988).

Adequate training and briefing of staff taking on the role of mentors was seen as vital for the success of the Norfolk Management Programme. A two-day mentor development programme has been established to develop and support a team of mentors within the Colleges and Services. The aims of the mentor development programme are:

- To induct mentors into the framework and process of the Norfolk Management Programme;
- To ensure a common understanding of management skills in Further and Adult Education and the Youth and Community Service;
- To explore the role of the mentor in relation to:
  (a) The identification of management development needs and the review process;
  (b) The development of management development plans which meet both individual/team needs and corporate needs;
  (c) The formulation of appropriate learning programmes and facilitation of access to college learning opportunities;
  (d) The development of the Management Development Portfolio and the production of appropriate evidence;
  (e) The assessment and accreditation process.

Mentors participating in the mentor development programme have raised a number of interesting questions which have implications for the mentor role:

- What expertise/experience should a mentor bring to the role?
- Can the line manager also act as a mentor?
- Should the mentors and participants choose each other?
- What support do mentors need once they are operational?
- How are mentors to record their contacts with participants?
- How should the mentor/participant relationship be monitored, reviewed and evaluated?

The system of mentorship established by the Programme also allows for the enrichment, referred to in the NASD (1984) booklet on mentorship, of experienced managers of long standing within organisations for whom opportunities for mobility within the service are limited. Mentors can also be accredited for their learning in taking on this role within the Programme. The report in *Personnel Today* suggests that it is difficult clearly to evaluate the effectiveness of mentoring but notes that it is generally appreciated over the long term and that those who have been mentored will remember their experiences and feed them back into the process when they become mentors themselves.

TARGET GROUP

Fifty middle and senior managers in the Colleges and Services were targeted for participation in the Programme in its first year. Recruitment and selection were the responsibility of the individual organisations, based on the following criteria:

- The organisation's management development policy statements;
- The development needs of the individual/team in relation to the organisational need;
- Career and experience of individuals to date;
- Career aspirations.

One college targeted all of its Heads of School in the belief, first articulated by Drucker (1983), that a manager needs to stay challenged and have the opportunity to reflect on his/her experience in order to sustain work satisfaction. This is especially important for many of our managers in colleges who have achieved what Drucker refers to as their 'terminal' positions; participation in the Norfolk Management Programme should provide the opportunity to find a new challenge and make a new contribution. For such participants the chance to acquire a management qualification will be of secondary importance.

ACCREDITATION

Norfolk LEA sought and gained an agreement with Sheffield City Polytechnic for a process of accreditation for the Norfolk Management Programme which recognised learning achieved through work-related management tasks. There is no requirement to attend the Polytechnic. All participants must attend the Introductory Unit but apart from this no other 'course' attendance is required.

Accreditation is based on the accumulation of credits, under the Credit Accumulation and Transfer Scheme (CATS) for participants' prior achievement and the fulfilment of learning contracts as documented in the Management Development Portfolio and endorsed by the Assessor. The assessors have been appointed by the Polytechnic and are expected to meet participants on a termly basis and be involved in the formulation of learning contracts and in assessing the learning outcomes presented as evidence in the Management Development Portfolio. Participants have the opportunity of achieving the award of the Sheffield City Polytechnic Certificate in Educational Management (sixty points) and the Diploma in Educational Management (120 points). The accreditation scheme and the possibilities for the accreditation of prior learning are shown in Figure 11.4.

The provision of an accreditation scheme was felt to be vital to the success of the Norfolk Management Programme, first to provide a quality assurance

	ROUTE 1	ROUTE 2
	ACCREDITATION ROUTES **CERTIFICATE/DIPLOMA IN EDUCATION MANAGEMENT** **Sheffield City Polytechnic**	

ROUTE 1	ROUTE 2

PART 1
 	
CONTRACT LEARNING or UNITS   CONTRACT LEARNING UNITS
                   30 Credit Points
                   +
                   APEL (50%)
 	
                   up to 30 Credit
                   Points
 	
    =   =
 	
60 CREDIT POINTS
 	
AWARD OF CERTIFICATE IN EDUCATION MANAGEMENT
	PART 1
	
	APEL (50%)
	
	up to
	60 Credit Points +

PART 2 a substantial learning contract = 60 Credit Points or by negotiation with course tutor two smaller contracts of 30 points each = 120 CREDIT POINTS **AWARD OF DIPLOMA IN EDUCATION MANAGEMENT**	PART 2 a substantial learning contract = 60 Credit Points (see note ii) or by negotiation with course tutor two smaller contracts of 30 points each = 120 CREDIT POINTS **AWARD OF DIPLOMA IN EDUCATION MANAGEMENT**

Figure 11.4 Norfolk Management Programme: accreditation scheme

mechanism and second, to meet the professional development needs of participants by providing access to the CAT scheme which has national currency.

The infrastructure developed by the Norfolk Management Programme is sufficiently flexible and adaptable to take on new developments such as the Management Charter Initiative (MCI). The MCI management competences, based on the National Vocational Qualification model, were published in

October 1991 (Day 1991). The Further Education Staff College's Pilot Diploma Programme in Education Management is based on the MCI Level 2 standards (NVQ Level 5) and covers the following key roles: Managing Operations (Curriculum), Resources, People and Information as well as personal competence. Those participants on the Norfolk Management Programme who wish to seek MCI endorsement for their management competences will be well placed to use the evidence documented in their Management Development Portfolios to demonstrate competence against the national standards, using an accreditation of prior learning route.

MONITORING AND EVALUATION OF THE NORFOLK PROGRAMME

A systematic approach to monitoring has been adopted in which data relating to efficiency, quantity, effectiveness and quality is collected. Data required includes:

- Numbers and details of participants and mentors;
- Development needs identified;
- Learning outcomes planned and achieved for each component of the Programme;
- Content and methodology of learning programmes as specified in learning contracts;
- Structure and organisation of development in Institutions or Services;
- Support available to participants;
- Costs;
- Impact and effect of development on individuals and their Institutions or Services.

EVALUATION

The Programme has been kept under constant review since its inception. During 1992, in addition to questionnaires issued to participants, an evaluation was conducted by an experienced in-service provider on behalf of the Programme Committee. This evaluation consisted of interviews conducted with participants, mentors and senior managers of involved institutions.

Senior managers were generally very supportive of the programme, and described it as 'a good concept' and 'a positive force', for example. Some institutions had not valued the Programme as much as others, and courses of short-fall ranged from institutional failure at strategic planning for management development to the inevitable lack of adequate information during the first pilot stage.

Participants are claimed to have gained from the Programme, but to different extents. Some attributed most of their development to it directly, but others felt that the Programme was only one factor among several. Participants were usually more positive about the role of their mentors when they had selected them themselves; imposed mentors were a source of ill-feeling in some institutions. When it worked well, the mentor system was viewed as valuable.

Mentors were very positive about the role and its effects. Most felt that they had gained as much as their mentees. It helped to establish trust and good working relationships; and the success of the system was seen in the keenness of other staff in the colleges to become participants: 'the Programme sold itself'.

In more general terms, the pilot scheme threw up problems and issues that have been addressed. The credit accumulation scheme was insufficiently clear at the outset, and participants would have welcomed clearer deadlines. Most participants requested a more extensive core programme of training events to support the group as a whole and to assist in facilitating contact with other participants. Mentors needed more time to function in role, and for their institutions to recognise formally the time they gave. All these issues have been taken on board by the Programme Committee.

THE FUTURE

[Staff] cost money to acquire and maintain and they should provide a return on that outlay; their value increases as they become more effective in their jobs and capable of taking on greater responsibility.

(Armstrong 1988, p. 125)

Armstrong argues convincingly that the rate at which the value of staff within an organisation can be increased is related not just to their natural ability but also to their motivation and their opportunities for promotion. He presents the time it takes an individual to become effective in his or her job as a learning curve. Developing people is about accelerating this rate of increase in value and hence steepening the learning curve.

Those presently involved in the Management Development Programme receive the support and guidance which enables them to make an effective contribution to the development of the organisation and this should increase their value to the organisation in the manner described by Armstrong. As more managers join the Programme, management development will be seen less as a discrete activity engaged in by a few staff but part of the overall development and effectiveness of the organisation and its staff. The opportunity is there to ensure that an organisation is able to make the most of its principal asset – its human resource. This process is crucial to meeting the government's aspirations for effective colleges in a climate where their traditional links with Local Authority management processes have been severed.

REFERENCES

Armstrong, M. (1988) *How to be an Even Better Manager*, London: Kogan Page.

Belbin, R.M. (1982) *Management Teams: Why They Succeed or Fail*, London: Butterworth and Heinemann.

Day, M. (1991) 'Management competences come out', *Competence and Assessment* 13: 3–7.

Department for Education (1992) *The Further and Higher Education Act*, London: HMSO.

Department of Education and Science (1988) *Education Reform Act*, London: HMSO.

Department of Education and Science (1990) *Developing School Management: The Way Forward*, A report by the School Management Task Group, London: HMSO.

Drucker, P. (1983) *Management*, 6th printing, London: Pan Business Management/Heinemann.

Falconer, H. (1992) 'Bowing to experience', *Personnel Today*, 7 April, pp. 25–7.

Jones, J. and Woodcock, M. (1985) *Manual of Management Development*, Aldershot: Gower.

Leicestershire Management Development Project (1990) *Shaping Management Development in the Education Service for the 1990s*, Task Group Report, Leicester: Leicestershire LEA.

Mumford, A. (1989) *Emphasis on the Learner: A New Approach*, Learning to Learn series, IMC International.

National Association for Staff Development in Further and Higher Education (1984) *Mentorship*, Papers of one-day joint conference of NASD/Standing Committee of In-service Certificate in Education tutors, Loughborough, October, Colchester: NASD.

Pedler, M., Burgoyne, J. and Boydell, T. (1986) *A Manager's Guide to Self-Development*, 2nd edn, Maidenhead: McGraw-Hill.

Quinlan, K. (1991) *CEMP: An Organisation and Management Development System*, London: Further Education Unit.

Woodcock, M. and Francis, D. (1982) *The Unblocked Manager*, Aldershot: Gower.

Chapter 12

Evaluating INSET
The search for quality

Trevor Kerry

THE PROBLEM

As far as education is concerned we live through increasingly quality-conscious times. Local Management of Schools, the imposition of British Standard 5750 in FE institutions (FEU 1991), the government's White Paper *Education for the twenty-first century* (DES 1991a) and new assessment arrangements in schools (DES 1991b) are all evidence of this; however, it has to be remembered that being quality-conscious does not guarantee instant success in delivering quality or even defining it adequately in any given situation. So it is opportune that those who are concerned as managers and providers of INSET should not be left behind in the overall 'quality movement'.

Nor is the initial picture of quality in INSET provision necessarily optimistic. Cowan and Wright (1990) took Baker Days as the example of this. They calculated that Baker Days account for about 20 million teacher-days per year but, in a survey of 110 Baker Days which they conducted, the majority of teachers questioned expressed dissatisfaction with Baker Day programmes. Cowan and Wright concluded that:

> Schools are managing INSET programmes in an arbitrary way, taking little heed of the long-term needs of individuals or schools or account of alternative ways of developing staff.
>
> (Cowan and Wright 1990, p. 118)

Manifestations of this conclusion were listed as failure to match the INSET to actual school needs, lack of evaluation of programmes and failure of evaluation to inform forward planning, and the disjointed nature of many Baker Days in the overall context of school development.

Perhaps the whole blame should not be laid at the door of schools: the government has, through the Grants for Education Support and Training (GEST) scheme, through legislation and also indirectly, set imperatives and agendas which have interfered with schools' plans, in particular in the period 1990–1. But Baker Days represent only a small fraction of total INSET provision nationally. Total national expenditure for INSET through the government's GEST scheme runs to £377 million, and much INSET programmed by university departments of education, polytechnics and others is not GEST-supported. So, the question must be asked: does the quality match the cost? While the answer is probably negative, this chapter attempts to explore criteria of quality which could be used as yardsticks against which performance could begin to be assessed.

MEASURING QUALITY

Measuring quality in INSET is usually described as evaluation, a term which will be used here. Of course, some evaluation is formative and some summative. At the formative end of this spectrum the concern may be to define or describe quality processes rather than 'measure' outcomes. Oldroyd and Hall (1991) go further and identify four kinds of quality control in INSET, each exemplified by a question.

- Monitoring: are we carrying out our plans?
- Formative evaluation: do we need to adjust our plans and how are we carrying them out?
- Summative evaluation: was the process successful and were the outcomes worthwhile and valuable?
- Review: should we change our assumptions, aims, priorities and approach?

Implicit in this model is its coherence, by which is meant that the audience for the answers to all four questions is, or could be, the same audience. In practice this is often not the case.

WHO MEASURES?

Part of the problem of making judgements about the quality of INSET events is that several different stakeholders exist, and each may come with different perspectives and hence different questions (or, at least, different emphases in the way in which the questions are put). This is rapidly obvious when one skims the literature of INSET evaluation. This point is exemplified in the articles which form just one edition of the *British Journal of In-service Education* (vol. 17.1 Summer 1991) as follows:

- Gill writes on the government's role and expectations as seen in recent training literature from the Schools Examinations and Assessment Council (SEAC) and the National Curriculum Council (NCC);
- Poulson and Merchant discuss the need of LEAs to be assured of delivering effective INSET;
- Roberts emphasises the need to satisfy the course participants as a whole;
- Simmons notes that individual teachers may have personal aspirations and that these will have a role in their judgements;

• Busher identifies the course tutor as a stakeholder.

To those listed above, one could add that, increasingly, with devolved INSET funding and Grant Maintained status, school governors and headteachers will want to be assured of quality in the sense that training leads the involved teachers the more effectively to meet the aspirations articulated by the school. Institutions (universities, polytechnics, colleges and professional associations) need quality assurance in relation to events which they offer. So the audience for answers about quality in INSET is diverse, and the answers may be less than clear-cut because of the nature of the 'hidden agendas' of each stakeholder. It is even conceivable, if not probable, that for any given INSET event what epitomises quality for one stakeholder may spell dissatisfaction for another.

CRITERIA OF EFFECTIVENESS

What is the range of possible criteria of effectiveness against which INSET can be judged?

Recently, cost effectiveness has become a fundamental criterion. This is implicit in the Grants for Education Support and Training (GEST) literature already quoted, and it featured too in the Report of the government's Efficiency Unit (Glickman and Dale 1990). This Report was especially significant in that it made overt the political dimension of INSET provision in this country: 'In this regard, Local Education Authority Training Grants Scheme (LEATGS) can be seen as a policy in its own right rather than, as is the case with Education Support Grants (ESG), a mechanism to advance policy priorities as they arise.' In other words, by limiting or targeting the funds effectively available for INSET – including those provided as the LEA's required contribution – it is possible for politicians to control teachers and their work. An implicit criterion of effectiveness here is the match between what the politicians believe teachers should learn about professional practice and what they actually learn. This criterion is unacceptable to many teachers because it flouts professional freedom, ignores professional wisdom and begins from a 'template of excellence' which is neither fully articulated nor, therefore, available for testing.

The contextual (i.e. political) reality, therefore, of INSET provision leads to quite other criteria of effectiveness than those proposed by Hopkins (1985), who argued for teachers to be 'accountable to professional codes of practice or principles rather than to examination results or arbitrary product criteria' and saw accountability in terms of professionalism and a professional ethic. This approach tends to view the teacher as an autonomous researcher, professionally dedicated to improving his or her performance through an investigative classroom approach but bound by the professional conventions already noted. Often the view is linked also to an emphasis on action research as the appropriate investigative style. Of these approaches Elliott (1989) concludes:

> In the final analysis the ultimate validation of specialised knowledge about education is that it enables educational practitioners to discover better solutions to the complex practical problems they confront in realising educational values in action.
>
> (Elliott 1989, p. 86)

Thus, the effectiveness criterion of these approaches is improved teaching performance or more effective teaching skills. Though views of how these are to be achieved might vary (contrast, for example, Glaser and Strauss 1967 with Altrichter and Posch 1989) the differences are more of perspective than principle. Neil (1985) investigated what marked in-service experiences as worthwhile by interviewing in-depth experienced educators who were also participants in INSET events. From these interviews he concluded that the underlying criterion of success was a factor which he labelled 'civility'. In this context, civility means:

- Devotion to sustaining the teacher–student relationship;
- Personal conscience and careful assessment of the needs of others;
- An outer expression of civility: how we say or do things.

Further, civility is operationalised in INSET activities through assessment of individual professional need, both short-term and long-term, and the accommodation of the programme away from the provider's goals towards those of the participant. This small-scale American research may vary in detail from our UK experience because of the different educational context, but it is borne out by similar small-scale in-depth studies here, such as that by Cowne and Norwich (1987) where the term civility was replaced by the concept of partnership. The emphasis in these studies is towards criteria of effectiveness which take into account the degree to which the individual needs of teachers are met – though Cowne and Norwich acknowledge, too, the legitimate aspirations of other partners.

Hodgson and Whalley (1985) deal with course evaluation in the context of a Diploma in Education programme. They argue that evaluation in INSET is valid only if the criteria chosen are appropriate and relevant, and if the list 'is complete in that it consists of all the appropriate and relevant criteria' (p. 44). These criteria have, they claim, to be derived rather than invented, e.g. by brain-storming. In summary, they find that Diploma courses of the kind described must meet two major criteria: that they bring participants up to date, and that they use the up-to-date knowledge and skills. Under the first criterion they point to four sub-criteria:

- The course must provide information;
- It must provide expertise, techniques and methods;

- It must give comprehensive coverage;
- It must encourage critical analysis.

On the second main criterion, use of updated knowledge, a distinction is drawn between reaching an awareness of the need for change and achieving change. Both are to be evaluated by reference to appropriate sub-criteria; first, awareness:

- The practical relevance of the course;
- Wide experience, e.g. through visits, speakers;
- Thought and reflection; e.g. through personal tutorials;

then, achievement:

- Innovation by development of a theoretical basis for working with colleagues;
- Local and national context;
- Keeping up to date via the literature.

So far we have tried in this section to look at criteria for measuring INSET quality from the point of view of various audiences: the government, the LEA, participant teachers and providers. But schools – in the person of the head or of the governing body – may wish to establish criteria that have more to do with curriculum change. A model such as Stake's (1977) may be more in tune with these aspirations. This model takes into account antecedents of INSET (factors which pre-exist), examines transactions (what happens in the teaching/evaluating situation) and seeks outcomes (summatively evaluating the learning in progress and modifying forward behaviour). A headteacher may thus be able to monitor change through INSET; but it is likely to be a long process of continuous evolution or development, and time-consuming to monitor.

Finally, Churcher (1990) is right to draw attention to the need for teachers to 'be concerned to evaluate the impact of in-service education on the education of children' (p. 37). Criteria here must relate to learning rather than teaching, to the improvement in pupils' perceptions of classroom processes and to pupils' attitudes towards their work and towards schools and to teachers. But the connections between teachers' INSET and pupils' learning are difficult to research and are mentioned in the literature mainly as problems rather than as solutions. The use of pupils or students as sources of evaluative data is sensitive and controversial.

EVALUATION AND CHANGE

This overview of evaluation as a means of quality assurance in INSET has so far identified some motives for evaluation, some kinds of measurement, the audience of evaluation and some problems in establishing satisfactory criteria against which to make evaluative judgements. This section moves on to what might be regarded as the purpose of evaluation: the need for change, and the assurance that desirable change is taking place.

Whoever is the audience for quality assurance through evaluation, the context of desired change is almost always the school. In other words, evaluation tends to seek an assurance that teachers are effecting change in curriculum, classroom practice, teaching and learning process or the organisation and management of learning. Eraut *et al.* (1987) suggest that this kind of school-based evaluation to support decision-making requires:

• Evidence of how things are;
• The presentation of arguments about desired practice;
• Clarification of issues;
• Suggestions for (new) ways of thinking;
• Recommendations.

Radnor (1990) pursues this further to develop a model for evaluating INSET in order to produce change. This model sets out three stages in conducting evaluation:

• Setting up the evaluation brief;
• Carrying out the evaluation process;
• Disseminating the evaluation findings.

The model presupposes the existence of an internal evaluator appointed to carry out interviews, to design and administer questionnaires and to compile a case-study. The evaluation process itself is designed to help teachers to identify with it by being communicative and participatory, and by extending teachers' knowledge base about what is happening in the school. Pupils can be involved. The evaluative process is intended to result in a summative report, which is concise and readable but which identifies recommendations for future process. Dissemination is through access by staff to the report.

Radnor's sample of teachers saw the process positively in that it provided recommendations for future ways forward, reflected on current practice in an analytical (not critical) way, encouraged staff and students to listen to each other, was systematic, broadened teachers' perspectives beyond narrow subjects, and gave teachers a sense of ownership.

Clearly such an evaluation of INSET requires an investment of both time and resource, but it may go some way to quality assurance in terms of matching achievements to objectives through any given INSET activity.

THE NATURE OF EVALUATION

Radnor's approach to evaluation has attractions (its detail, task-orientation, and sense of ownership) but some drawbacks (particularly those related to resources). Nevertheless, Parsons (1990) would clearly applaud the overall methodology. However, Parsons is also conscious of the hidden curriculum of evaluation:

> There are powerful forces to contend with in evaluation and the evaluator cannot proceed as though involved in a technical exercise alone. It is a socio-political activity and the supportive and formative nature of reporting is vital.
>
> (Parsons 1990, p. 6)

For the supportive and formative nature of this kind of evaluation Parsons coins the term 'palatability'. This term recognises the susceptibilities of all those, from teachers to elected members, who may be looking at quality assurance through evaluation. He argues that external evaluators will often be used, and that they can maintain palatability and a high professional standard by discussing the brief carefully, communicating accurately with schools, making the evaluation processes rigorous, providing feedback and keeping the distinction between inspection and evaluation. Reports can be discussed in draft form and the contractor's horizons broadened by negotiation.

Some might have doubts about this kind of commissioned evaluation, which appears to be not quite independent but rather subject to amendment of report or interpretation. It is interesting to debate whether such a view is merely triangulation under another name.

THE AGENT OF EVALUATION

In everything which has gone before it has been implicit that quality assurance through evaluation will be carried out by an 'evaluator', though this person has not been identified. Traditionally, one form of evaluation has been by inspection, as was implied by Parsons (1990). In this case the evaluator was usually an LEA inspector or adviser, or an HMI. Recently, some evaluation has been built into the GEST regulations, though much of this is limited to statistical data of debatable value in assurance either of quality or of change. In-school evaluations have been carried out commonly through 'happy-sheets': low-level questionnaires about enjoyment of the day but yielding extremely limited data on how training has altered attitudes or practice.

Increasingly there is an emphasis on the role of an external agent either to oversee the evaluation (Radnor 1990) or to conduct it. Thus, Churcher (1990) talks of the 'itinerant evaluator' as a recognised class of educational specialist. This is a move away from traditional views which hinged on the concept of the teacher as researcher, monitoring his or her own classroom practice (Stenhouse 1970, Elliott and Adelman 1976).

McGowan (1989) goes further and argues that schools cannot manage and evaluate their own INSET without outside help from support agents such as advisory services and teachers' centres, and that quality cannot be delivered unless the contact between support agencies and schools is continued for a significant period of time. In the new climate following the 1992 White Paper these services may be increasingly provided by private consultants.

SOME PROBLEMS FOR EVALUATION

Oldroyd and Hall (1991) asked a group of staff development co-ordinators to identify things about evaluation of INSET which they saw as problematic. This process produced a list (op. cit., p. 160) of person concerns on the one hand, and task concerns on the other. Person concerns were about how to motivate one's self to undertake evaluation, to find the time for it, and to encourage colleagues to participate and respond.

Task concerns were focused towards deciding on methodology for evaluation, on prioritising what needed evaluation, on identifying quality criteria and on measuring the long-term classroom-based effects of INSET.

Despite the difficulties, however, it is clear that the task has to be attempted; and Lowenstein (1990) goes so far as to identify INSET – or rather, the lack of it – as one cause of teacher stress leading to burn-out.

SUMMARY

Within the context of the kinds of considerations that are outlined in the research reported in this paper, an attempt was made to begin to assemble some criteria by which quality assurance by a team of INSET specialists working for Norfolk LEA could be judged and which could be used by both school-based evaluators and others. The remainder of the paper goes on to look at those criteria, to provide a rationale for their selection, and to place them in a wider context.

JUDGING QUALITY

As we have seen from the research, the judgement of quality in programmes of in-service training will inevitably operate on a number of different levels. In this section we look from the perspective of a provider as opposed to looking at criteria for judging individual in-service events, which is dealt with below. The basic question to which we are seeking an answer here is: what are the criteria of effectiveness which a provider must operate in making broad judgements about its INSET provision? All that can be achieved here is to probe the 'onion layers' of criteria which go to make up effective INSET provision on this broad front.

The following items might be included as factors in overall effectiveness of INSET provision:

- Sound theory;
- Modelling or demonstration;

- Simulated classroom practice;
- Feedback on performance to participants;
- Hands-on experience.

Clearly, a school or local education authority must assure itself that the training which it buys, and encourages, is based on a sound theoretical grasp of where it wishes its teaching and learning to be. The provider will have to take into account the desires of government and legislation, and also of schools and teachers. Theories cannot exist in a vacuum, and therefore it is essential that those who are charged with the management and leadership of in-service training are able to supply models of practice and demonstrations of how good classroom practice operates. This is quite definitely not to suggest that providers should identify one acceptable method of teaching for any given subject or phase of education: quite the opposite. The alternative models should be available for trial and scrutiny. In the process of trialling, both those charged with delivering the INSET and those participating in it should scrutinise and thus obtain feedback on both the theory and their performance. This can be done only when the work is practically based.

Wherever LEAs attempt to remain major providers of INSET in the new climate, the process of in-service training might need to be judged against the authority's ability to deliver on criteria such as the following:

- Opportunities provided by the LEA for teachers to share professional wisdom;
- The status and credibility accorded to participants in in-service training;
- The stimulus to confidence resulting from LEA programmes of training;
- The structure and focus given to the job of teaching by the LEA;
- The impact on the culture of schools of the in-service education provided by the LEA.

In so far as it is possible, it is desirable that local authorities share with their teachers an opportunity to exchange views on professional practice, and provide fora within which teachers can also exchange views. It is in such contexts that teachers feel that they have status and credibility. Through these means, too, the confidence of teachers is boosted: a commodity sadly lacking since the onslaught by the government of rapid and sustained innovation on the teaching profession. Through its in-service training, the LEA can provide both structure and a focus to the role of the teacher and to the process of teaching and learning, yet can do this without removing from teachers the whole of their professional autonomy and judgement. In-service education which is successful will have inevitable spin-offs into the culture of schools, which will not only value the process of in-service education but will also be more professionally self-conscious in going about the business of teaching and managing learning. Grant Maintained schools will need to assume the responsibilities outlined on behalf of their own staffs – or perhaps in small groups or federations, though the trend to competitiveness for pupils may militate against this.

If these overall criteria are a reasonable summary of some of the main concerns which need to be brought to bear when judging the effectiveness of an LEA's in-service training programme, then it is possible to deduce from them some criteria for quality assurance which can be applied to INSET programmes. At a recent DES conference the author asked a group of senior LEA advisers and officers concerned with in-service training to attempt to articulate some of these criteria, and the following list represents a slightly amended version of their suggestions:

• Whether the intentions of the in-service training are clearly formulated;
• Whether the INSET is contextually relevant;
• The rationale and structure of the programme;
• Whether the learning methods are appropriate;
• Whether there is evidence of improved culture and morale in schools subsequent upon the programme, and ownership of the programme itself;
• Whether there is evidence of a willingness to innovate and experiment;
• Whether the LEA has effectively identified and then met the needs of the teachers involved;
• Whether the training contains within itself opportunities for participants to obtain qualifications or promotion to which they aspire;
• The effect of the training on the learning of pupils in the classroom;
• Whether there is an increase in professional confidence;
• Whether there is an improved effectiveness in management of schools and classrooms following the in-service training;
• Whether the progress of participants in in-service training is effectively profiled and recorded.

These considerations form the basis of a possible methodology which could inform an evaluative investigation into the work of the in-service and support structure of a school or LEA, whether this was carried out by a wholly independent evaluator or through internal mini-evaluations. Frequently, internal evaluation relates more to the effectiveness of individual events than it does to an overall training programme and rationale. It is to this topic that we turn next.

Increasingly, individual schools or groups of schools are taking over the role of INSET provider in respect to their staff. In these cases the heads and governors of schools will have to assure themselves that precisely these criteria have been met. It seems likely that, to achieve this, resources will be increasingly devolved by the government to schools – but so will accountability.

JUDGING THE QUALITY OF INDIVIDUAL INSET EVENTS

In practice most in-service training is delivered through a series of discrete INSET events, each of which has a short-term life of its own. Criteria for judging the effectiveness of individual events would include the need to discover whether the events provide the following:

- Updating for participants;
- Appropriate information;
- Expertise in the person of the deliverers;
- Critical analysis by the participants;
- A broadening of participants' horizons;
- An awareness of the need for change;
- The ability to achieve a change.

Within this overall context, much of which relates to research already reported in this chapter, the group of senior in-service officers and advisers referred to above identified the following criteria, which may form a check-list for judging the effectiveness of an individual INSET activity:

- The rationale for the event (including the needs identification process);
- Pre-event preparation and the quality of information provided;
- The clear intentions of the event provided to participants;
- The opportunity for participants and organisers to negotiate;
- The clear articulation of the intended objectives and outcomes of the event;
- The quality of organisation, administrative arrangements, environment and facilities provided;
- The coherence of the event in a series of coherent programmes;
- The quality of presentation and materials;
- The balance of activity within the event;
- The flexibility of the programme and opportunity for its review;
- The opportunity for action planning as a result of the event;
- The degree and quality of feedback and support given to participants;
- A realistic assessment of where participants would go next, e.g. in terms of resources;
- The coherence of the link between the individual event and other related events which follow.

At the beginning of this section it was suggested that what was needed was the ability to peel back the 'onion layers' of criteria and to see those layers as inter-related within a whole scheme. In terms of methodology for pursuing such an aspiration to measure quality in terms of pre-articulated criteria, it would be necessary to generate a consistent methodology for collecting data both at the micro-level of individual events and at the macro-level of overall provision. Such a process requires a good deal of organisation and management.

It remains to be seen whether this is possible: in particular, in the context that schools are being encouraged to be more independent of the LEA, more competitive with one another, and to opt for increasingly devolved systems of funding. It may be that these aspects of change in the educational system are actually inimical to effective INSET delivery, and it is also highly debatable (though this is not the context in which to debate it) whether such competitive independence is in the best interests of schools, the teaching profession, and pupils.

CONCLUSION

The overriding conclusion of this chapter has to be that quality assurance through evaluation of in-service training is enormously difficult to achieve. The criteria for judgement might be deduced from the intentions of those involved in the training; but they will certainly vary from one situation to another and are subject to forces operating upon them from a variety of directions and often in a context of conflict. Not only are the criteria themselves unclear but also the system within which they operate is in a state of flux, the methodology by which they can be instituted is by no means simple or lacking in resource implication, and it seems to be becoming increasingly difficult to pursue a policy of linking in-service training with classroom practice directly. Perhaps what is needed now, in the context of recent rapid educational change and legislation, is a clear and unambiguous statement from the Department for Education of its view of quality in in-service provision. So far, as we have seen in this chapter, the DFE has not so much led as followed: it surveys practice and produces a critical analysis of it. It would be interesting to know the dimensions of the template against which the DFE officers make their judgements of quality and the methods of evaluation which they regard as appropriate in order to achieve quality assurance.

In the meantime schools, LEAs and other providers of professional development and in-service training would do well to take the messages of this chapter. First, there has to be a coherent institutional plan. Second, the plan should be judged against the criteria list above. Third, each individual event should be monitored for quality using the criteria on page 175 above. Fourth, while evaluation is costly in time, human and financial resource, without systematic and continuing evaluation no quality assurance can be achieved.

REFERENCES

Altrichter, H. and Posch, P. (1989) 'Does the "grounded theory" approach offer a guiding paradigm for teacher research?', *Cambridge Journal of Education* 19 (1): 21–31.

Churcher, J. (1990) 'Evaluating the effectiveness of in-service education and training', *Education Today* 40 (2): 37–41.

Cowan, B. and Wright, W. (1990) 'Two million days lost', *Education*, 2 February, pp. 117–18.

Cowne, E. and Norwich, B. (1987) 'Lessons in partnership', Bedford Way Paper 31, London: London Institute of Education.

Department of Education and Science (1991a) *Education for the Twenty-First Century*, London: HMSO.

Department of Education and Science (1991b) *Assessment, Recording and Reporting*, London: HMSO.

Department of Education and Science (1991c) *Grants for Education Support and Training 1992/93*, AN/06/43, London: HMSO.

Elliott, J. (1989) 'Educational theory and professional learning of teachers: an overview', *Cambridge Journal of Education* 19(1): 81–101.

Elliott, J. and Adelman, C. (1976) 'Innovation at classroom level: a case study of the Ford Teaching Project', in *Unit 28, Open University Course E203*, Milton Keynes: Open University Press.

Eraut, M., Pennycuick, D. and Radnor, H. (1987) *Local Evaluation of INSET: A Meta-Evaluation of TRIST Evaluation*, Bristol: National Development Centre for School Management Training.

Further Education Unit (1991) *Quality Matters: Business and Industry Quality Models and Further Education*, London: Further Education Unit.

Glaser, B. and Strauss, A. (1967) *The Discovery of Grounded Theory*, Chicago, Ill: Aldine.

Glickman, B.D. and Dale, H.C. (1990) *A Scrutiny of the Education Support Grants and the LEA Training Grants Scheme*, London: HMSO.

Hodgson, F. and Whalley, G. (1985) 'Evaluation of in-service education: a question of criteria', *British Journal of In-service Education* 12 (2): 44–7.

Hopkins, D. (1985) *A Teacher's Guide to Classroom Research*, Milton Keynes: Open University Press.

Lowenstein, L. (1990) 'Teacher stress leading to burn-out – its prevention and cure', *Education Today* 41 (2): 12–16.

McGowan, P. (1989) 'What's the use of INSET? – the role of external support', *British Journal of In-service Education* 15 (2): 95–101.

Neil, R. (1985) 'How in-service teachers' education can be made worthwhile – Civility', *British Journal of In-Service Education* 12 (2): 22–7.

Oldroyd, D. and Hall, V. (1991) *Managing Staff Development: A Handbook for Secondary Schools*, London: Paul Chapman.

Parsons, C. (1990) 'Evaluating aspects of a local authority's in-service programme', *British Journal of In-service Education* 16 (1): 4–7.

Radnor, H. (1990) 'Evaluating change processes promotes change: school-focused evaluation – A professional development model', *British Journal of In-Service Education* 16 (3): 150–5.

Stake, R. (1977) 'Countenance of educational evaluation', in D. Hamilton *et al.* (eds) *Beyond the Numbers Game*, Basingstoke: Macmillan.

Stenhouse, L. (1970) *The Humanities Curriculum Project*, London: Heinemann.

Chapter 13

Looking forward

David Bridges

In the preceding pages we have seen that the changes which government has introduced in recent years into education in general and teacher education more specifically raise more questions than they ever begin to answer. They present us with a formidable professional and research agenda. It is perhaps worth noting in conclusion some at least of these question.

Who will feel a real sense of responsibility for the quality and delivery of the initial and continuing education of teachers?

The role and the ethos of the traditional teacher training institutions have been steadily and quite deliberately undermined by a government paranoid in its conviction that here lay the roots of an ideological subversion of its educational policies. And yet here too were to be found communities of people with a strong sense of professional vocation (which persistently drove them to exceed the more limited and mechanistic obligations imposed under, for example, Polytechnic and College Employers' Forum conditions of service); a highly professional body with a single-minded commitment to the quality of teacher training and to service to students in training. LEAs, particularly over the period of GRIST and GEST funding, developed a strong sense of their responsibility for, even proprietorship over, the in-service training of teachers. Indeed, for many advisers this was their main function and *raison d'être*. But this too has been eroded first by the increasing focus on the inspectoral role of 'advisers' and more recently by changes in LEA funding which put LEA advisers in the role of competing suppliers of in-service support responding to the priorities of schools.

Some responsibility for initial training continues to lie with higher education institutions which will be accredited for this purpose, but, as we have seen, a major part of the exercise of this responsibility is to shift to schools. However, the primary business of schools is to teach their pupils. It remains to be seen what sort of priority they will be able to give to their growing responsibility for the initial and continuing education of teachers and how they will exercise that responsibility individually and collectively. Will schools be able to ensure that they have at least one person whose first priority is students/teachers undergoing training?

How will a strategic vision of, and response to, the needs of the profession be developed and sustained?

At national and regional levels LEAs and higher education institutions with representative teachers and headteachers have for a number of years provided a collaborative forum for both the identification of needs of the system for training and re-training and the mechanism for the delivery of the training which was required. The best of the old DES Regional Committees (on which were represented HMI, LEAs, HE staff and teachers) were able to carry out this function collegially, sensitively, and even with foresight and imagination. LEAs subsequently set up their own more local apparatus for the same purpose. As this role slips from the hands of LEAs, we have to ask where this same wider grasp of the future as well as present needs of the system at local and regional level will be developed and whether the short-termism which appears to characterise the developing marketplace response to training will really meet these needs. How will schools operating in an increasingly competitive environment be able to develop that wider systemic view – or will this be yet another responsibility pulled more firmly into the grip of central government?

How will continuity and progression in teacher training be developed?

There is nothing to look back on with great nostalgia here. The history of what was until recently called the 'probationary' year is undistinguished; discontinuities between initial training and induction have been aggravated by the variations in initial training provision, the geographical mobility of teachers between training and first appointment and by the failure of higher education, LEAs and schools to get their act together in any really co-ordinated policy. Likewise theoretical, let alone practical, models of career-long professional development of teachers have been in short supply – as indeed have the finances and conditions of service necessary for this notion to be taken really seriously.

But if the old HE/LEA nexus was not outstandingly successful in delivering this kind of continuity and progression, schools are not very well placed to provide it either – unless, that is, teachers come to spend more of their careers (from initial training to senior post) in a single school or some national agency takes control. This would probably be the institution which emerges from the merger of the National Curriculum Council and the Schools Examinations and Assessment Council, judging from its early ambitions for aggrandisement. There is a considerable will to develop a more coherent career-long approach to the professional development of teachers which is reflected, for example, in increasing interest in professional records of achievement and derived from the implementation of regular programmes of appraisal. It remains to be seen how and whether this might be achieved.

How will teachers' professional knowledge become the property of the professional community and how will it be communicated to new generations?

Developments in school-based training offer new and intriguing possibilities for the unpacking and articulation of the craft knowledge of teachers. The challenge of the new programmes is to succeed in this task. We should expect to see new approaches emerging to the processes which give a new teacher access to the craft knowledge of a colleague: to whatever patterns of observation, co-working, discussion, reflection, analysis and action research make this possible. We should also expect substantive new insights and understanding to emerge out of these processes – understanding which will not merely add to the competency of the new teacher but contribute to the wider stock of professional intelligence.

There are very exciting possibilities here which merit the combined attention of colleagues in all corners of the education service.

How close will be the association of teacher training and higher education – and what are the consequences of a weakening in this relationship?

There is little question that government measures designed substantially to remove teacher training from the hands of higher education have to be seen as part of a wider programme to undermine the influence of all those bodies – HMI, LEAs, teachers' unions and higher education – which have stood in recent history to challenge its own hegemony in educational policy and practice. The fact that successive Secretaries of State have also taken a whole gamut of new powers into their own hands adds to the sense which professional educators have of working under a new kind of educational totalitarianism legitimated by a succession of Conservative administrations.

Schools have been bought off in this transition by being thrown sufficient tokens of local power to give them the sense of being self-governing. This is, of course, an illusion already in respect to many fundamental aspects of their policy, most notably on curriculum and assessment which are at the heart of the educational enterprise. The new patterns of control mean that schools are more amenable than at any previous time to government directive on teaching, on assessment, on levels of finance, on forms of organisation, on the values which are represented – on virtually anything required by the policy of government or even the whim of a Secretary of State, who in most respects can now act without even reference back to parliament.

The purpose in rehearsing these observations is that they provide one important reason why schools and HE institutions should sustain and indeed strengthen their traditional association in the education of teachers. They need to cultivate and fortify in any way they can the independent mind and voice of the professional educational community under an increasingly autocratic administration which is daily, it seems, more separated from the common sense of that community.

But how realistic is this aspiration? The conditions which government is imposing on higher education partnership in initial teacher training in particular are leading higher education institutions themselves to ask whether it is worth the candle. Indeed, some have questioned whether they can, with integrity, any longer acknowledge as their own courses so closely formulated and controlled by government and delivered in a setting (i.e. schools) which will inevitably have difficulty in providing the context for adult teaching and learning (the libraries, the strong association with research, the mental space for reflection, the support for divergence of thought and argument) that is the proper hallmark of higher education.

But schools and universities (and not just Schools of Education in the universities) need to work closer today than ever before, not least because the transition from school to university will shortly be one which is part of the continuing educational experience of a third of all school leavers. Nearly all new teachers will enter teaching on the basis of a university degree. University Schools of Education have an important role as mediators between schools and higher education; helping universities to come to terms with the changing character of education in schools; helping teachers to interpret what they have learned in universities (as well as the rich wealth of experience gathered from other sources) in the classroom; supporting teachers in their own determination to advance the integrity of their subject(s), their pupils and themselves in an environment of increasingly monolithic political control.

Whether and how higher education is able to carry out this role in the next decade and what are the consequences of any diminution of the function are issues which merit careful and continuing attention.

Index